ORO

ORO

Cizia Zykë

Translated by Stanley Hochman

St. Martin's Press
New York

TRANSLATOR'S NOTE

Tico and *Tica* are nonpejorative terms often used by Costa Ricans in referring to one another. The custom has its roots in the national habit of adding the suffix *-ico* or *-ica* to nouns, so that, for example, *momento* becomes *momentico*, and so on.

The Costa Rican unit of currency, the *colon*, changed in value due to inflation during the time period of the narrative. As a rough guide, at the story's beginning (1981), a *colon* was worth one-twentieth of a U.S. dollar. At the end of the story (1984), a *colon* was about one-sixitieth of a dollar.

For obvious reasons, the names of people, places, and companies have sometimes been changed.

ORO. Copyright © 1985 by International Book Production. English translation copyright © 1987 by St. Martin's Press, Inc. All rights reserved. Printed in the United States of America. No part of this book may be used or reproduced in any manner whatsoever without written permission except in the case of brief quotations embodied in critical articles or reviews. For information, address St. Martin's Press, 175 Fifth Avenue, New York, N.Y. 10010.

Library of Congress Cataloging-in-Publication Data

Zykë, Cizia.
    Oro.

    Translated from French.
    1. Zykë, Cizia.   2. Adventure and adventurers—
Costa Rica.   I. Title.
G530.Z95   1987   917.286'0453   86-26298
ISBN 0-312-00093-6

First published in France by Hachette Publishing Inc.

First U.S. Edition

10 9 8 7 6 5 4 3 2 1

PROLOGUE

THE TROPICAL SUN burned overhead. My feet plodded rhythmically through the sand. I had been walking along the beach of Punta Burica, the southernmost point of Costa Rica, for several hours.

Except for my Magnum in its shoulder holster, I was wearing only a bathing-suit. My leather boots were slung around my neck by the laces. Stuffed into my boots was everything else I owned: my passport, a shirt, a pair of jeans, four sticks of dynamite, and about three thousand grams of gold.

I'd got a ride that morning from San José to Río Claro, where the road came to an end. If I kept walking at this pace, I would be in the mountains near the Panamanian border by nightfall. Tomorrow I would cross the mountains and enter Panama at Puerto Armuelles. It wasn't the normal route, but going through the Customs station was too risky. I had to get out of Costa Rica before the authorities knew I was gone.

It was 21 February 1984. I had been in Costa Rica for about three years, but it seemed longer. A lot had happened since Diana and I stepped off the bus in Golfito. The port of Golfito is the embarkation point for the Osa peninsula – so, you might say, it's where this whole adventure began.

Part One

ONE

WEARY IN BODY AND SPIRIT, we got out of the bus. For more than ten hours we'd had the salsa drummed into us; with the deafening music, the suffocating heat and the forced intimacy of three people to a seat, the ride from San José to Golfito had been like a journey through hell.

Diane, sitting next to the window, had been fine, but I'd been pressed up against the smelly gelatinous mass of a big Tica who'd spread herself all over me. Luckily, she'd left the bus at the halfway point – only to be replaced by a toothless old man who proved a little too affectionate: using my shoulder for a pillow, he immediately went to sleep. My friendly little jabs in the ribs must have been painful, because his moans lulled me into a half-sleep until we got to Golfito.

At my request the driver let us off in front of the Hotel Delfina, which looked like all the other houses in the place – an old wooden building with a zinc roof. We climbed the steps to the reception-desk. Nobody. The only evidence of a human presence was the blaring television. My shout brought a little old lady.

'Hi, beautiful. A room for two, please.'

'That'll be fifty colones – payable in advance.'

'OK, gorgeous. . . .'

She showed us a few rooms, all squalid as usual. Diane chose one with a balcony because it was the coolest and the least dirty. The bed was in pretty bad shape, and the sheets were just disgusting. I had the bedding changed, and Diane asked for some soap and towels. The old woman grumbled a little – something about gringos; she wasn't too gracious, but she did as she was told.

While Diane was getting undressed, I slipped off my gun and its holster, the new leather straps of which had been killing my shoulder.

9

Then I took the Bible from Diane's bag, tore out a page, and rolled a joint of Mango-Rosa – a terrific local marijuana – so that we could smoke in the shower.

It was a shower in name only: more like a dark little stall with damp and sticky walls and a trickle of water flowing from just above our heads. No clothes-hooks – not even a nail; it was only the delicious feeling of the water running over our tired bodies that made it a little less depressing.

Calmer and more comfortable we went out on to the main street to find some place to eat.

Bordered on one side by whorehouses and on the other by buildings perched on pilings and crowding against the sea, the railway tracks and the pothole-covered road took up all the available space in this little port wedged between the Golfo Dulce and the hills. Golfito is nothing but a loading-port built by the American banana companies, and its only residents are the company employees, a few shopkeepers, and the usual fauna of these little tropical harbours. The choice of a restaurant was easy since they all offered the same casado, a national dish made of rice, frijoles – black beans – a boiled banana, and a little sliver of meat, also boiled.

After dinner we enjoyed the evening cool and the spectacle of street life: a few characters with nothing much to do, some drunks, and plenty of whores.

As a matter of fact, one of them was dragging herself along in front of us. She was enormous.

'Like her?' asked Diane with a smile.

'I think she's very sexy – but what happens when one of these little Ticos gets his scrawny head stuck between those giant thighs?'

Our burst of laughter brought a 'Que pasa?' from the lady herself.

'Nothing, beautiful.'

She walked off, but we kept her in view. A few yards further on, she was stopped by some guy who'd obviously put away a few. The way he grabbed her left no doubt about his intentions: he wanted to jump her right then and there. The girl gave him a whack that sent him sprawling against a café table, and the whole street came to life; people were laughing and yelling 'Go to it! Kill the son of a bitch!' The whore flipped the crowd the finger, then disappeared into a bar.

'The girl's got spirit,' said Diane.

She was radiant that evening. Her pale green eyes, her long Venetian-blonde hair, her skin – tanned and healthy as only the skin of a girl born and raised in the tropics can be – made a pleasant contrast with the cruddy landscape around us.

I wanted her, and she knew it.

'Let's go back to the hotel,' she said, kissing me.

Night. Diane was alseep. I couldn't doze off, so I went out on to the balcony. There, leaning against the railing, a big Mango-Rosa cigar in my hand, I started to think.

Two years ago, when we'd left the Caribbean islands, where I had met Diane, we'd had no worries; the future seemed crystal-clear. A year later, the death of our son had been a blow to our happiness, and since then – gambling, doing drugs – we had travelled all over the world looking for the right deal. From the opium-dens of Asia to the casino in Monte Carlo by way of Macao, Bangkok and Las Vegas, I had looked for it everywhere – and ended up here in Central America, flat broke.

Some quick profits in the import–export business had put me back on my feet for a while: it's easy enough to make fast money by arranging an exchange between a co-operative arms-seller and an equally co-operative coke-dealer. Unfortunately, my passion for gambling had caused me to lose those twenty thousand dollars at the casino just as quickly and easily as I'd made them, and I had exactly twelve bucks on me when I crossed into Costa Rica.

Unlike most people, I don't find the lack of money a problem. I've been knocking around since I was eighteen, and I've never worried about money – if it wasn't in my pockets, it was waiting for me in other people's. I didn't have a nickel, but that didn't matter; somehow or other, I'd find a way of getting some dough.

I'd been a millionaire several times over, but the money had always gone as easily as it had come. I never thought about money when I spent it. If I'd had to economize, I wouldn't be what I am, and I wouldn't have had any of my extraordinary adventures: over-cautiousness doesn't make for a very exciting life. My last cent will always be spent for a splurge, for comfort, for never having to do things by halves.

My only real concern, the motivation for all my behaviour, what makes me roam around the world, is the search for increasingly ambitious projects. After a great adventure, only a greater one will satisfy me – and that's not always easy.

In this over-regimented world it's hard to be an adventurer and to follow your own rules. So far as I'm concerned, nothing is forbidden: I *want* to do it, therefore I *can* do it. Unfortunately, this modern world is no longer big enough. It's impossible to carve out a kingdom, to live an adventure, without being stymied by laws, because the struggle is now unequal. Everything is done for the weak, who have gathered

11

together under the banner of law and order, and everything is weighted in their favour against those who want to get away from the control of laws. It's no longer a struggle of man against man. In all my adventures I've come up against governments – in Africa, in Asia and in the Caribbean – and when that happens you can't win. I'm a hundred times less corrupt than the Third World leaders I've come up against, but they always have credibility and international recognition on their side. Would Costa Rica provide me with what I had been looking for so long? I'd tried everything in Central America – been a leftist guerrilla in El Salvador and a rightist guerrilla in Nicaragua – but the fact is that I'm too independent and no longer naïve enough to maintain the sacred fire of a revolutionary. It's Utopian to hope for a better world; there will always be exploiters and people who are exploited – and, if it's not nice to be an exploiter, it's even worse to be one of the exploited. In any case, I fight for one person only – myself.

At first glance, Costa Rica didn't look like a suitable place for wheeling and dealing. A tiny little country wedged between Panama in the south and Nicaragua in the north, it had undergone a 700 per cent devaluation in a matter of months. Poverty was beginning to put in an appearance, but it was still discreet; even though the average Tico had no money, he could satisfy his basic needs: rice, beans, bananas and coffee. There was no starvation in Costa Rica yet, but there was no more luxury, either. My first experience there had been a dig of a pre-Columbian burial-ground in the middle of the country. I'd done the same kind of thing in Peru fifteen years earlier, but under different conditions. Here, though the forest was luxuriant, it was by no means pleasant; and, while the lack of food had been a drawback, what was worse were the colloradillas – microscopic insects that slide by the dozen under your skin, race towards your crotch and itch like hell. But the toughest thing was to sell the pre-Columbian artefacts, because art had no value in Costa Rica, and the antiquarians were interested only in objects made of gold or jade. Sometimes they would only offer me three or four dollars for things that were more than a thousand years old! A beautiful ceramic vase that survived centuries might accidentally get smashed against the mug of one of those arseholes who ran a pre-Columbian art gallery. . . .

Fortunately, Diane had taken over and sold several items to members of the French embassy. And it was also thanks to her that we met Shlomo.

I had to hope that this likeable small-time operator hadn't lied to me. He told me that I was wasting my time, that there were more profitable things to do in this country. In the south, he said, there was a place overflowing with gold – the Osa peninsula. To hear him talk, all you had to do was bend and scoop it up, though he let me know that the area was unsafe, full of adventurers and criminals on the run.

His story interested me. Not the part about the gold, because I knew that people always exaggerated about that, but the life he described. The Osa peninsula seemed to be a forgotten spot – pretty much out of touch with the rest of the country, dangerous, and to some extent beyond the law. In other words, the kind of place I liked.

And that was why two days later, after using my last pots for target practice – fifteen hundred years exploding against the wall – we had boarded the bus for Golfito, from where you took the boat for Osa.

A few good restaurants, the acquisition of a .38 Smith & Wesson long-barrelled revolver from the said Shlomo, and the purchase of two hundred grams of Mango-Rosa and some dried hongos – mushrooms – had put a serious dent in the proceeds from the pots we had sold. The day after arriving in Golfito we were going to take the boat for Puerto Jiménez, the only village of any size on the peninsula. I counted my money. I had eighteen dollars left.

The boat was anchored some ten yards from the loading-dock, and the passengers were quietly sitting on the quay under a burning sun. I was told that the departure was imminent, but I knew the habits of the country, and we went off to wait in the cool of the same hash-house we'd been to the day before. A transistor was playing 'Capri, c'est fini' – unlikely music for this corner of the world. An hour went by without anything happening except the sun beating down even more strongly on the little group seated on the quay. Another hour and the sailors began to shuttle back and forth in cutters, transporting first the passengers and then the luggage. The boat, a little tub about twenty yards long, half of it shaded by a tarpaulin, was loaded to the gunwales.

Everyone had crammed into the seats in the stern, but we were comfortably settled up front, smoking some dope and watching the dolphins that came to play around the boat. Then I went back and mingled with the crowd to see what was doing. There were lots of women – sturdily built, big cows – and some very lean men carrying tools and obviously ready to try their luck in Osa.

All the way in the rear, a small weasel-faced guy was bustling around among the others, who were listening to him. He showed them a gold nugget, the first I had seen there. I went up to him, and we started to talk. His name was Jeremy, and he was a former banana company pilot who had opened a bar in Puerto Jiménez and trafficked in gold, like everyone else over there. He invited us to come to his bar

13

if we wanted some leads. Two hours later we were in Puerto Jiménez.

Landing in Puerto Jiménez is kind of funny, since there's no port and no jetty. The boat simply stops when the water becomes too shallow, and everybody gets ashore however he can. I had to take off my boots and roll up my trousers to carry Diane to the beach. Shouting, laughing, everyone saw to the unloading of his stuff as best he could. The three sailors carried the women, each of them slyly trying to palm off the old ones and take the young ones – a task that had its compensations. We went to Jeremy's bar, the Rancho de Oro, set back off the beach, to check it out and have a drink, because the heat was suffocating.

The bar was pleasant enough. Built entirely of bamboo and well ventilated, it didn't stink the way some of them did, and it was practically empty because it was siesta time. In a corner I spotted a guy who looked a little unusual. He was seated alone at a table on which were a small set of scales and an impressive number of beer-cans that he was emptying at regular intervals. About forty, blue-eyed, he had a baseball-cap screwed down on his balding head; there was enough blond hair sticking out for me to tell he was a gringo – one of those Americans who'd come to try his luck in Costa Rica.

I went over to him. 'My name is Juan Carlos,' I said.

'Hi, I'm Wayne.'

'Mind if I sit down?'

'Go right ahead.'

Wayne was a former Marine who'd been living in Costa Rica for several years. He'd knocked around just about everywhere before coming there, and it turned out we'd been in a lot of the same places – Asia, Africa, the usual hellholes. We got on well.

He lived in Golfito, was married to a Tica, and did three-way trading: he bought gold cheap on the peninsula, and once a month he went to sell it in Miami, from where he brought back dollars, which he exchanged on the black market, also for a profit. This kind of set-up, in which you turn a profit twice, was one of the easiest things to do with gold, because the Costa Rican bank didn't buy at the world market price. He told me that he used to take his scales into the mountains, where he could buy the gold even more cheaply directly from the prospectors scattered in various corners of the jungle, but an ambush – which he had only survived thanks to a bulletproof jacket he always wore – had cooled his enthusiasm.

'Now I buy here, in Puerto Jiménez. I come on Sundays, when the men are down from the mountain. The profits are slimmer, but there's less risk. I have to think of my family,' he said with a smile.

14

From his tone, I got the feeling that he was sorry to have been trapped by life with a wife and child in a country that was falling apart.

When I told him my plans, he asked: 'Are you armed?'

'Yes, I'm all set.'

'Do you have tools, equipment, a horse?' he asked, glancing at my worn boots.

'No, but that's no problem. I'll take care of that here.'

'If I can give you a hand, if you need dough. . . .'

'I'm fine, thanks. But it would be helpful if you could steer me to someone who's leaving for an interesting spot.'

'I'll look around. Come back this evening.'

'OK. Until then.'

The choice of a hotel was simplified by the fact that there was only one, right in the middle of the village. Puerto Jiménez extends for about half a mile along a wide dusty road on which the sun beats down mercilessly. There was nobody on the streets; everyone was taking a siesta behind closed shutters. Across from the bank – a building about the size of a public urinal – a cop sprawled on a chair, his rifle resting on his knees. A drunk, a pitiful relic of last night's bender, was stretched out in front of the door of a bar. Three guys were snoozing in chairs in the shade of a porch roof. Those were all the signs of life in Puerto Jiménez.

Walking down the centre of that interminable street, battered by the sun and breathing the dusty motionless air, I felt as though I'd come to a ghost town. At the end of the street was a police station, whose inhabitants I would unfortunately get to know all too well.

That evening I went back to the bar, where I had no trouble getting information, because gold prospectors – poor drunken oreros – are blabbers. They stand everybody to drinks and are only too happy to treat gringos. But how could I figure out how much of their drunken babble was true?

Puerto Jiménez is a village that only comes to life at night. The whores search out the oreros to relieve them of their gold, and the bars fill up with poor prospectors looking for pleasure and something to buy; the whores and the con men are there to help them. All night long, Puerto Jiménez is filled with the noise of their carousing, their laughter and their brawling. At dawn they end up in the gutters, their pockets turned inside out by kids looking for their last colones.

Later Wayne showed up with another European, Hans, and a Tico called Memo. Hans was a German who lived in Puerto Jiménez, and he was also looking for gold. Memo was leaving the next morning for

15

Carate, a village on the other side of the peninsula. We agreed to meet, and he went back to his buddies.

'If you go to Carate, look up Brett. He's a nice guy,' Wayne told me.

After a few drinks, we went back to the hotel.

Memo, accompanied by a dumb-looking giant, came to get us at about four in the morning. A quick cup of coffee, and we were ready. Diane carried her make-up kit; I lugged our mutual knapsack. By the time we had gone a few hundred yards, it began to weigh me down, and I called to Memo's friend. A rapid parley, and in exchange for my last five dollars he agreed to carry the knapsack as far as Carate. All I had left were a few coins, but at least I could walk comfortably.

After about half an hour Memo took a short cut into the mountains. The pleasure trip was about to begin. The jungle was a real oven, damp and suffocating, and we were covered in sweat. The ground was rain-soaked, and the vegetation retained the humidity. There was no real path, and sometimes we had to cut our way forward with a machete. Unlike the little Ticos, I couldn't run along without sinking in the mud and, when I fell, I fell with all my weight. (Though the Ticas are big, the Ticos are small and thin; they're adapted to racing through the woods.) Diane, who was ridiculously light and agile, looked as if she were out for a country stroll.

Because there was so much mud, I walked barefoot, my boots slung around my neck. In level areas I sank up to my knees, and when we went uphill or downhill I slid. We could manage because we had our hands free, but it wasn't so easy for the poor bastard carrying my heavy knapsack. Despite his brute strength, he was having a hard time, constantly stumbling and falling, and soon he was coated with mud. That annoyed me because he was getting the knapsack filthy. Suddenly he slipped and went spinning away, sliding for more than thirty yards before he was knocked half-unconscious by the pack, which had conked him on the head. Everybody laughed – though *he* didn't find it quite so funny, because he'd really hurt himself. But then an idiotic smile spread across his big dumb face and, still thinking of my five bucks, he picked up the knapsack and went on. We walked like that all day, stopping occasionally to refresh ourselves with some bitter oranges gathered along the way, or to smoke some dope. I'd told Memo not to wait for us, and he had disappeared long ago.

It was ten in the evening when we came out on to a beach; we were at Río Oro, about two hours from Carate. My last few coins bought us some biscuits and sodas, which the three of us shared. Diane and I decided to sleep there, and to get rid of our porter – whose growing affection was beginning to get a little embarrassing – I pointed out the route with a friendly tap on the shoulder and told him we'd meet the next day in Carate. A little confused, but happy to have made some money and some friends, he went off into the night.

We tried to sleep on the beach, but in spite of our exhaustion it was a long night. The heat, the mosquitoes and the damp sand made it hard to sleep, and we were relieved when it began to get light. I wanted some coffee and a cigarette, but we didn't have another centavo.

At dawn we started for Carate. On the way I spotted some turtle-tracks in the sand. The eggs were buried about a foot beneath the surface. I scooped up about ten of them and covered the others up again. We ate them raw for breakfast, and we were still sitting on the sand when a native on horseback came up. He looked about fifty or sixty.

'Hi!'

'Hi! Where are you headed for?'

'We're going to Carate.'

'So am I.'

'That's a lucky break, because my wife is really exhausted.'

And without giving him time for too many questions I asked him to get off the horse, made Diane climb up and gave her the knapsack.

Once he'd got over his surprise, the guy was happy enough to walk along beside me. He slung his spurs around his neck and began a monologue that went on until we reached Carate.

It was eleven o'clock when the old man pointed to a European-style wooden house and said: 'Carate. That's the house of the Canadians who run the mine. My stepson lives about fifty yards behind it. Come with me and we'll have some coffee.'

We got to a zinc-roofed shack made of palms and wood. In front of the door, two naked children were playing with a pig. A man stretched out in a patched hammock got up as we drew near and greeted the old man.

'Hi, Pop, how are you?'

'Fine, Saltarana, thank God. Look, I've brought you two French people from Jiménez.'

'French people? Great, come in and have a seat,' said the stepson. He got out two rickety chairs and called his wife. 'Hey, Negra, make some coffee. We've got company. Are you hungry? Would you like something to eat?'

While I was helping Diane get off the horse with the knapsack, Saltarana bustled about, pushing aside the kids who were watching us open-mouthed. Exhausted, we sat down in the shade.

17

Saltarana was a lively little guy with a likeable air about him. His inquisitive eyes darted from one to the other of us as we drank our coffee.

'What are you doing here, looking for gold?'

While I was talking to him, the señora invited Diane to take a shower.

Saltarana had been here for two years, and he more or less worked for the Canadians, doing odd jobs for them.

'The gringos don't have much contact with the oreros, so I'm a kind of go-between, and Negra does their housekeeping. There are two of them – Mr Bill, the manager, and Fucking, the chief mechanic. They run the mine.'

'Fucking?'

'Yes. We call him that because he uses that word every time he opens his mouth. He's a real arsehole,' he concluded.

A little while later, he got out some scales and a small bottle. He produced some gold from the bottle and weighed it while his step-father counted out some banknotes. Saltarana explained to me that they were in business together. The old man bought from him the gold that he in turn had bought from the oreros. In Osa everything revolved around gold.

Saltarana invited Diane and me to stay at his place.

'There's room,' he told me.

He swept aside a greasy hanging and showed me two bunk beds. I turned to Diane, and we looked at each other. It wasn't the Ritz; in fact it was probably the dirtiest place she'd seen since we'd been together. But we didn't have much choice, and the life we lived made some concessions necessary. We accepted the invitation.

'Swell,' said Saltarana. 'Now I can leave.'

I looked at him in surprise.

'I've been wanting to do some celebrating,' he explained, 'but I can't leave the place alone for too long or they'll steal my stuff. One day I found the door broken in, and all my kitchen equipment was gone. But with you here I can go off to Jiménez without worrying. Make yourselves comfortable – there are plenty of supplies.'

A few minutes later they left – he, his wife and the two kids – all four on an old motorcycle. They had known me only a few hours.

I spent the rest of the afternoon relaxing and picnicking on the beach with Diane. In the evening, while she was getting dinner ready, I went to the pulperia, the nearby general store and bar. Where there's alcohol there's nightlife, and I could hear the sounds of drunken cries and shouts coming from the big well-lighted building. As I went in, a

18

staggering Tico brushed past me to heave his guts into the street. The bar was jammed, and there were already a few men sprawled on the floor, dead drunk. The pulperia was fairly large. One part was a warehouse in which were stacked sacks of rice, frijoles and other basic necessities. This was separated from the rest of the place by a bar, stocked with bottles of guaro, a sugar-cane liquor. It all stank of vomit and spilled alcohol. I made my way to the bar, on the other side of which a gringo, helped by a pretty little barmaid, was serving out drinks and yelling at the drunks. He was tall, blond and about forty; the marks of alcohol showed in his face. When he saw me he came from behind the bar.

'Are you the Frenchman who just got here? Glad to meet you. I'm Brett.' He extended his hand.

'Good to meet you. I'm Juan Carlos.'

'Are you alone? I heard you had a very beautiful woman with you. News travels fast here, you know, and it always makes its way to the pulperia.'

He stopped to bawl out a Tico who was making obscene gestures to the barmaid, who was apparently his wife.

'I can't stand these bastards any more. Each one is crazier than the next. About the only thing they can do is drink and yell. I've been here three years now, and I'm sick and tired of them. Luckily, they spend all their gold in my place. What's brought you here? Going to try your luck with gold?'

'Yeah, Wayne told me about Carate. Said it might be interesting. Incidentally, he sends his regards.'

'Wayne! That crazy bastard! Still dealing in gold? He's going to end up a corpse. Can I give you a drink?'

'Sure.'

Brett was glad to have a European to bitch to.

'Look at these wrecks,' he said, pointing to two skinny old men who'd just walked in sporting a battered cassette-player. 'They come here every evening with their fucking music. They've got only two cassettes, and I have to listen to them all night. They live upstairs. They must be at least ninety, and they've been together for about ten years – they fight like an old married couple.'

The two old men were skinny and wrinkled, their skin blackened by the sun, their arms and legs distorted by prospecting for gold; their hands looked like spatulas.

'I hear there are two Canadians here. What are they like?'

'Those bastards? I rent the pulperia from them. They don't want any strangers around, because they're afraid of competition. In the beginning they told me they were going to close the mine, because

19

there wasn't all that much gold. That's why I took over managing this place. A lot of hot air! They work like animals and pull out about a kilo every day. You'll never see them here. They live a way off, and they never mix with the others. They won't even let their workers come here.'

The noise in the pulperia was getting louder, and I was beginning to feel my lack of sleep. Just as I was about to leave, Brett stopped me.

'I imagine that if you've come to this hellhole it's because you're broke. Don't let that worry you. I give credit to everybody here, because it's the only place where they can pick up supplies. So, no matter what you need, don't be shy about asking. We white men have got to stick together. . . .'

'See you tomorrow.'

I went back to Diane. The filthy shack had been transformed! A little shifting of furniture and two judiciously placed candles had spruced it up. Diane had made a good simple meal: boiled spiced turtle-eggs, some rice and fried beans, and flamed bananas and coconut. I told her what I'd learned: there was gold, a fair amount of it, and what we had to do was figure out the best way to profit from the situation. We went down to the beach, but the mosquitoes, tiny and voracious, quickly forced us back inside.

Early the next morning I was awakened by a loud banging at the door. A voice was calling Saltarana's name. I opened the door, and a fat little man looked at me in astonishment.

'Where's that bastard Saltarana, and what the fuck are you doing here?'

What was this arsehole's problem? I was about to sock him when another guy intervened.

'Hey, cool it. All we want is Saltarana. My name's Bill, and he's Fucking.'

I explained that Saltarana had left and that I was living there temporarily.

'We're the managers of the mine. Drop by some day,' he said as he left.

Bill seemed nice enough, but Fucking was obviously a bastard, as Saltarana had said.

Diane and I decided to rearrange the house. If we were going to be there for a while, the place might as well be habitable. I broke up the two bunk beds and made one big bed out of them, then while Diane was stuffing the gaps between the planks with palms I got rid of the hanging and replaced it with a screen of interwoven bamboo and leaves.

When it was all finished, Diane began to laugh. It was true that I had taken over most of Saltarana's living-space, but I like to feel at home. Anyway, the Ticos are used to living all squeezed together.

The house belonging to the Canadians, Saltarana's place, the pulperia with the upstairs occupied by the two old men, and four shacks along the Carate river pretty much made up the whole village. Higher up the river was the encampment of the Carate Mining Company, with its machine shops and its workers' dormitory; a little farther away was the orero camp. It had been slapped together out of cardboard and plastic – a real shanty-town, built by the prospectors who had grouped together so they could help one another.

About a hundred of them lived there with their women and children, in cramped, muddy, uncomfortable quarters – never imagining anything better for themselves. I was familiar with the scene. Gold was nothing new to me. I'd already seen prospectors' camps in Gabon and in Brazil, on the Venezuelan border. You find the same lousy miserable conditions everywhere. These guys work all day and then drink up their profits in a few hours. If I was going to launch myself in this adventure, it certainly wasn't to do that. But first of all I wanted to learn as much as I could so that I could make the most of my opportunities.

We went back to the house. I knew Saltarana would return in a few days, and I wanted to take advantage of our privacy to relax with Diane.

That evening I went back to the pulperia by myself. It was the focal point of Carate, because all the news passed through there: one guy had found a nugget of such and such a size, another had died in a landslide, someone had discovered a fantastic pocket at such and such a place. . . . As the night advanced, the news became more and more fanciful, the size of the nuggets increasing with the number of bottles drunk.

Brett, who had become a racist, hated the natives, and I had to admit that the local Ticos, because of the conditions under which they lived, were neither nice nor intelligent. They were brutalized by their workhorse labour, their brains were destroyed by bootleg alcohol – many of them were barely human.

Sometimes Brett had trouble controlling the situation. He was married, but the locals didn't respect him enough to leave his wife alone. He also made the mistake of occasionally getting drunk with the men, which tended to lower certain barriers. The Ticos couldn't distinguish between courtesy and familiarity, and before long they crossed the line – especially in this pulperia, where once night had fallen nobody could stand upright. Fights were common: Brett frequently had to use his fists, and he often had to take guys who lay half-unconscious on the filthy floor and drag them into the gutter, where they spent the night with their noses buried in their vomit.

The atmosphere was rotten, but it was the only place where I could gather useful information and meet the oreros.

'See, that's the way they live,' Brett told me. 'They work for a few days, then spend everything in one night. But I'm not complaining – it all ends up in my pockets,' he added with a smile. 'And what about you? What are you planning to do – go with them?'

'No, I don't have a slave mentality. I plan to learn as much as I can about gold, then find some way to profit from it without working like a maniac. I just need to learn some of the local panning techniques – after that I'll manage. No problem.'

'Nothing could be easier. All you have to do is offer one of these bums a drink, and he'll tell you everything you want to know. Would you like me to introduce you?'

'No, I'll take care of that myself. But thanks.'

The next day I picked up a few bottles of guaro on credit from Brett and went to see the two old men. They were in the middle of a heavy argument, but they were so surprised by my visit that they called a halt to their domestic squabble. The sight of the bottles made them smile from ear to ear.

'Listen, friends, I've got a proposition for you. I have to learn all about panning, and I'm willing to supply the drinks while you're making me an expert.'

They thought this was a great deal and took my proposal very seriously. Swollen with importance, they walked solemnly down to the river. My method was simple: a turn at panning, then a swallow. The pan – they call it a catiadora – looks like a big saucer, with a slight depression in the middle. After you shovel in some gold-bearing gravel, you have to crouch, with more then ten pounds in your hands, and bend forward. It's an awkward position, and hard on the back as well.

Standing in the water, the old men rotated the half-submerged pan. The current this created, together with the help of centrifugal force, little by little carried away the sand and the stones, which the men had to stir frequently so they didn't pile up; then, by a right-to-left movement, they made the gold, which was heavier, slip to the bottom of the pan. The movement is simple, but it takes a lot of practice. A little too much water or too sudden a gesture, and the tiny grains of gold jump out of the pan.

I practised for a while, but my back began to kill me. When I decided to call it a day, the two bottles were empty and the old men were filled to the brim. I left them collapsed on the banks of the river and went back to spend the afternoon on the beach with Diane. Later, convinced I was their gravy-train, my two professors came back, and I had a hell of a time getting rid of them. Now that I knew the basic movements, I just wanted to perfect my technique. I didn't have to be the world champion – if the catiadora was going to be part of my future equipment, I'd always be able to find some poor son of a bitch to break his back in my place.

When Saltarana returned with his little family, he was a bit surprised by the renovations, but he accepted them. We had started on a diet of avocados and turtle-eggs. The turtles, generous little animals, would crawl up on the sand in front of the house to do their laying. I'd get up and go to the beach early in the morning, follow their tracks, and return with a good supply of eggs. I tried to fry them, but the whites remained liquid. The best thing was to boil them with spices, which could penetrate the soft porous shell. The menu was further improved by the coconuts you could find all along the beach. Scraped and mixed with frijoles and the water the rice had been cooked in, their taste helped to keep you from getting tired of the boiled vegetables too quickly. Saltarana's wife tried to follow my suggestions for varying the menu, but she never understood the point of it. The Ticos live on boiled starches from childhood on, and culinary refinements mean nothing to them.

Every morning I walked along the river and watched the oreros. In Osa they work the gold along the river-bank, working in the rivers under the open sky. The gold, which has been carried along the current, is mixed with the alluvial material of the river-bed. All of this has to be washed until you reach the bedrock, and there's only one way to do it – get rid of everything.

After choosing a spot whose potential richness has been determined by a few preliminary catiadoras, you have to clear it of its big rocks, which is insanely hard work. Rocks weighing up to several tons have to be broken up by pounding on them all day under a broiling sun with nothing more than a miner's bar. Amazingly, the Ticos take to this job without batting an eyelid. Small and spare, they jump on the rocks and beat away for hours on end.

At the same time you have to change the course of the river – or at least a part of it – to get just enough current for the canoa, a simple gadget typical of Osa. It's a sort of three-sided box: usually about a foot and a half wide and three feet long, with two boards about six

23

inches high that form a channel for the water and the gold-bearing gravel. The entrance to this sluice is completely open; the exit has a two-inch lip that cuts the current. One or two people load the canoa with gravel, which is then washed by the current. A man squats near the canoa and lifts out the largest stones while constantly rocking the canoa to prevent the gravel from piling up. This movement is very important, because the current carries off the pebbles, whereas the gold, because of its density, remains behind; but, if the soil and the gravel are allowed to cluster, the gold rolls over the stones and escapes. The trick lies in the regularity of the movement, combined with just the right amount of current and a good slant to the canoa. From then on, all you have to do is keep feeding in the gravel so that the force of the current remains unchanged.

Seated comfortably on a rock and puffing away at a Mango-Rosa joint, I watched one group of oreros bust their balls. After a while, the hole they were digging was too deep to allow them to keep shovelling without swallowing water, at which point they closed the canoa and extended the deviation several hundred yards so that the water-level sank. It was real coolies' work, a job for loonies. I went from one group to another, and they all used the same method, just with more or less energy.

In the early afternoon, when they lifted out the canoa, I went over to inspect the results. They spilled the residue of the canoa into the pan and the gold appeared. I couldn't believe it: there was no more than ten grams! A day of unbelievable labour for almost nothing. . . .

A little later I told Brett about what I'd seen. He laughed and said: 'All those guys are hopeless. There's not a real orero in the lot. It doesn't make any difference to them whether they grow bananas or look for gold. Some of them don't know any more about it than either of us and, besides, the river's already been washed and rewashed hundreds of times. The real oreros, the ones who really find gold, live in the mountains. They don't come in very often, but when they do their pockets are always full. They're easy to recognize, too – they have the biggest celebrations.'

'Are those guys far from here?'

'Well, some are a few days away, others only a few hours. But to get there you have to have rubber boots,' he said, with a glance at my bare feet. 'I doubt if I have your size, but ask the company pilot to bring you some from San José.'

I forced myself to go to the pulperia every evening to glean information. Eventually, I became known as the Frenchman who wanted to go prospecting, and some of the men would come over and talk to me without being asked. I also met the local dope-dealer, who showed up

24

regularly with his horse loaded down with as much grass as it could carry. Pot was cheap, but he sold so much of it he made as much money as if he'd been selling alcohol. But since he wouldn't give credit nobody liked him, and he was in a dangerous business. His predecessor had been found in the jungle with his head split open by a machete and his pockets turned inside out.

The Ticos were naturally peaceful, but they sometimes turned violent when they'd been drinking. They were quick to whip out their machetes, and the pulperia would heat up with their brawls. One night while I was talking to Brett two guys grabbed at his wife. He punched one of them, but the other took out his machete. I went over and hit him in the face with a bottle, then beat him around the ears for good measure. He didn't seem to appreciate the free beer, and he collapsed on the floor with his face all bloody. The two of them had had it, and while everyone laughed Brett did a little housekeeping by dragging them outside. He left them there unconscious, but I wasn't very worried – they had thick skulls.

The next day I met my previous night's victim. He grinned, and I could see that all his teeth had been knocked out by the impact. As usual he had his machete, and I expected trouble – but his smile was sincere.

'Hi, Frenchie, how's it going?'

'OK. How about you?'

'Great! That was some night last night! You really hammered us, but it was fun. Now I'm going back to the mountains, because I'm broke. See you later.'

And he went off into the jungle. That little celebration had cost him his teeth, but he had had fun. The Ticos are like that. They don't bear grudges.

A few days later Juanito, Saltarana's brother, came to see me.

'Since you're interested in gold, why don't you come work with us? I'm in a very rich spot.'

He showed me the thirty-two grams of gold three of them had harvested the day before. Out of curiosity I went with him. I don't really like teamwork but, if the site turned out to be a good one, maybe I could talk him into doing the humping for me. . . . He worked at the bottom of a very steep bank that rose like a cliff. The current and the shovelling had undermined the foot of the wall, which had already been eaten away by the violent seasonal rainstorms.

'Listen, Juanito,' I said to him as I pointed to the cliff. 'Aren't you afraid that's going to come down on you?'

'Oh, that kind of thing happens from time to time,' he said with a big smile that exposed his snaggle teeth. 'But there's always a warning – some falling sand and pebbles. All you have to do is run like hell. It's a little dangerous, but it's worth it.'

And in fact, except for a few false alarms that made everyone break into a mad gallop, the morning went off without incident. Then, around noon, when the rain had stopped, the collapse came without warning. We barely made it to shelter. The whole cliff had come sliding down; hundreds of cubic yards of earth covered all the work we had done. A big rock had rolled right towards us, but had been stopped by a tree-trunk.

I surveyed our demolished labour. Juanito, still laughing at the scare he'd had, was talking about hiring a company tractor to clear the ground, the way he usually did. I realized that he could never make a profit in this location, because every time he dug there would be a landslide. The stupid bastard! I wanted to sock him for making me risk my life so stupidly for a profit that was lost in advance! I left the arsehole to his dreams of being a millionaire and went home.

I was beginning to get sick and tired of it all. What the hell was I doing there? I'd come ready for anything to make my pile, but everything I had found was just chickenfeed. All I could do was scratch the earth like a mole and dig out a few shitty grams: even if I conned everyone else into working for me, I wasn't sure I could keep myself in cigarettes.

I had nosed around pretty much all over the place, I was well known by then, and several oreros had come to make me propositions. None of them was worth a damn. The mining company would have been glad to see me go; Mr Bill was polite enough, but Fucking made his dislike evident.

And yet I still felt that the peninsula could be the point of departure for something big. I'd noticed that some of the gold prospectors who came to the pulperia brought only nuggets, instead of the gold dust the local oreros usually found. Saltarana, with whom I often spent my evenings, explained it to me.

'Those oreros are not like the ones here. They go to the jungle, where they've got a camp set up. They're on their way to Corcovado, the forest reserve – it's illegal, and there's nobody around for miles on end. Here, everything's been pretty much worked over for the last forty years, and there's nothing left. Over there, it's virgin territory, with the nuggets lying right on the surface. Life is harder, but it's more profitable.'

Finally, some *real* gold prospectors! Sultarana told me they went up into the mountains alone or in groups of two or three, loaded down like mules but only with bare necessities: rice, flour, sugar and coffee. They'd stay in the jungle for several weeks, generally working the same spot, which they covered up when they left. They lived there without any comforts, sheltered by a roof of leaves or plastic. Sometimes they were never seen again – victims of a jaguar, a snake, a landslide, or an unscrupulous partner. There are no witnesses in the jungle. Nobody knew how many of them there were up there, and nobody cared. I had the feeling that would be the place for me.

I'd been waiting several days for my rubber boots, because I couldn't go very far while I was still barefoot. The pair that the pilot had brought me back were too small, and about the only thing I could do with them was cram them down his throat. (I had stowed my leather boots in Saltarana's house – you can't wear leather boots in the jungle.)

I had decided to move on, but I could neither leave Diane there nor take her along. I needed to be alone, to have my hands free, to be ready to seize any opportunity, so I spent a lot of time with her because I knew we would soon have to separate. One of the things we did was go off together to try our hand at some panning. Diane had a better feel for it than I had. Working an area Juanito had told us was untouched, she found her first nugget: eight grams – seven in refined gold. In an area about a foot and a half square we found twenty-five grams in an hour. When Juanito had pointed the spot out to us, it had probably never occurred to him that we'd have such luck.

On the beach that evening Diane asked me what my plans were.

'Do you think there's anything here for us? Saltarana is nice, but I assume we're not going to spend the rest of our lives with him.'

'It seems to me that in the beginning the only way I can make any money out of gold is to buy it in the mountains and sell it in Panama. But to do that I need some capital. I'll never pull it off with the gold available in Carate. I hear there's a lot of gold in Corcovado National Park, so I'm going to go up into the mountains there.'

'Fine. It'll feel great to be moving again. When do we leave?'

'No, baby, I don't want to take you up there. The living conditions will be brutal, and you've already had a hard enough time. I'm going to try my luck alone – you can wait for me in San José.'

I could see the disappointment in her eyes. I took her face between my hands.

'It's only a matter of two or three weeks. You can stay with Jean-Paul, the queer. He's a decent guy and he won't bother you. We'll use

27

the Hotel America as a mailbox. . . . But we've still got some time. We'll be together for a little while yet.'

We spent a lot of evenings talking with Saltarana. He asked a lot of questions about the countries I'd visited, and their different customs. In an old school atlas that he knew by heart I showed him where I had travelled. Sometimes it was difficult to explain things to a Tico who had never been out of his country.

Diane had taught Negra to like swimming in the ocean, and it was fun to see them together on the beach: Diane, tall and blonde, wearing a pareo – a piece of cloth worn like a sarong – and Negra, as small and wrinkled as a prune, wearing a bathing-suit that went up to her belly-button.

But one evening Saltarana seemed ill at ease, as though he had something on his mind. He circled around it without being able to say a word, so I decided to help him.

'What's bothering you?'

'It's the Canadians.'

'What about the Canadians?'

'They don't want you around any more, especially Fucking. I don't think they like the idea of there being another foreigner who's interested in gold. Until now they've had it all to themselves – no competition. They told me to tell you to go.'

The news about Fucking didn't surprise me. He hadn't said hello since the time I almost slugged him, and he even arranged things so that we didn't run into each other. Mr Bill had always been polite, but never more than that. I could understand how they felt: when they were the only foreigners in the gold business it was easier for them to impose their authority. They weren't comfortable with the Ticos; in a few weeks I had become better known than either of them, and the oreros kept dropping by with proposals for working together. The Canadians were feeling left out.

Saltarana continued: 'You know I'd like you to stay on, but they're my bosses and. . . .'

He was uncomfortable. He liked me, but he had to think of his family, his work. Those sons of bitches knew that and took advantage of it to put pressure on him rather than deal directly with me.

'Don't worry, Salta. I don't want you to have any problems because of me. Besides, I've already decided to leave.'

He lowered his voice and indicated that I was to come closer.

'I've got an idea. I know you have a revolver,' he said with a smile and a sparkle in his eyes. 'Every week they take the gold to San José. Sometimes there's as much as ten kilos. There'd only be three people to kill: the pilot and the two guards. We could share when we get to Guanacaste. What do you say?'

The plan couldn't have been simpler. He was obviously proud of it, and he was surprised when I smiled and refused: that kind of thing just isn't my style.

The new development had made my decision easier. I would go up into the mountains, and Diane would take the company plane back to San José. I'd leave her all the gold we had managed to pan – thirty-five grams, worth about $450 – since I was sure I'd find more up there.

I was still barefoot, but what the hell – I was glad to be moving again: alone and with only myself to worry about, it would be easier to pull something off. But, first, I wanted to be sure Diane was safe. She was the only woman I had ever loved, and for the last five years we had lived a wonderful life. Born in the islands, the daughter of one of the last of the Caribbean adventurers, she had the natural class and force of character I appreciated in a woman. Though she was rich, she had left everything to follow me. But our recent adventures had taken their toll, and her health had suffered. She had been born to live in luxury – this stinking jungle was no place for her. Our love was too precious to let it be spoiled by this kind of life. Crammed into a shack, without any privacy – that wasn't what I wanted to offer her. It would be better if she regained her strength in the capital while I plugged away in the mountains; later – in a few weeks, I thought – I could go back to her with something to offer.

I went with her to the plane.

'Have a good trip and enjoy yourself in San José.'

'It's going to be hard without you. . . .'

'Don't worry, baby. I'll be in San José in a few weeks.'

Still barefoot, I left early in the morning, wearing shorts and a shirt, carrying twenty-five cartridges in one pocket and some hongos – mushrooms – and plastic-wrapped Mango-Rosa in the other. I made sure to bring along my precious Bible, which was crammed under my holster. That was all the equipment I had.

Juan's shack would be my first stop, but his directions had been vague. He told me to go along the beach until I got to the Madrigal river, then follow that to the fourth place where it branched off. At that point, I was supposed to take the first tributary to the left, which should theoretically lead me to a small stream marked by a lightning-struck tree – and from there to Juan's place.

It's not exactly easy to go up the Madrigal. There was no marked path, because I was now in Corcovado National Park – off-limits to gold prospectors. That meant I had to walk on pebbles and rocks in order to avoid leaving footprints that would attract attention. The river was high, so I was rapidly soaked from head to foot, but what I was worried about was my revolver; I didn't have any grease to protect it, and in these regions my .38 was a must. The fourth fork seemed far away, and I began to have some doubts about its location, because this was the middle of the rainy season and the torrential downpours had formed a lot of small streams. I decided to follow one of them, but I walked for hours without coming to any lightning-struck tree. The banks became steeper and steeper, and the river had narrowed to a trickle that was about to disappear. I must have made a mistake somewhere; I'd been walking for six hours.

I knew I was completely lost. I had no idea of which direction to follow. My feet, bruised and bleeding from the stones, hurt like hell. Sudden rock barriers forced me to make wide detours. Without a machete I had trouble moving ahead. Night was beginning to fall when I finally spotted the tree that served as a landmark – and none too soon. I continued up the river to its source without seeing anything; it was only when I began to backtrack that I heard the rhythmic sound of an axe. Finally, I was there.

I sat down on a boulder right in the middle of the river and gave the cry I'd heard used by Osa prospectors, a sort of coyote howl. I waited a few minutes, then repeated it. The sound of the axe had stopped, and I sensed that I was being observed. I had to give them enough time to identify me. When I heard a slight crackle behind me, I turned and saw Juan.

'Greetings, Frenchie. How's it hanging?'

'Hello, Juan. Are you all right? I've come to see you – and, believe me, I've had a hell of a time finding you.'

Juan's face broke into a grin. He was a sturdy little guy of about thirty, and his toothless smile made him look sympathetic.

'We're pretty well hidden, but you have to be careful – the park rangers pass this way sometimes and they're real sons of bitches. Come with me!'

I followed him, walking carefully so as not to leave a track that might lead the rangers to his shack.

'It's not that those arseholes are all that smart,' Juan told me, 'but every once in a while they spot a few oreros, and when they do they confiscate everything – gold, tools, the works. If you argue, they toss you in the clink, and since most of the guys here are on the run they don't want to be captured.'

The shack was very simple: a plasticized tarpaulin resting on four stakes, a corner for the fire, and a common bed, about a foot off the

30

ground and made of branches tied together and covered with leaves. Two other people lived with him. A young man – a vicious sneaky-looking little faggot whom I instinctively disliked – and a taciturn old man who cooked the meals. They didn't seem happy about my visit.

'You can sleep here,' Juan said as he showed me the bed. 'We'll squeeze together a little.'

'Thanks, but my religion forbids me to sleep with other men. I'll build my own bed. Lend me a machete, will you?'

'I'll help.'

I couldn't very well tell him that this greasy meat-sandwich promiscuity was too much for me – he'd never have understood. Hygiene is something unknown to them, and in any case, since they spend days on end submerged in water, they feel perfectly clean.

Working quickly, we put together a bed near the fire. It was made of four forked branches stuck in the ground with a wooden framework supporting balsa trunks cut lengthwise. Unlike the Ticos, I removed the bark, to keep insects from setting up house in it. Then I covered it all with palm leaves.

It was night by the time we finished. Feeling tired and filthy, I went down to the river to wash up. I found a natural little basin, and although the water was chilly it felt fine and did me a lot of good. While I was at it I washed my shorts, underpants and shirt. I climbed back up to the camp naked. The young faggot was standing in front of the shack and watching me. After hanging my clothes over the fire, I settled on the bed and started oiling my revolver. I was so busy that it was a while before I noticed the little queer openly taking me in.

'The show's over, you little fucker, so beat it,' I said, covering my cock with a handful of leaves.

'Hey there, Frenchie, aren't we touchy!' he said, wiggling his arse.

I could see I'd been right about the vicious little pervert, who obviously wasn't going to leave me alone. It's not that I have anything against faggots – it's just that I'd rather they kept their distance.

After a frugal meal of rice, frijoles and coffee, we began to talk. The pages of my Bible had dried out, and I rolled a Mango-Rosa cigar and passed it around. Soon the atmosphere relaxed and tongues loosened. The old man and the young one, who I now realized formed a couple, never left the jungle – Juan brought them whatever they needed from Carate. There must have been some reason for them to end up here and have to lie low like that, but I didn't find out what it was. Juan had fallen asleep and was snoring noisily. The little faggot kept peppering me with questions.

'Where's France?'

'Far from here.'

31

'How many days on horseback?'

The old man, who was slightly less ignorant, explained to him that you had to take a plane or a boat to go there, and I took advantage of the discussion this started between them to get a little shuteye. In the middle of the night, while I was snoozing, a sudden touch made me jump. The little faggot was there, his hand on my belly. I was so disgusted that I punched him in the face with everything I had. He fell down and started to scream. The old man came right over to help him; he lifted him up, kissed and caressed him, and examined him by the light of the fire. His little slut, mouth bleeding and lips split, looked at me with eyes blazing with hatred. I'd have to be careful around these two.

It was still raining when I got up at dawn, numb with cold. It rains all the time in Osa, and that day it rained so hard it was impossible to work. I put on my still-damp clothes. The day was grey and depressing.

The next day, taking advantage of a break in the weather, we went down to the river very early. The same shit over and over again – move the stones, smash the rocks, fill the canoa with shovelfuls of earth. In the afternoon we stopped after having screened a few cubic yards of gravel. Juan lifted out the canoa.

'Look, Frenchie, look how it shines!'

I looked. A few scattered grains, three grams at most. . . . I felt like calling it quits then and there.

Juan could see I was disappointed. 'Not much today. We haven't got down far enough yet, but tomorrow you'll see. . . .'

And the next day I saw. The endless rain had caused the ground to slide, and the hole was completely plugged up. Back to square one.

Another whole morning lost. I was wasting my time, and the atmosphere there was just getting worse. I had another run-in with the kid, who got a slap when he tried to send me for water.

In the afternoon, tired of listening to them babble, I went off into the forest. I soon noticed a bunch of monkeys high up in the trees. They were howler monkeys – you could hear their cries for miles. They had cute little faces, and they stopped to watch me. But, cute or not, I was hungry for meat and I would have shot one in a second, except that the rangers might have heard the detonation. Too bad.

A little farther off I came across an iguana perched on a branch. Unfortunately, my stone missed its target, and I continued my stroll. That same afternoon I saw some weirdly coloured small frogs – red, green, platinum and gold. I had never seen anything so strange, not in the Amazon or in any other tropical forest. Later I learned that they were loaded with poison and just touching the skin of one could send you reeling. Finally, on the way back, I was lucky enough to run into a boa. Meat at last! This time I didn't let it get away: a whack with a machete and I went back to the camp a happy man. I'm carnivorous; my body needs more than starches.

Unlike most of the snakes that infest the peninsula, the boa isn't dangerous. The others, especially the ones that live in the national park, can be deadly, and a good number of prospectors die from snake bites. There were thousands of them – from the coral, a minute little snake, to the cascabel, a rattler that can be as long as ten feet; not to mention the fer-de-lance, known here as the tercio pello; the most common, the bocaraca; and various other kinds of slime whose names I still didn't know. The bastards usually go for the extremities – your hands or your toes. When a guy is bitten on the finger, he cuts it off with a machete. Sometimes that will do the trick, but many men die from it. Like the oreros, I learned to inspect my bed before getting into it, and I also was careful when I walked, because I was still barefoot. You see a lot of snakes during the day, and at night my companions, rather than take the chance of stepping on one, would piss from their bed, despite the odour that settled down in the shack. The previous day, while piling up some rocks to divert the current, I had found a tercio pello under one of them and had jumped back just in time. The tercio pello is poisonous, and its fangs can pierce any pair of boots.

Back at the shack, I quickly gutted the boa and cut it up into small round slices. We had a feast, and that evening I was treated to their usual bullshit – stories like: 'One day when I was hunting, I saw a place with lots of nuggets.' 'And what did you do?' 'Nothing, since I was hot on the tracks of a wild boar.' To tune it out, I smoked a lot of Mango-Rosa, which is a great soporific.

The fourth day was a repetition of the first three, and by then I was really getting fed up. Juan left in the afternoon for Carate and was due back the next day; I gave him my part of the gold so he could buy me some jerky. The night was hell. I was awakened by a big bite on my finger, and I was so obsessed by the fear of snakes that I was about to cut my finger off. The old man stopped me.

'It's a scorpion. The bite's not deadly.'

Maybe not deadly, but so painful that it was impossible to sleep; I spent the night sitting in front of the fire. At dawn, since those two wrecks were obviously not going to do any work today, I went back to bed and finally got a little sleep.

Several hours later, having drunk some coffee, I decided to do a few

catiadoras in the river. After panning for a while with no results –
only a few grains that I didn't even set aside – I gave it up. On the way
back I saw a disgusting sight. On his knees in the mud, his pants
around his ankles, the old man was cornholing the kid, who looked as
pleased as punch. Christ! What the hell was I doing here with these
perverts? Disgusted, nauseated, I went back to the shack. My mind
was made up: I'd wait for Juan to get back with the meat and then
blow this shithole. I knew that two hours farther upstream Miguel
had a shack that he shared with two whores he'd brought back from
Jiménez. (I'd seen them go by when I was in Carate – two enormous
masses of flesh, each one crushing a poor mule.) I was busy reheating
the frijoles when Juan appeared – with no supplies: nothing but a
half-empty bottle of guaro.

'Where's my meat?'

'Listen, Frenchie, there was a celebration in Carate, so I had a lot to
drink – and, anyway, I don't think there was any meat left.'

He got all balled up in his drunken lies.

'You fucking pig, you got drunk on my gold.'

In a burst of alcoholic tenderness he put a hand on my shoulder and
blew his malodorous breath into my face.

'Don't get angry, Frenchie! Look, I brought some guaro, and that's
better than meat.'

Blind with rage, I picked up the pot of boiling beans and threw it at
his face. Juan fell to his knees, shrieking in pain. The way he screamed, I began to feel sorry for the arsehole. Meanwhile the noise had
brought the others on the double. They were surprised, but they
didn't say a word. My distrust of the kid saved my life. He rushed me
with his machete, but I already had my revolver out.

'Drop that, buddy! Drop the machete or I'll blow your head off!'

He stopped, terrified. Reluctantly, he obeyed and let it fall.

'Lie down with your hands and feet spread out.'

He did as he was told without a murmur. The old man never
budged. He was scared, too.

'And now you, you old faggot. Take care of Juan.'

Then, picking up the machete, I methodically destroyed the camp,
ripping the plastic tarpaulin, breaking up the beds, scattering the fire.
While I was at it, I gave the still spreadeagled queer a kick in the head.

'Don't move, you son of a bitch!'

Juan, his face buried in his hands, was still moaning. The poor
bastard wasn't really malicious, just pathetic.

Keeping my revolver trained on all of them, I backed away. I was
feeling calmer now; I had let off some steam.

The road to Miguel's place was easy. I couldn't get lost because all I had to do was follow the river for two hours. My feet were killing me; the cuts still hadn't healed, and I had to keep stopping to remove the tiny pebbles that lodged in the gashes. But I felt free, and the jungle didn't seem all that bad to me now. A tribe of howler monkeys kept me company for a while, deafening me with their cries. The rain had stopped, and the Mango-Rosa made the road almost pleasant. I'd just about lost track of time when I spotted Miguel's hut. To my great surprise, it was right at the edge of the river, with no camouflage at all. Maybe because it was deeper into the jungle than Juan's place, there was less chance of unwanted visitors.

As I got closer, I heard bursts of laughter, and then a serenade in a falsetto voice. I walked a few feet farther and stumbled on an unexpected sight. Seated on a tree-trunk in front of the shack, the two big women I had seen in Carate were encouraging Miguel, who was kneeling in front of them, to sing. One of the women noticed me, and stopped him with a gesture. He climbed off his cloud and looked at me.

'*Hola*, who are you?'

'I'm Juan Carlos, and I've come from Carate.'

'Ah, you're the Frenchman, aren't you? You were living at Saltarana's place, right? I heard about you. Come on in. Welcome. He's the French guy who's looking for gold,' he added for the benefit of the women.

Miguel was small, solid and likeable; there was a feeling of good humour in his camp. His shack was simple, just like the others. With busy nights in mind, he had made himself a king-sized bed, and in full view, hanging from the ceiling by four cords, was a cardboard box with a few leaves of Mango-Rosa sticking out. We spent the evening smoking and laughing. I do a lot of dope, but even I was impressed by how much we smoked that night. We didn't make cigars so much as big grenades wrapped in newspaper and passed from hand to hand. I got very friendly with Miguel, who even offered me one of his fiancées. Pleading exhaustion, I declined the offer politely, and we settled down in the big bed for the night. There was plenty of room for me and, given Miguel's size, I wondered if he hadn't planned to bring some more women along. He slept between the two girls and, small as he was, he all but disappeared between the two mountains of lard who seemed to be blanketing him to keep him warm. I could see his laughing happy face half-hidden under a gelatinous breast. Then I fell asleep, making sure to keep my distance. I had no desire to be buried under an overflow of nocturnal affection.

35

In the morning Miguel showed me his work-site. It was impressive: tons and tons of stones weighed each other down and formed a wall several hundred yards long. Everything had been very carefully thought out, and he was proud of it. His method was simple: first he took all the stones from the stream; then, when the water had become clear, he put on an old mask, dived, and gathered the nuggets.

I noticed that my questions bothered him. He wasn't the happy and carefree Miguel of the night before, and I soon found out why.

'How many grams do you get out every day?'

'Depends on how clear the water is. . . . Listen, Frenchie, I'm going to level with you. You're welcome here – you like a good time and so do I. But I'm a loner, and I'm used to being on my own. All this is mine. I've been working here a long time and—'

I stopped him right there.

'No problem, Miguel, I understand you. I'm a loner, too, and I'm not going to stay here. I just want to let my feet mend.'

He relaxed.

'I'm glad you understand. Thanks.'

He was smiling again. 'As for your feet, you can stay as long as you want. As I said, you're welcome. Stay with us, smoke with us, eat with us, fuck with us – that's fine with me.'

Then he called over the younger of the two whores.

'Rosa, take care of Frenchie's feet. Do a good job.'

Rosa went off and came back with a handful of leaves that she boiled down to a paste. She applied the unguent to my skin and covered it with clean rags that she wrapped around my feet. I felt as though I were walking around in space-shoes, but it soothed the pain. Rosa was pleased with her work, and I thanked her with an affectionate whack on her enormous arse.

The two whores quickly became my good friends. I baptized the bigger one 'Slutbucket' and told her it was the French name for a beautiful flower. She was a big cow, but an ambitious and professional whore. I got along better with Rosa, who was almost as big but had a pretty little face. She soon told me her life-story. No, she hadn't always been a whore, but problems with her stepfather had forced her to leave her home, her family and her studies in Panama. She had sunk lower and lower, until she ended up in a Jiménez whorehouse where she serviced sixty clients a day. When Miguel came along with his proposition, she followed him into the jungle.

'I plan to stay here a year and save enough money to go back to Panama.'

I almost felt sorry for her and found myself thinking it was too bad she was so huge.

Miguel the Loner had obviously had a brusque flash of desire one day after a particularly successful harvest of nuggets. Since he never felt comfortable in town, he preferred to take his pleasure at home, so one morning he went to Jiménez – and came back a few days later with these two beasts. Since then they'd had an easy life sitting all day on a rock and watching Miguel work. Their tits in the air, dressed only in enormous panties that came up to their belly-buttons, punctuating their bursts of laughter with loud farts, they spent their time eating, smoking and shitting. They gave him a hard time, ate up his supplies, and took all his gold. They even made him sing. They persuaded him that he had a beautiful voice, so he sang every evening. I got a kick out of seeing that little guy, one knee on the ground, his eyes clamped shut, singing a love-song to those enormous sausages who repaid him with affectionate slaps on the back of the head.

I made myself a separate bed because, although Miguel worked hard all day, he fucked like a rabbit for a good part of the night.

One afternoon, Slutbucket, turned on by my gringo wallet, offered her services.

'Thanks, Big Girl, but you're really too ugly.'

'And are the French women beautiful?'

How could I ever explain to that cow the difference between the *svelte* body of a European woman and her own mass of hairy lard? On the other hand, I let Rosa give me a blow job and was surprised by her gentleness.

My feet were better. Rosa's unguents, renewed several times a day, had done the trick. I was busy cleaning my revolver when she came over to me.

'You're leaving?'

'Yes, tomorrow morning.'

Without a word she turned to the box hanging from the ceiling, took out two big handfuls of Mango-Rosa, wrapped it all in a piece of plastic, and handed it to me.

'Here, this is for you.'

'Don't you think that's too much? There are three of you smoking here.'

She smiled and signalled me to follow her. We walked about five hundred yards to a flat cleared stretch, where a surprise awaited me. They had planted marijuana in an area about ten yards by twenty; some of the plants were as high as twelve feet.

On the way back I asked: 'Isn't Miguel afraid of problems with the rangers?'

'Miguel has lots of friends among them, and enough gold to keep them friends.'

So that was the explanation for the uncamouflaged shack, the Mango-Rosa out in full view of everybody, and Miguel's carefree manner. He'd been there a long time and he had learned how to make his nest comfy.

That night after his serenade, I asked Miguel a few questions about the oreros in the neighbourhood so I'd know where to go.

'In this ravine there aren't any more. I'm the last one. There are some in the valley on the other side, but they're not very good ones. There's just El Gato. He's good, and his spot is pretty rich.'

'El Gato, the old man who works with Chato? They're around here?'

'Yes, do you know them?'

'I met them several times in Carate. That's good news. I'll go see them.'

At dawn I said my goodbyes. Rosa, who had grown fond of me, asked me to take her along.

'Sure, but only if you agree to carry me until we get to El Gato's place.'

Everybody laughed but Rosa. I didn't want to hurt her feelings, but I couldn't see myself in the mountains with anything as big as that. I patted her cheek.

'You know it wouldn't work out. After all, you're not unhappy here, and sooner or later you'll get back to Panama.'

'I guess you're right. Good luck, Frenchie.'

The night before, Miguel had given me some complicated directions. He'd lived in the jungle for so long that he was just as much at home as other people are in the streets of a city, and it was hard for him to understand that to me one tree looked pretty much like another. Now he repeated his directions for me: I was supposed to go right up the mountain, follow along the crest until the next valley, then go down again. That's where I'd find El Gato. It seemed simple enough when he said it, but once I was in the jungle, with the same vegetation in front, behind and on either side of me, it was a little different. 'Follow the crest.' Fine – but, first, you had to know you were on the crest!

Anyhow, I climbed up the first mountain, went down it, climbed up another mountain, followed one crest, then another, and – hell! I was completely lost. I didn't even have a river to follow. Not a single landmark. I went down, climbed up, circled around. The ground was slippery, and a couple of times I went tumbling downhill. Hours went by like this. I was tired of the whole mess, sick of seeing nothing but this fucking foliage, this fucking rain, this fucking mud! I'd never liked the jungle, and now I hated it. What the hell was I doing there? Why couldn't I have had an easy job, like a guard at a railway crossing or a civil service employee?

It was almost night when I decided to call a halt. That was enough for one day. I climbed up a tree and settled myself on a big forked branch a few yards off the ground: snakes are nocturnal, and I wanted to avoid them if I could. Since my matches were wet, I couldn't even smoke a joint but, luckily, I still had a few hongos. In any case, what with the rain and the mosquitoes, I knew I wouldn't get any sleep. The hongos were mildewed, they tasted rotten, and I ate them all. I spent the night hallucinating wildly and screaming 'Follow the crest'. The animals had quietened down, and my bursts of laughter sounded weird in the jungle. By dawn I was voiceless and bruised, because on top of everything else I'd fallen out of the tree – and I was still tripping. When I started off again, I felt rotten and had the taste of bile in my mouth. Luckily, a little while later I stumbled across a creek. I drank my fill, and the fresh water did me good. I followed the stream for over a mile, but then it disappeared into a hole in the rocks.

All I had eaten during the past twenty-four hours was four raw fresh-water shrimp. There were plenty of cabbage palmettos around, but I didn't have a machete. I sat for a long time while my matches dried out on a stone, and then I smoked a joint. The first toke was delicious, and I didn't feel like moving ever again. When night came, I just cleared a square of ground to lie down on – the hell with the snakes and insects.

In the morning, I was still alive, but even hungrier and dirtier. I started off again, going downhill all the time, and heard the sound of water. I was saved. This time the water was too wide simply to disappear. I knew that all I had to do was follow its course and I'd come to human life or the sea. I washed, stretched out on a rock, and fell asleep in the sun.

I was still dozing when I was awakened by the feeling that someone was there. A bushy-haired little old man – dressed in rags, and carrying a machete and a large knapsack attached to his back with string – had come out of nowhere and was watching me. He looked as surprised as I was.

'Hi, how are you?'

He sat down in front of me without removing his knapsack and lit a cigarette.

'What are you doing here?' he asked.

'I'm looking for El Gato's shack. Do you know where it is?'

39

'Not far from here,' he said, pointing vaguely. 'Just follow the crest for an hour, and you're there. Couldn't be simpler.'

Another arsehole telling me to follow the crest. This pissed me off. I put my hand on my revolver and said: 'Listen, old man – if it's so close, you can come with me.'

He got up, looking more than a little irritated. I collected his machete from a rock. The old guy hadn't been lying; after less than an hour of slogging along, we reached El Gato's camp.

'Hi, Gato. How's it going?'

'Hi, Frenchie. Good to see you. Come in and sit down.'

'I was lost, and without the help of this gentleman I'd still be up to my neck in shit.'

'Have some coffee for your trouble,' Gato said to the old man, who gulped it down and left. Parting wasn't exactly sweet sorrow for either of us.

'Have you come to work with us?'

'Sure, why not? Where's Chato?'

'That poor bastard! A bocaraca bit him in the neck two days ago. He wasn't a pretty sight – his neck and face swelled up like a balloon. We buried him yesterday. The son of a bitch picked just the wrong time to die, because there's a lot of work. It's a good thing you've come along to replace him.'

In the mountains there's no more fuss than that about death. No formalities, no burial permits. Sometimes the authorities get to hear about it by chance several months or several years later, and by that time the bodies of the poor stiffs are already part of the Osa mud. Their families forget about them and no one else cares; some of them never had any identity papers, were never inscribed in birth registers, never had a legal existence.

Gato's camp was very well organized – three individual beds separated by foliage. I slept on Chato's bed, but I wouldn't have anything to do with his blankets. El Gato's helper – or, rather, his valet – was a pure-blooded but simple-minded Indian who took care of the shack. He wasn't exactly a gourmet cook, but he did pretty well. The camp was kept supplied with a variety of food that Gato had delivered at regular intervals. There were several kinds of beans, some jerky, and even coconut oil and spices. The Indian often went hunting in the jungle and brought back fresh hearts of palm, bitter oranges, and cassava roots.

I spent several weeks with them. Of all the prospectors who worked in a team, El Gato was the best I had seen. He washed the gravel systematically and, following the bedrock, slowly went down the river. We worked every morning, no matter what the weather was

40

like. Armed with a miner's pickaxe, the Indian broke up all the agglomerations and separated the large rocks from the auriferous matter. He worked rhythmically, without any sign of fatigue. He never spoke and never stopped. Sometimes I thought that his brain had slowed down, like a badly oiled machine.

Gato was always at the canoa, lifting the stones and helping the current wash away the gravel so the gold could sink to the bottom. You could see from the rhythm of his movements that he knew what he was doing.

At about one o'clock the canoa was lifted out; there was never less than ten grams a day – about $150 for each of us – and every evening I got my share. It wasn't a hell of a lot, but it was regular; I figured I'd have a nice bit of capital at the end of a few weeks – and there was always the possibility of a big nugget showing up. After all, why not?

The afternoons were quiet. I often went off with the Indian to hunt in the forest. He had a .22 carbine whose little cough didn't make much noise. It was old and rusted, it had a crudely sculpted wooden stock, and it was made up of pieces cannibalized from several other carbines; despite this, his marksmanship surprised me. I never saw him miss a shot; and, though he'd always leave camp with three cartridges, the first was enough to assure our meat-supply. The other two were just in case. Those Indians who have carbines are always very good shots, because their poverty – not to mention the difficulty of getting cartridges – obliges them to hit the bull's-eye every time. Gato told me he'd seen the Indian hunt a jaguar and kill him with a single .22 shot. Most often we ran into pavos – a kind of turkey – toucans, or monkeys. Once we brought back a pizote, a sort of arboreal fox. Though it's not very big, it's fierce: I've seen one fight with three dogs and come out ahead.

The Indian also explained that there were many 'chanchos del monte', carnivorous peccaries that eat everything they run into, including oreros. One afternoon, as we were returning from a hunt, I heard the loud noise of cracking branches. The Indian motioned to me to climb a tree as quickly as I could, and the next minute a herd of 'chanchos del monte' appeared out of nowhere. The Indian, up in his tree, took aim, and – bang! bang! – killed the last two. I wanted to climb down, but he indicated that I was to wait until the others were farther away. I asked him why he was being so cautious.

'The chancho is dangerous,' he replied as he lifted one of them on to his shoulders, 'and he's not afraid of anything. If he sees you, he'll try to uproot the tree so he can eat you.'

41

I'd have liked to know more, but this intellectual effort had exhausted him. Gato gave me additional information.

'If you're a yard or more above the ground, you're pretty safe because they don't see you – they never lift their heads. If you ever hunt them, be sure not to shoot the first ones of the herd – they're the leaders and, if they die, the others won't budge and you could spend days up in your tree. I know what I'm talking about because it's happened to me. They're dangerous animals, and even the jaguar is afraid of them.'

'Let's hope they don't decide to visit us.'

Gato shrugged fatalistically. 'If they do, we've had it.'

Charming little pets.

The evenings were calm. El Gato, who'd spent a lot of time in the jungle, was full of stories – both real and phoney. Though he'd been in Costa Rica a long time, he was a Nicaraguan by birth and often spoke of his native country, but he never really explained why he'd left it. Like most of the men you run into on the peninsula, he'd probably been involved in some sort of shady business. He was intelligent, and more educated than most of the oreros, and he was crafty – probably a bit too much so; he'd teamed up with this Indian, who looked on him as a god and had been following him for years, entrusting his share of the gold to El Gato and listening to him like an open-mouthed child when he told his stories. The fact is that El Gato was a born storyteller and could go on for hours.

'I wasn't always a prospector, you know. I used to be a huaquero – I specialized in breaking into tombs. I don't do that any more because the spirits of the Indians don't like it.'

'I did pretty much the same thing in Linea Vieja, and I never found anything except some worthless pottery.'

'You didn't choose a good spot. In the Talamanca range, north of the peninsula, there were a lot of Indians, and so there are a lot of tombs. Almost all of them have gold, and there are treasures in the mountains.'

He told me the story of a Spaniard, known to all the huaqueros.

'This guy used to go to Talamanca, where there are still some tribes of savage Indians, and every time he'd come back with unusual gold artefacts – things like masks and large statues. The rumour was that he'd discovered a legendary city to which the Indians had fled to escape the Spaniards. One day, he didn't come back. He treated the Indians badly, and they must have killed him up there. Nobody ever found the place.'

Most of his stories were legends, or tall tales, but sometimes they were true. He also told me about the Chocuaco lagoon, somewhere in the middle of the peninsula.

'There's a super lode there, but a Tico called Barbaroja – a really tough and dangerous bastard – won't let anyone else near it.'

The days passed, each one like every other one. The gold production was steady, but something was eating at me; we only came up with very small stuff, and an occasional tiny nugget. This surprised me, because since we were working high up the river we should have found more – and bigger ones, like the ones he'd shown me in Carate. I began having doubts about Gato. I'd watch him out of the corner of my eye from time to time, but he worked barefoot and in shorts, so I couldn't see how he could be stealing. It bothered me, but I didn't want to confront him because that would put him on his guard.

One morning, as I was carefully bringing the conversation around to this, a guy leading a mule showed up.

At the sight of him, Gato howled with pleasure; practically out of his mind with joy, he dropped everything and ran over to give him a hug. The Indian watched them uneasily. As I came up to them, they were about to conclude a bargain.

'How much do you have left?'

'Two gallons. They're the last, but it's good guaro.'

'Sell me both of them.'

'No, I can only let you have a litre. I have to see some other people, and they pay me well.'

'Christ! Name your price, and I'll pay – but let me have all of it!'

He ran off and disappeared into the jungle, where he'd hidden a flask in which he kept his gold. I watched the guy as he unloaded two pichingas – plastic bottles, each containing three and a half litres. All I had to do was sniff, and I understood: he was selling bootleg guaro – rotten and very strong alcohol secretly distilled by the peninsula's peasants, who would toss in just about everything and then hype it up with 90 per cent alcohol. This stuff would kill your brain in no time.

When Gato returned with his flask, he was even more excited.

'Name your price, and I'll pay it.'

After some masterly bargaining by the seller, Gato weighed out forty grams of gold in exchange for the precious bottles. It was an insane price – about fifty times the real value of shit like that – but Gato couldn't have cared less; he was ready to sell father, mother, wife, children, and himself if need be, in order to get his hands on that guaro. Even before the seller had left, Gato was sitting on a rock, swallowing big gulps.

In two days he slurped up the seven litres all by himself, since

43

neither the Indian nor I drank any. Two days during which he screamed, vomited, tripped, and pissed all over himself – in short, the kind of binge you wouldn't have thought possible. The first bottle didn't last the day. He stumbled around the camp, knocking over just about everything, and I had to fight off his affectionate drunken assaults; finally he collapsed, but then he came to, took another big swallow, staggered, and collapsed again. He spent a good part of the following two days heaped in a corner, hugging his precious bottle to his chest, raving and singing. From time to time he seemed to come to a decision and resolutely get to his feet, but luckily he couldn't stay upright very long.

Except for a little panning, I didn't work those two days. I was waiting for it to be all over. In my experience those old drunkards had an unusual amount of resistance, but this one beat all.

The Indian never took his eyes off him; in a way that showed long experience, he kept picking him up and making sure that he didn't wander too far away. The second bottle was emptied during the third day, and after a final hiccup Gato sank into a coma. The Indian carried him to his bed as if he were a rag doll. I was curious to see what he'd be like when he finally woke up.

The next morning, looking pale and still dressed in his soiled clothes, he called to the Indian in a hoarse voice.

'I feel like shit. Go get me a bottle.'

He went back to sleep, and the Indian explained that after a drunk like that the only way he'd ever get on his feet again was to have some of the hair of the dog – but very little, only a few swallows, just to fight evil with evil. He'd go to Carate and buy a bottle.

I decided to go with him so I could learn the road. To get to Carate, he had to pass by Miguel's camp, and for once I was going to walk through the jungle without getting lost.

He started off at a run, but since my feet had callused over and were in pretty good shape I had no problem keeping up. With an eye to some future trip on my own, I borrowed his machete so I could blaze a trail by marking the trees. Three hours later we were at Miguel's: it's a lot faster to travel in a straight line! But I was exhausted when we arrived, and I decided to wait there with Miguel and his two women.

The Indian took off again at the same pace. I grabbed a supply of grass, since mine was almost gone. They were happy to see me, and Rosa said that I'd lost weight. The picture I painted of Gato soaked to the gills amused them, but they were saddened by the news of Chato's death. It was almost night when the Indian came back. How had he made the trip so quickly? He didn't even seem winded. I suggested we spend the night there.

'I've got to go. My master is sick and he needs me.'

'But it'll be pitch black in ten minutes, arsehole! How do you expect to find your way?'

He asked Miguel for a candle and made himself a lantern out of an old tin can with cut-outs on the side. Holding his improvised beacon, he waved goodbye and disappeared into the night. If he could do it, I could do it, I decided. I followed him.

Gato took a whole day to pull himself together. Seated on his bed, glass in hand, he took a few sips from time to time but otherwise never opened his mouth.

The next morning he was better and we went back to work.

I humped away alongside Gato for three weeks and put aside almost 110 grams of gold. Everything was gong fine, but I was a little uneasy because, even though I was eating pretty well, my strength was going, and I could feel I'd lost a lot of weight. In addition, I slept very badly because of the humidity and because even when it's well prepared a log bed is still uncomfortable.

On several occasions I heard Gato return from the river with the catiadora and quietly slip back into bed. Early one morning, before daylight, I saw him leave camp with the catiadora. I let him get a little way ahead, then got up and followed him. It was still not dawn. Though I couldn't see very well, I tried to walk quietly. Once I thought I'd lost him, but suddenly saw him crouched about ten yards from me, shitting in the pan. I didn't need a blueprint: the son of a bitch was swallowing some nuggets on the sly while we were working, then getting them back via his arsehole! I was furious. If anything makes me mad, it's somebody trying to hustle me – and, on top of everything else, the bastard was using the catiadora in which we cooked our rice! I felt like killing him. I quietly unholstered my revolver, but some instinct that had remained on the alert made him lift his head, and seeing me, gun in hand, he jumped to the side. The bullet hit the ground between his feet, and he ran off, his trousers around his ankles. That's what saved his hide, because I never fire at a man's back. I walked up to where he'd been, not to see what was in the catiadora – I already knew – but because in his panic Gato had forgotten his precious flask of gold. I hefted it. There were easily 250 grams, all in nuggets. While we were sharing the flakes and dust, this bastard was keeping the big stuff for himself! I was sorry I'd missed him.

The Indian was awake and terrified when he saw me return to the camp carrying the flask and holding my revolver. He'd heard the shot and was convinced that I had killed Gato and that he was next.

'Don't be afraid. I didn't kill Gato. But tell him he was lucky. He'd better not let me see him again, and he'd better be sure that he never crosses my path – because next time I won't miss.'

'Sí, señor.'

'And don't stay with him because he'll never give you a centavo.'

'Sí, señor.'

The poor dope couldn't say anything else. Obviously, he was unable to understand what had happened, and my words were too complicated for his idiot brain to take in. He just stared at me, completely bewildered, convinced that I'd killed his god.

I'd had enough of the place, but before leaving I took his gun, broke the stock against one of the posts of the shack, and tossed him a twelve-gram nugget. It fell at his feet, but he didn't pick it up. Assuming his head didn't burst, it would probably take a few days before he began to understand what had happened. I left him to his brooding and started for Carate.

I'd calmed down, and soon I was laughing to myself at the memory of Gato scampering off, with his arse all shitty. When all was said and done, it hadn't worked out too badly for me. His cheating had made it possible for me to accumulate over 350 grams of gold, since I'd poured my original share into the flask. I'd been walking for about an hour when I suddenly got dizzy. In a few minutes I was soaked in sweat and my legs had turned to rubber. I had to sit down. My head was spinning, and I couldn't see straight. I lost consciousness and spent the rest of the day and that night stretched out on the ground, shivering. I was unable to stand, and the slightest movement was torture. I was burning up, in a sweat, and my teeth were chattering. In the morning, I felt a little better, and I slowly got under way again. Every step was an effort, and I was so dizzy I had to lean against the trees. And that's the state I was in when I got to Miguel's that evening after following the trail I'd blazed previously.

'What's the matter with you, Frenchie?' Miguel asked.

I couldn't talk. I wanted only one thing – to lie down. After hiding my gold under the leaves of the mattress, I collapsed on the bed. I trusted Miguel and Rosa, but Slutbucket didn't inspire much confidence.

Rosa, glad to see me but worried about my health, took off my sweat-soaked shirt and put several blankets on me before beginning to massage my arms and legs. For two days, while the crisis was at its height, I was delirious.

One morning, Rosa, who'd spent hours looking after me, asked: 'Who's Diane? The woman you love?'

I nodded.

46

'When you're delirious, you keep calling her name.'

It was true I was thinking about Diane a lot. I wanted badly to see her again.

Miguel wasn't worried. So far as he was concerned, all sicknesses were *mal de vientre* – indigestion – and you just had to wait for them to go away. Nevertheless, my arms were getting paralysed, and I did everything in slow motion. I couldn't swallow, and when I did I'd vomit up everything, even liquids. I sweated like the damned, and my urine was dark and foul-smelling. I recognized the symptoms of malaria, which I'd been suffering from on and off for over ten years, but this attack seemed more severe than the others I'd had.

On the morning of the third day I wasn't any better, and I was convinced that if I stayed there I'd die. I determined to try to get to Carate. The effort just to get up made my head spin, and I vomited bile. I could imagine the torture awaiting me. Kind-hearted Rosa offered to come with me but, given the speed at which she moved, she wouldn't be very useful.

It was hell – and it went on for two days. Every step hurt; I walked slowly, incapable of doing otherwise. I had to crawl up the smallest hill on all fours, constantly stopping to rest. At the first descent, my own weight dragged me downhill and I went spinning all the way to the river, where I was knocked half-unconscious and for a long time lay stretched out in the mud, my feet in the water, unable to get up. I hurt just about everywhere, and I kept losing consciousness. The first rays of the sun brought me to life and gave me strength enough to start off again. My shirt had long since disintegrated into rags, and I'd attached the remnants of my shorts with my holster straps – but despite all my falls I'd managed to hold on to my precious flask . . . At about noon the foliage became thin enough for me to be able to glimpse the beach, and I wanted to shout 'Victory'. But my suffering wasn't over yet.

I made my way along the beach in short stages. I'd set a goal – a coconut-tree, a big rock, a bush – a hundred yards away and force myself to reach it, going those short distances without once taking my eyes off the landmark, then stretching out to recoup my strength and begin all over again – a coconut-tree, a rock, a coconut-tree. Each stage was a victory that gave me the strength for the next one, but the rest periods became longer and longer. I forced myself to start again, because if I stopped too long I'd remain nailed to the spot. I was often tempted to give up, but the will to see it through and my desire to be with Diane again kept me going. Finally, I reached Carate.

*　　*　　*

Saltarana didn't recognize me. I hadn't shaved in five weeks, and I was dirty, thin, feverish-looking. He went for Mr Bill.

The Canadian took me to his place. Worried by my condition, he offered to send me to San José in the company plane the very next day.

In the morning I collected the stuff I'd left at Saltarana's. My jeans floated around my legs, and I had a hell of a time getting my leather boots on. I shaved painfully and studied my face in the mirror. No wonder Saltarana was surprised: I looked like a corpse. I gave him my revolver.

I boarded while Fucking looked on mockingly. The cocksucker was pleased to see me like that.

In San José a small company truck picked us up at the airport and dropped us at the main square, where the Canadians had their office – about fifty yards from the Hotel America. The last few yards seemed endless, and it took a long time for me to cross them. Surprised to see me in this state, the owner helped me up the stairs leading to the reception-desk. There I found a message from Diane telling me where to reach her.

I had the desk clerk call for me.

'Hello?'

'Hi, darling.'

'Where are you?'

'In San José, kid. Listen, don't ask questions – I'm not up to them. Take a taxi and come get me at the America. Hurry, baby.'

I hung up. Those few words had exhausted me, but I was happy. I was going to see Diane again.

A few minutes later she was there. Her smile disappeared as soon as she saw me.

'Darling, what's happened?'

'I've had malaria. Nothing serious, but I need to rest.'

Her beautiful green eyes were looking for the man she had left only five weeks earlier. She wanted to throw herself into my arms, but I held her away because I was filthy and I stank.

In the taxi that took us to Jean-Paul's place, huddled against me, she inspected me carefully, and I could see that she could hardly keep from crying. When we got there she helped me out of the cab, then made me sit down in an armchair, kissed my forehead, and went off to run a bath. On her return, she gently undressed me and carefully removed my boots from my painfully swollen feet.

Half an hour later I was clean and looked something like a human being again. Wrapped in a bathrobe, I drank some tea as Diane sat facing me and watched. There was an awkwardness between us because we hadn't the courage to talk about my illness. She'd noticed how thin I was while I was bathing, but could she even begin to imagine how sick I felt? I gave her the flask of gold and was getting ready to tell her about Gato when I felt a new attack coming on, and I began to shake so hard that I had to put down the cup.

'Come and lie down,' said Diane.

'Don't worry, it's just an attack of malaria. No problem.'

Then Jean-Paul showed up, and he was shocked, too. Lying under a heap of blankets, I must have looked even thinner. Signalling to Diane, he took her aside; he didn't quite dare to ask any questions with me looking on, but like many homosexuals he had a deadly fear of illness.

He went for a doctor, a friend of his, who lived right across the way. He was a nice guy who took my temperature and listened to my heart. He concluded that I had a fever brought on by infection, and wanted to have me hospitalized immediately, but I refused. I'd already had some experience with Third World hospitals in Africa, Asia and South America, and I had no desire ever to set foot in them again. I knew what was wrong with me, and I could take care of myself; in the hospital they'd finish me off.

'You're not being reasonable,' he said. 'You need round-the-clock care, and we have to run some tests to identify the virus. It might be contagious, and you have no right to refuse hospitalization.'

Eventually, I was convinced – not by the good doctor's sensible explanation but by Diane's eyes begging me to agree.

At the Calderón Guardia Hospital the doctor took care of the formalities while I said goodbye to Diane. Lying on a stretcher, my hands in hers, I tried to comfort her. Her beautiful face was tear-stained, and once again I was aware of how much I loved her. Yet no sooner had I returned to her than we were separated again. It hurt like hell.

'Don't worry. I'll pull through.'

The doctor was speaking to one of his colleagues, and I could see in the eyes of the attendants who came for me that they already considered me a goner. So far as they were concerned, I was a dead man on reprieve. They put me on a wheeled bed, and Diane, weeping uncontrollably, watched me being rolled away. I waved one last time before she disappeared from sight.

One of the two attendants gave me an antispasmodic shot to relax me – the only treatment I got during ten days of hospitalization. While a young intern filled in my chart, I was weighed: not quite 137 pounds. I'd lost over sixty pounds in five weeks!

I was put in a private room across from one that was large, dark and silent. In the evening a chubby little nurse brought me dinner; I swallowed a few mouthfuls and immediately vomited them up. When she gave me some tranquillizers and sleeping-pills I asked for more, because I knew that my body, accustomed to a lot of drugs, would be able to resist soporifics. Well loaded with tranquillizers, I fell asleep to the sound of her babble.

The next day she woke me for lunch. She was nice, but a constant talker. Pleased to have a foreigner at her mercy, she bombarded me with questions about Osa and Paris. I stopped listening after a few minutes because I became aware of a strange noise coming from the room across the way – a sort of amplified rattle.

Interrupting her flood of words, I asked: 'Who's making that noise?'

With a big smile, she opened the door of the other room. There were a dozen dying patients lying in a dozen beds surmounted by crucifixes. From one of those beds came the rattle that had intrigued me – a gasping breath. It was the anteroom to death, the room into which they put patients who weren't expected to live.

Now I understood why I wasn't in a ward in the other wing of the hospital where most of the patients were: the cocksuckers had put me here to save themselves some trouble. I was lucky they hadn't shoved me in with those other poor bastards. Well, maybe I'd had it, but one thing was for sure – I wasn't going to croak here. A bullet in my brain would be a better solution. The next night I slept very little; just as I'd feared, the sleeping-pills weren't strong enough. I thought about Diane, about our dead son, about all the bad luck that had stuck to us for more than two years. Diane had been born to be happy, but life had dealt her blow after blow.

I was lost in my thoughts when I heard some noise in the corridor. I was also immediately aware that the old man's gasping had stopped. Out of curiosity, I got out of bed.

The old man had kicked off, and was surrounded by two attendants who were removing his pyjama bottoms as they chatted. Then, still talking, with a routine gesture they pressed down on his belly to empty his bowels and – quite casually despite the odour – wrapped him in a sheet and tossed him on to a trolley. And – *wham*! A present for the worms. There was no humanity, no sign of feeling in their gestures; probably desensitized by the hundreds of people they must have packaged that way, the two morticians worked without a hint of emotion.

But what shocked me the most were the crosses over the beds. Poor bastards! As soon as that cruddy cross was raised over their heads they'd had it. They were denied the right to a possible miracle. 'OK, buddy, here's your cross. Now hurry up and die.' Later some hypo-

crite in a cassock would shed a crocodile tear over their 'exemplary'
lives. I went back to my room more determined than ever to get out of
there alive.

The next morning, after a breakfast I was finally able to keep down, I
was visited by the priest. The skunk came right to the point.
'My son, do you speak Spanish?'
I didn't answer.
'Are you ready to appear before your maker?'
He, too, had already given me up for lost. I quickly interrupted him.
'Listen, you son of a bitch, I've fucked six nuns and a mother
superior, I've fornicated, pissed and shit in churches, but I've never
fucked a priest in the arse. Since I don't much care for your face, I'll
make do with a blow job, and maybe that will open the gates of
paradise to me.'
The skunk drew himself up, offended.
'My son, you're delirious!'
'Beat it, bastard, you stink.'
I picked up one of my boots and aimed for his face, but my action
had no force or speed; I barely got his shoulder. Inspired by rage, I got
up to finish him off, but he retreated to the door, making a quick sign
of the cross which I just about managed to duck. He disappeared
while I was searching for something else to throw. I felt pleased at
having got the rotten bastard to take to his heels. I'd beaten the devil.
I don't give a fuck about religion, and it's never bothered me. I know
that the weak need something to grab on to, a carrot to make up for
the stick. Suffer, my brother, shut your trap and work, your place in
paradise is certain . . . It's not for me.
But it's those jackals in cassocks that I hate. Except for half a dozen
or so missionaries I'd run into during my travels, I had found nothing
but hypocrites, exploiters and profiteers – especially in underdeveloped countries, where the credulity of the masses was greater than
elsewhere. In drought-stricken Africa, while kids were dying of
hunger and dropping like flies, I've seen priests traffic with food –
exchange a bowl of rice for favours from starving kids. While people
were dying all around them, those modern priests, safe inside their
mission, stuffed themselves, guzzled, and fucked like rabbits. And
while they did all this they went on saying mass and preaching
abnegation and repentance.
Word of my encounter with the priest spread, and I became popular
in my wing of the hospital. Patients and interns came to see 'el
frances', the insane prospector. The doctor brought me a chess set. He
worked in another department, but he'd slip away whenever he could

51

to check on me and play a game of chess. A practising Catholic, he couldn't understand my behaviour towards the skunk, and we had many long theological discussions. He was a good guy, and I owe him for what he did for me there.

I still wasn't getting any treatment, but every day the vampires would take a blood specimen for analysis. At this point, however, I was able to keep my food down and had begun to eat regularly, so I knew I was going to make it.

Every evening I'd play chess with a little old man, a former professor. A cardiac case, hospitalized for two months, he knew that for all practical purposes he was a dead man. He was nice, but his story was familiar: married when he was very young, he was the father of two children and had worked hard all his life. Though a fervent Catholic, he was scared shitless by death. His wife had always cheated on him and had already forgotten his existence; his kids never came to see him, and he was left to die all alone in the hospital. One day he started crying and complaining about his fate, but I cut him short.

'Listen, Prof, you've had the life you chose, so don't expect me to feel sorry for you.'

I don't like people who whine.

That evening he didn't show up for our chess game, and later I went looking for him; he'd been put in the dead men's room. He was unconscious, and I knew it was all over for him. Death had check-mated him before I could.

In the morning, feeling more depressed than usual, I saw the skunk giving him extreme unction. He looked like a vulture keeping an eye on his dinner. I couldn't stand it; I grabbed a water-pitcher and tossed it at him with a curse. Unfortunately, I still wasn't co-ordinating very well, and it was the Prof who caught it. The priest left on the run. From the look on the attendants' faces, I could see that I'd probably gone too far. They might very well decide I was a lunatic!

I was more than a little uneasy when the director came and said: 'I don't know how they do things in French hospitals, but here in Costa Rica we respect the dying. You're discharged as of this afternoon.'

The head nurse, when she gave me my clothes, made me promise to return for a check-up. I agreed, but I knew I'd never come back. So far as I was concerned, it was all over, I was cured; the only thing that bothered me was a persistent headache. I phoned Diane and asked her to come and get me.

Half an hour later I was outside. I'd survived one more time. But for how long?

Part Two

TWO

Y<small>OU NEVER REALLY APPRECIATE</small> the small things in life until you're deprived of them, so we spent the following four weeks in San José in pursuit of agreeable moments, small joys, the pleasures of the city.

When I left the hospital we moved into the Grand Hotel of Costa Rica, a luxurious spot right in the centre of San José: after so much filth and discomfort I needed cleanliness and a normal life.

We'd sold the gold very quickly, without handling it, without even weighing it. The Second Avenue jeweller at whose place we'd carried out the transaction did all that for us: he didn't understand our reluctance to touch the gold but, then, he didn't know the tortuous path along which it had travelled!

When I finally went out into the hot sun of the capital I had $3800 in my pocket.

Though it's neither as clean nor as lively as a European capital, San José offers more pleasures than any other city in Central America. While its streets are laid out and numbered like those in American cities, it retains a Latin flavour. Noisy and animated during the day, it's deserted at night; it's not the capital of vice or violence, and it's not for those who want danger and thrills. Compared with its neighbours – Managua or Panama City – it deserves its reputation as 'the Switzerland of Central America'. You can find just about everything in San José, but only in small doses. The whores are in bed by three in the morning, the bars that are open twenty-four hours a day can be counted on the fingers of one hand, and in the Zona Roja, the red-light district, the worst that can happen to you is to be jolted by some drunk coming out of a crummy bar. It's a peasants' capital, and there's an agreeable if surprising sense of security and calm when you arrive from one of the neighbouring countries. That suited me

55

fine, since I'd had my share of excitement and needed some peace and quiet.

Diane and I celebrated our reunion physically, and no pleasure could compare with having her in my arms again. We spent entire days in the room, far from the world.

I should have stopped smoking, but I couldn't.

Diane felt well. She appreciated this moment of calm, when I was at her side and far from the dangers of Osa. Without her telling me, I knew that she'd rather not go back there, that she'd rather live a city life. Jean-Paul mentioned that his American neighbour, who'd been in the country a long time, was selling his nightclub. The price was right and the club well located – right opposite the hotel. If it were fixed up, it would be a good deal. Diane was interested, but I wasn't.

I'd run a few nighclubs – the first, at the age of eighteen, in Argentina, then two others in Toronto when I was twenty-one. But I didn't like cities any more, and the possibilities of a nightclub were limited. The fact is I was convinced that Osa was in the cards for me. I hadn't done all that suffering, spent weeks learning about gold, put up with the stupidity of the oreros just to let it all drop now. For the moment, I was still convalescing, but my inactivity was already bothering me, and I wanted to find something to do.

So I began to wander around San José in search of some kind of deal, and I quickly found four interesting places to hang out. First, the Manolo, a centrally located combination bar and cafeteria that attracted almost all the tourists, which meant you could make some interesting connections. Then the Soda Palace, the city's oldest bar and always a lively spot. Most of the European residents of Costa Rica went there; generally speaking, they were older people who knew the possibilities offered by the country since they all lived on more or less legal little deals and business arrangements.

The only café with a terrace in all San José, the bar of the Grand Hotel, was also one of the best spots in town. The gringo investors generally stayed at the hotel, and a lot of big deals – the sale of anything from real estate to cargos of arms or drugs – were arranged between dessert and coffee. Finally, there was the Esmeralda, the meeting-place for dealers in pre-Columbian art, whom I'd met while trying to sell my pots on my first trip through town.

It was Diane who turned up the kind of deal I was hoping for when she went to the French embassy to pick up our mail. Because of our previous business with the artefact, she was well known there, and a member of the embassy staff asked her to get in touch with a friend of his, also a government employee but at the Italian embassy. (I won't mention the names of those corrupt officials.) The next day, I went there and spoke to a rather interesting couple.

'What did they want?' Diane asked when I got back.

'I think there may be something here for us. The little chisellers want to buy half a kilo of pre-Columbian gold, in the form of easily transportable pieces. Of course they say they're collectors, but I don't believe them. They don't want to pay more than forty dollars for a gram of antiquarian gold.'

'What do they want for that price?'

'Phonies, obviously. But they have to be perfect imitations. These people are too cautious to come right out with it but, given the price they want to pay, they know they can't get the real thing. It would be up to me to find good imitations.'

'You think you can do that here?'

'Wherever there's a strong market for the real thing, phonies inevitably turn up. I've seen counterfeiters of pre-Columbian art in Peru, Ecuador and Colombia, and there must be some here. I'll scout around – it'll keep me busy.'

The Esmeralda is one of the few bars open day and night. In the evening it's the meeting-place for the mariachis, those Mexican singers that you can recognize by their big sombreros, their tight trousers with triple rows of brass buttons on the sides, and their ugly pusses. During the day it's the headquarters for dealers in pre-Columbian art.

You might think they'd look suspicious, but you'd be wrong: they're all nice old guys who look like respectable heads of families – but deep down in their pockets are gold and jade artefacts just waiting for a customer. Only one of them tried to give himself an image by wearing black glasses and patent-leather hair. He looked like a Marseilles pimp from the fifties.

As soon as I sat down in this joint I ran into an old friend, Carlos Finca. A short, chubby and jovial man of about fifty, he was always trying to palm off valueless items on me at an exorbitant price.

'Listen, Carlos, I've got a buyer for some little gold huacas. . . .'

I hadn't even finished my sentence before he was emptying the contents of his pockets on the table – bits of pottery, jade, and worthless pieces of gold. I could already foresee the moment when he'd throw in his watch and his socks and make me a price for the lot.

'No, Carlos, that's not what I'm interested in. I want to buy half a kilo of gold figurines. Small things if possible, and at no more than twenty-five dollars a gram. There'll be a good commission in it for you if you can help me. Classy imitations will be fine.'

At the word 'imitations' he played indignant. He was being cautious, and I could understand why: he was only a go-between, and if he revealed his sources he ran the risk of being cut out of the deal. The promise of a nice percentage was what made him decide to help me.

I intended to let him stew a while. If, as I suspected, there was a group of counterfeiters, my offer to buy should smoke them out.

Carlos had finally been able to get some information. When we got to the Esmeralda he still wasn't there, and we were visited by a few other sellers. The rumour had got around that I was in 'the business', so they came to try their luck. We were shown some very expensive but not very impressive stuff. There'd been too many middlemen taking a cut along the way.

I kidded around with one of the sellers for a while.

'Look, Frenchie, it's beautiful, isn't it?'

'Very, very beautiful.'

'It's yours for five thousand colones. A special price, just for you.'

'Actually, that's not expensive at all.'

'Then, you'll buy it?' he asked, his eyes gleaming with hope.

'No.'

I always got a kick out of that kind of dumb dialogue. When the arseholes pushed their trinkets a little too insistently, Diane would tell them their stuff was ugly, and that would put an end to the discussion.

Fortunately, Carlos Finca came looking for us. He'd been able to contact several people, and we went off to visit Colman, boss of the Casa del Cacique on Second Avenue; Big Sergio, the proprietor of a gold-buying shop; the director of the Pre-Columbian Gallery; and Julio Nargas, who had a currency-exchange place on Central Avenue.

I couldn't come to any agreement because they all kept insisting that their things were real – and therefore expensive. They probably didn't run into many foreigners looking for imitations. Professional con men, it never occurred to them to sell phoney stuff as phoney stuff; to do business without lying went against their code of honour. Too bad. I was getting a headache, so I called a halt to these useless discussions. If those little chisellers at the embassy phoned, I'd tell them they'd have to find their own sources! In any case, I was still convalescing and didn't feel like knocking myself out.

That was pretty much my state of mind when old Carlos showed up at the hotel again.

'Frenchie, Chocho wants to see you. Your proposition interests him.'

I didn't really believe it, but I had nothing to lose and went to meet him. And that's how I got to know Chocho Verde, the biggest counterfeiter in Costa Rica.

Since it might sound repetitive if I say that he was another fat guy, let's just say that down here prosperity rhymes with obesity; a big belly is an outward sign of wealth, just as in Asia.

Chocho Verde was smiling. He was more intelligent than his colleagues: he came right to the point.

'Hi, Frenchie. Carlos told me what you're looking for. At that price I can only offer you phonies.'

Finally, someone who understood.

'OK, but the gold has to be better than twenty carats, and they have to be good imitations that can pass in Europe.'

'Are you going to sell them over there?'

'No, I've got an order. But I think my buyer is going to trade them in Europe.'

'OK. I'll show you a few things from my factory. Unfortunately, my production is limited because the work has to be done carefully. Still, I pretty much cover San José.'

'I've seen Julio Nargas and the others, and they kept talking about authentic pieces.'

'I supply them,' he said with a big smile. 'If they've ever got their hands on even one authentic piece, it's been by accident. Let me explain. When huacas are found, they don't remain on the local market for long: either they're shipped to the United States, or they find their way to me. These original pieces serve as models. We use the same method as the Indians – the lost wax process. If you'd like, I can show you a few of my things in the Gold Museum here. There are also some in American and European museums, and I'm pretty proud of them! To tell the truth, I've even bought back some items I thought were authentic, and they turned out to be stuff I'd manufactured years earlier.'

'Are the experts as bad as that?'

'There are no real experts in pre-Columbian gold. I've managed to pull the wool over the eyes of the guy who claims to be the best of them. His name is Noli and he lives in New York. When I send him an important lot, about a tenth of them are real – and half of the time the arsehole sends the real ones back to me because he thinks they're imitations! As for local experts, there's no one – except for old Carlos Holtzer, who's beginning to go blind.'

Fat Chocho struck me as a boaster, but his reproductions were very good. It wasn't easy to convince him to sell me his stuff at twenty-five dollars a gram, but finally, after a very long discussion, we came to an agreement. I was to pay him $12,500 – $7000 up front as a deposit, and $5500 after the sale.

It would be a good deal, but I was in a bind. Where could I find the deposit money? All I had left of the Osa gold was two thousand dollars. I couldn't very well bring my customers to Chocho's place; first of all, they wanted to remain anonymous and, second, I knew the old fox would try to deal with them directly. Some French-speaking tourists I met at Manolo's helped solve my problem.

I should have mentioned that a few days earlier I had met some guys at the Esmeralda. They liked my boots, and we got to talking. Two of them were Canadians, and there were also a North African Jew and a Spanish Basque. Two days after my meeting with Chocho, I again ran into the North African, David, and the Basque, Roberto, who asked me how he could make some quick cash. David, the younger of the two, was a nice enough guy who had picked up street sense in Paris. Roberto was cleverer, but nowhere near as nice: he was a little thug. They'd come to the right man. I was about to see how much guts they had.

'You want to make a quick thousand dollars?'

'Sure,' said Roberto. 'What do we have to do?'

'I've got a deal going, but I'm short of cash. I need a loan of five thousand bucks for a few hours. If you've got that much, I can give you a thousand in interest.'

They glanced at each other. David was enthusiastic, but Roberto was suspicious.

'What kind of guarantee do we have? What's your deal? After all, we don't really know you.'

The questions were justified, but they annoyed me. I didn't like the big Basque.

'Look, buddy, I have no guarantees for you. You asked me how to turn a quick buck and I told you. As for the deal, it's just a sale of some pre-Columbian stuff.'

At this point David intervened.

'Don't get your back up, Juan Carlos. Roberto is worried about the dough. We've got the five thousand, but that's our entire stake. We had to work some shady deals with traveller's cheques to get that much together, and we took a lot of risks.'

'If it'll make you feel any better, I can do it all at the America Hotel in a room right next to your own. That way you can keep an eye on your precious dough. But that's the best I can do.'

'I'll buy that,' said David.

Roberto was less enthusiastic, but eventually he agreed.

60

The next day I concluded the deal with the Italian, who was beginning to get impatient. The funny thing about it was that he thought he was remaining anonymous, while in fact he was being spied on from every corner: on the one hand, there was Chocho's lieutenant, who'd been ordered to keep an eye on me and was doing sentry duty in the lobby; and, on the other, there were my two clowns. At the end of an hour the Italian left with five hundred grams of gold artefacts – eagles, frogs and Indian chiefs – all of them excellent reproductions and sold as such.

After everyone had been paid off, I had a profit of six thousand dollars. It wasn't exactly El Dorado, but it would give me enough to return to Osa and begin buying and selling. I decided to complete my convalescence there because I didn't want to spend my capital in San José.

That same evening David and Roberto invited us to a restaurant so that we could celebrate. During dinner I told them about Osa and about my plans. They quickly got excited and asked if they could come with me. Like the good opportunist he was, Roberto suggested he could put his dough at my disposition in a sort of joint venture. They were so eager that, for reasons I'll never understand, I made the mistake of agreeing. They saw it as a little diversion, something to remember with pleasure in their later years, and if things turned out badly they could always go home to Papa and Mama. For me, living by my wits was a life-style, and the least mistake could be tragic. There's no such thing as unemployment benefit for people who do my kind of work.

Maybe that fucking headache kept me from thinking straight, or maybe I was just feeling soft towards them because they'd helped me out – but, whatever the reason, I agreed to take them on.

The visas of all four of us were about to expire, and we had to leave the country. The simplest thing would be to take the plane to San Andres, a small Colombian island about an hour by air from San José. We decided to do that the following day.

When we were alone that evening, Diane, somewhat uneasy, asked me: 'Why do you want to get mixed up with these young kids? Dave's all right, but he isn't really on the ball. And Roberto's just a little thug who doesn't exactly inspire confidence. He's a user and a hypocrite.'

'OK, I know they're not exactly top-notch recruits, but after the favour they did me I just couldn't refuse. If they get in the way, we can always split.'

'It would be better if we split right now.'

'Look, baby, I know you'd rather be alone with me, but what's done is done. I gave my word, and I won't go back on it. Let's see what happens.'

Even now, the only way I can explain my mistake is to say I was still sick.

The stay in San Andres did us good. I knew that in a little while we'd be back in the muck of Osa, and the time we spent in this resort was pleasant: the beach in the afternoon, the casino in the evening, and coke all day long.

For one of the few times in my life I watched my step in the casino. I knew there was another deal in the offing, so I didn't want to take any risks. The fact is it's inactivity that makes me gamble; as soon as I feel bored, I find myself at the green-baize tables and then there's trouble. The last two years had been terrible: the casinos in Macao, Vegas and Panama had cleaned me out of about $150,000 – all I had.

Diane pointed out to me that our croupier was keeping the big bills instead of putting them into the till. He was very skilful and could deal out an entire deck of cards with the note folded in the palm of his hand. He knew that we'd caught on to his little trick and he discreetly augmented our winnings; he must have paid off the guy supervising the table. Roberto, excited by the coke and the gambling, his head filled with the idea of his coming trip to Osa, wanted to put the bite on him. Poor little European punk, thinking he could stand up to those Colombians! When I refused, he cooled off. He wanted to play tough guy, but he hadn't quite lost his head and preferred to take advantage of the protection I could offer. Definitely a less than top-notch recruit.

We got back to San José without running into any trouble, and when we got there our buddy at the French embassy gave me a magnificent present – a chrome-plated .357 Magnum – to thank me for helping his friends in the Italian embassy. It was secondhand, but a beautiful piece none the less.

Once we'd made a few purchases, we took the plane to Golfito. Because there was some kind of trouble there, we had to land in Coto 47, a little banana depot about twenty-fives miles away; from there we rented a taxi-van.

An innocent-looking little Tico asked if he could come along. When we got to Golfito, the taxi was stopped by demonstrators blocking the streets. I had to hire a lighter to take us to *China*, with the silent Tico still in tow. The trip to Puerto Jiménez was uneventful. Dave and the Basque were excited by the proximity of adventure, but I was exhausted by the events of the day and spent the time resting in the front of the ship in the company of Diane. Before I fell asleep, it occurred to me that I still didn't have any definite plans about how to proceeed in Osa – but we'd see when we got there.

As soon as we docked in Jiménez, all of us went to Jeremy's bar, the Rancho de Oro. There I found Wayne, still sitting at a table covered with beer-cans. He didn't seem to have moved since the last time. I was glad to see him, and he said he'd heard about my sickness. The Ticos tend to exaggerate, so he was surprised to see me alive.

'I thought you were dead. What happened?'

I told him about Carate and Madrigal. The story about Gato, whom he knew quite well, made him laugh until tears rolled down his cheeks.

'Is that your team?' he asked, pointing to Roberto and Dave.

'Not really. They're two tourists who want a few thrills and are going into the mountains with me. We got some money together, and I plan to make it work for me by buying gold and reselling it in Panama.'

'Where do you think you'll go?'

'I'm not sure yet.'

'I'd try Cerro de Oro. A lot of gold comes from there.'

'Is it far?'

I still hadn't seen a map of the Osa peninsula, and it was probably time for me to buy one.

'You follow the route that leads north, the one that crosses the Tigre river, then you go on till you reach the landing-field at Las Palmas. After that, you'd better ask, because you have to go on from there along small trails.'

'Is there a plane that goes there?'

'You can rent one. But it's not far, and you'd be better off with a truck.'

At this point the little Tico who'd been with us in the taxi came over and asked if he could join us. He was small, fat and dark-skinned, and he proudly sported a ridiculous little musketeer's beard. But his eyes had a certain vivacity. I stopped Roberto from sending him packing and invited him to sit down.

'My name is Manuel Sanchez Riviera,' he said, shaking hands. 'I was listening to you. I'm also here to buy gold, and I can see that you know the area. If we go to Las Palmas together, we can share expenses, and once we're there each of us can buy on his own. That way we'll cut down the risks.'

He struck me as pretty smart. In addition, the presence of a Tico in the group seemed a good idea. Anyway, since I'd been dumb enough to take on the other two would-be cowboys, why not add this Sancho Panza to the team?

'OK. I intend to leave for Las Palmas by plane tomorrow morning. If you want to come along, you're welcome.'

While Sancho was busy phoning Golfito to arrange for a plane, Roberto came over to me.

'Why are you taking on this turkey? There are enough of us without him.'

'Listen, I'm the one who makes the decisions. Either keep your mouth shut, or take your money and beat it.'

'Don't get angry, Juan Carlos, I was just asking!'

Roberto is the kind you have to keep a tight rein on if you don't want him to get out of hand. The venal side of the big Basque was as nasty as the eager-little-boy side of Dave was appealing.

The next morning we were having a big breakfast when the pilot of the rented plane came searching for us. He didn't look like much. Small and pot-bellied, he wore a cap that was way too big for him and made him look really dumb. Still, you can't tell anything from looks, and he was probably a good pilot.

To my great surprise, we hadn't been in the air five minutes before the plane started down.

Thinking there was a problem, I asked: 'What's up, friend?'

'Nothing. We're here.'

I had just enough time to give him a big whack on the cap – temporarily blinding him – before we landed, all of us laughing.

I paid him and added a hefty tip by way of apology for my little joke – but mostly so he could buy a smaller cap. I made him promise to come for us in three days.

We were loaded down, so I sent Dave and the big fellow to Las Palmas for a taxi.

While they were gone, Sancho proudly showed me the weapon he'd kept hidden in his belt. It was a little .22, a toy for a kid. The sight of my .357 Magnum gave him a terrible complex – the poor bastard had been so proud of his rod!

Las Palmas, the last village before the mountains, consisted of five or six houses and the café we went into. The owner, eager to be of service, hurried to make us some coffee. His name was Alfredo, and he confirmed that the oreros were at Cerro de Oro, about four hours away on horseback. It was too late to make a round trip that day, but I learned that there was a small camp about an hour and a half away up the Rincón river. Alfredo, who seemed to like our money, agreed to rent me some horses and even suggested putting us up for the night.

We went up to the camp, but there weren't many people there and we bought only about thirty grams of gold. I'd made the trip mostly so we could get right back into action, but when it came to action it was Sancho who saw most of it. The river was swollen, and you had to be careful crossing it. On the return trip, as he went up the bank his horse slipped and both of them fell into the water and were immediately swept away by the current. Completely panicked, Sancho spun around in the whirlpools and screamed bloody murder. We fished him out when he got caught on some branches. He was half-naked and had lost his boots.

'My sack, my sack,' he shouted. 'All my money is attached to the saddle.'

There was a moment of panic, but luckily his horse had managed to free himself from the current and climb up the bank. The saddle was upside down, but the sack was still attached to it. Dave, who'd gone to get the animal, told me that Sancho's wallet was filled – and with nothing but thousand-colon banknotes.

After this incident we went back to Alfredo's place. I'd decided to settle in there: I preferred to spend eight hours a day on horseback rather than live in the mud.

Alfredo was a little surprised to find that he was suddenly in the hotel business, but he didn't make too much of a fuss about moving his stuff so that he, his wife and his kids were all crammed into a small room and the bedroom was free for Diane and me. After all, he had to take good care of his first customers. The others in our group bedded down wherever they could in the common room. I could see that Roberto didn't care for that and would have liked to get special treatment, too, but he was afraid to shoot off his mouth.

That night I realized I'd been right about Sancho: he'd told Alfredo that I was very rich, that I was going to buy up a storm, and that he'd better see to it I was treated right. He expressed himself with the kind of cultivated ease that made a big impression on peasants, and in the blink of an eye he had his prey in the palm of his hand. He was a cheat, but crafty and quick. His dumpy physique made you think he was a fool, but it wasn't true; his only weak point was that he was easily frightened, and that was why he'd instinctively put himself under my protection.

Unlike the other two, who played at being cowboys, and teased him mercilessly, he was a valuable member of the team. We soon came to a kind of understanding: I appreciated his quick intelligence and his usefulness, and he felt safe with me; he liked the way I had taken over the place. I continued to put on an act for Alfredo and kept spending freely to shore up my image. When I decided, later in the evening, that we needed fresh horses for the next day, no one was enthusiastic about venturing out into the night, the mud and the never-ending rain; but Carlito, the proprietor's son, a sturdy simpleton, was eager enough when I offered him two hundred colones.

I spent a good night, nice and cosy. At dawn Alfredo, helped by his better half, brought me breakfast in bed. Agreeably surprised, I complimented him, and he blushed with pleasure. He had obviously taken his new profession to heart. Outside, the weather was lousy, still raining every bit as hard.

A last kiss for Diane, and I left. We had been brought three horses and a little mule. My horse, the strongest, was already saddled and waited in the shed. I watched my buddies artfully manoeuvring to avoid the mule. Eventually it was Sancho, not quite as fast or maybe just a little more timid, who found himself perched on the beast. He looked as funny as hell trotting alongside us, and everybody began to laugh – but we were going to learn that he was the lucky one.

The young fellow who'd rented out the horses came with us because he was the one who supplied the Cerro de Oro pulperia. He was on foot and jogged ahead of us. The rain fell harder and harder, and the road, completely soaked, had turned to muck, so it wasn't exactly a pleasure trip. The horses sank deep into the red sticky mud, but they struggled on valiantly. We went on this way for about an hour – an hour of moving along the river in the mire that exhausted the horses. After that, we started up the hills. The Rincón meanders a lot, so you have to cross and climb the slippery bank, traverse a few hundred yards of flat and muddy underbrush, then begin the process all over again; we repeated the routine about twenty times. The river was high and deep, and the current was strong. Several times Sancho and his little mule were almost completely submerged. All of us were wet past our knees, and the tree-trunks kept rushing by so rapidly that any one of them could easily have done for both horse and rider.

The climbs and descents weren't easy, because the slopes were terribly steep. In the final analysis, Sancho had the better of us – his mule was sure-footed and had no problem, while the horses kept slipping and falling, sometimes tumbling for many yards. Soon, with the exception of Sancho, we were all covered with mud from head to foot. It would have been hell if we hadn't all remained good-humoured.

Every tumble provoked a storm of laughter. Little Dave had an enormous bump on his forehead, but he was enjoying the trip.

'This is terrific,' he announced as he rode along beside me. 'It's the kind of adventure I've always dreamed of. As soon as I can, I'm going to buy myself some spurs and a hat. Got any idea where I can get a secondhand revolver?'

'No, Dave, better forget that idea. Once you're armed, you have to assume a certain responsibility. If you had a revolver, you'd probably use it, wouldn't you?'

'Sure.'

'And suppose you shoot somebody and there's a witness. What then?'

'I guess I'm in deep shit.'

'Exactly, and so are the rest of us. As long as you're with me, no gun. We can behave like arseholes and argue among ourselves as much as we want, but there are limits. OK?'

'OK, Boss.'

After four and a half hours of this leisurely ride, we finally reached Cerro de Oro, at the edge of Corcovado National Park. The village consisted of some twenty wretched filthy shacks. We stopped our horses in front of a rancho somewhat less dilapidated than the others and a little apart from them.

The owner, Andres, an old man with a pirate's face, received us very amiably and offered us some coffee. He liked to talk, and he told me all about the area. I learned that there were already two people buying up gold – one, a European, Patrick, who'd been in Osa for about fifteen years, and the other, a Tico called Cartago, who ran the only pulperia around. Andres didn't seem particularly fond of him.

'He's a son of a bitch and a thief! He buys up the gold for almost nothing and sells his goods at five or six times the usual price. He's the richest man around here. Nobody likes him, but everybody needs him.'

I borrowed a table and a chair from Andres, and a few minutes later we were ready to buy gold. I set myself up under a plastic roof in the centre of the village. On the table in front of me was the scale, to the right of it my revolver, and to the left a pile of thousand-colon notes and a calculator. Dave and Roberto stood alongside me, and Sancho went off to scare up customers.

The first was a small toothless man. He approached cautiously, and I could understand why: the sight of our group didn't exactly inspire confidence.

'I hear that you buy gold.'

'That's right. If you have any to sell, I'll buy it.'

'Oh, I don't have much. Just a gram or so.'

He removed from his pocket a bit of aluminium foil in which a few grains were wrapped.

67

'How much does Cartago the pulpero pay?'

'A hundred and fifty colones a gram.'

'The thief! I'll pay a hundred and seventy-five a gram – and since you look like a nice guy I'll throw in something extra,' I said, handing him 180 colons.

He was as pleased as Punch when he left. By buying gold at 175 colones (seven dollars and fifty cents) a gram I was making a good profit, because on the outside it sold for twelve or thirteen dollars a gram.

A few minutes later the old man returned with two oreros.

'They've got some to sell, too.'

I bought it – seven grams from one and ten from the other.

The old man took a flask from his pocket, and this time he had almost twenty grams. The liar! Actually, he had just been cautious – and rightly so.

As soon as those men returned to camp and spread the news, other sellers began to stream in. They came from everywhere, and I had to make them line up or there would have been complete chaos. Some of them had very little gold – maybe one or two grams – others considerably more.

I stayed there all day. Sancho kept doing his act and calling me 'Don Juan Carlos' as though I were royalty. He had just the right touch for dazzling the peasants. Knowing Cartago's prices, he'd talk to them about co-operatives, joint buying, guaro at half-price. He was so persuasive that after a few hours they were all convinced that I was their saviour, that thanks to me things were going to change. Actually, about all they'd understood was that alcohol was going to cost less.

From time to time, I'd tell him – in a voice loud enough to be overheard – to add a little more money because I liked the way the man looked, or because he struck me as being a nice guy. That contributed to my image, too. Everyone now called me 'Don Juan Carlos'.

I wasn't doing this so much for the profit as to get myself known. Sancho, who tried to put the bite on the prospectors when it came to weighing the gold or calculating the price, was worried by my generosity.

'Are you sure we'll end up with a profit this way?'

'Don't worry, it's the "Zykë" method. All I want right now is for everyone to know me, and to know that I'm generous. After a few days of this kind of buying, my word will be as good as cash.'

'But it's a little dangerous. We could lose our capital,' said Roberto.

'Listen, buddy, you're looking at eighteen years of experience in underdeveloped countries. Results guaranteed!'

'But suppose it doesn't work?' he asked.

'If it doesn't work, you're ruined! But, if you gave me your dough, I suppose it's because you had confidence in me. Well, just keep on having confidence in me. Still, if you have a way to pull one of your traveller's cheques cons with these prospectors, don't let me stop you. To each his own.'

The big pig didn't know his place, and that really got to me. A couple of times he even tried to interfere in a transaction, and I had to put him down.

In the afternoon a guy who looked like a gringo came to see us.

'It's Patrick,' whispered Sancho, who'd nervously drawn closer to me.

By raising the price, we'd siphoned off his customers. I was expecting a sharp reaction, and I was ready for it.

'So you've come to buy gold?' he said.

'As you can see.'

'What are you paying?'

'A hundred and seventy-five colones a gram.'

'OK, but try not to raise the price too much – that'll make it possible for me to keep buying some of it.'

And that was that.

That's all it meant to him. He wouldn't be the one to get in my way, I thought. As for Cartago, he never put in an appearance.

By the end of the day I'd bought two hundred grams.

It had begun to get dark when I gave the signal to leave. The trip out had been hard; going back through the jungle at night was even worse. You couldn't see a thing, but luckily the horses knew the way. You had to bend down over the neck and withers or the branches would swat you right in the head. It was after ten when we got to Las Palmas, soaked, muddy and exhausted.

We quickly ate an excellent meal prepared by Alfredo's wife under Diane's supervision. Alfredo was still eager to be helpful, and he brought some pitchers of hot water to the room so I could wash. Then everyone collapsed into his own corner since we'd be leaving again at four.

The next day at Cerro de Oro the sellers flowed in from everywhere. Cartego didn't show himself, and I mentioned the fact to old Andres.

'That coward won't come. He's got no balls. You should open a general store here,' he said.

'I was thinking of that. I'm going to have to build a little house.'

'You can have my rancho, if you want.'

'Great! How much will you rent it for?'

Old Andres, who must really have hated Cartago, replied: 'You can have it for nothing. As long as it's a pain in that bastard's arse, I'll consider myself well paid.'

That evening, after Dave and Roberto had collapsed into bed, Sancho took me aside.

'I like the way you do business, and I wouldn't mind making a deal with you. Right now I've got six thousand dollars, a few tractors I inherited from my father, a land-rover and a boat. If you can use any of that, it's all available to you. Think it over.'

I did a lot of thinking that night. What I'd learned during my few days there, together with what Sancho was offering me, made me see the future in a different light. Things were falling into place, and a plan was beginning to evolve.

In the morning I had a talk with Sancho.

'I spent the night thinking, and I feel it's time to shift into high gear. It seems to me we've got to think big and act fast. If you're up to it, we can expand our operations very quickly. Are you seriously ready to go in with me?'

'I've got complete confidence in you. If you go on the way you've started, I'm ready to follow you and push ahead. There's just one thing: I'm interested in doing business with you – not with the other two.'

'I haven't made them any promises, but I like to be fair, and they've helped me out. I'll keep them on for a month so that they can make a little something. Then I can get rid of them.'

'I'd just as soon they went now, but I understand what you mean.'

'Fine, that's settled. Now, tell me – can you get the land-rover and the boat immediately, and what's the boat's horsepower?'

'They're mine, and I can have them right away. As for the boat, it's forty-five horsepower. I'll have to ask my mother about the tractors, since she's the one who takes care of family business now. But there won't be any problem once she understands.'

'OK. Then, what I suggest is that we join up and form a company to exploit the gold resources of the Rincón. You contribute your machines, and I contribute my knowledge of gold and my general know-how. Forty-five per cent for you.'

'Why not equal shares?'

'Simply because it's not my style to go fifty–fifty with anyone. I'd have the feeling I was being cheated, and that's no good for business. You'll just have to understand that.'

'Well, since you don't act like anybody else, I'm not surprised that you don't think like anybody else. OK, it's a deal,' he said, holding out his hand.

'Good! Now that that's settled, give me your cash and go wake up the two clowns. We've got a lot to do.'

Ten minutes later, all five of us were sitting around the table with the day's first cup of coffee. I explained my agreement with Sancho to Dave and Roberto.

'But you're going to earn your dough. The two of you will be taking care of the pulperia I'm going to open in Cerro de Oro at Andres' place. We'll decide together about the prices we'll charge. Mainly, we're going to sell alcohol, and that's the way we'll make our pile. Does that suit you?'

'We don't seem to have much of a choice,' replied Roberto.

'True. But don't worry – you're going to do all right this way.'

Dave was both sad and happy: sad because the adventure would be over in a month, happy that it wouldn't end the next day. Roberto grumbled a little because he knew he was being cut out of something good and was sorry he couldn't deal himself in. I summed it all up for them.

'Diane and I will stay here. You three will be on the move. You'll grab this morning's taxi-plane to Golfito, and from there you'll take the Samsa plane to San José. Sancho and Roberto, you'll buy the supplies for the pulperia – I'll give you a list. Sancho, here's the dough – you're in charge of it. Once you've done your buying, Roberto will rent a taxi-plane and bring all the stuff back here. Sancho and Dave, I want you to bring back the boat and the land-rover. Make sure you reserve a place on the barge for the land-rover. Three days should be enough time to do all that. Now get a move on, the plane should be here soon. Everything clear? No problems?'.

'No, everything's fine!' they chorused.

'Good. Sancho, come to my room so I can give you the money.'

When we were alone, I said to him: 'You're responsible for this cash. Keep an eye on Roberto, and see that he doesn't buy a lot of useless junk.'

Since they hated each other, I was sure that by sending them together each would keep a close watch on the other. An hour later they were gone, and I was finally alone with Diane.

I spent the afternoon teaching her to fire the Magnum. The Ticos, who were used to the snap of the .22, were frightened by the detonation of the Magnum, which sounded like a cannon going off. Two days later we went to see an encampment about two and a half hours from Cerro de Oro. Diane was an excellent horsewoman and rode at a good

71

clip, and with Sancho's .22 stuck in her belt she impressed the Ticos considerably more than the two cowboys did. Though she was very feminine, she radiated a strength of character that the men, accustomed to big floppy cows, found intimidating; they could see she knew how to make herself respected. She was the perfect back-up for me, and we bought about seventy grams of gold that day.

In the evening we returned to Cerro de Oro to spend the night in what would soon be our bar. Old Andres lent us two hammocks.

I caught a glimpse of Cartago, the storekeeper, who seemed eager to avoid us. To tease him, Diane greeted him with a sweeping gesture to which he felt obliged to respond. I could tell he would be a wonderful neighbour. . . .

Early the next morning we went back to Las Palmas. I hoped everyone would be punctual so we could get off to a quick start. The first to show up was Dave, sitting at the wheel of the land-rover. Everything had gone well, and he'd even brought back a 'bomb' – a small motor for pumping water and washing the auriferous rock. We then went to pick up Sancho, who landed the boat at Playa Blanca.

The taxi-plane bringing Roberto arrived shortly afterwards. He had almost a ton of merchandise, and we had to make several trips in the car to unload it all. More than half the stuff was alcohol, and the rest was a bit of everything: rice, frijoles, toothpaste, and even some of the dumb picture magazines the oreros liked so much.

We were unpacking the stuff at Alfredo's place when Sancho came to see me, looking a little embarrassed.

'Juan Carlos, I don't know if I did the right thing, but I let Roberto buy himself a gun,' he told me.

'Christ! I don't believe it! You must be as dumb as those others! You know it's going to mean trouble. We're not here to play around, damn it!'

'Sure, I know, but he bugged me all day long, saying he had his own dough, that he'd take the responsibility, that it would be useful to have in the mountains, and so on and so on. And he pretty much made me think that you knew about it.'

'No way! OK, now that it's done, let's try to limit the damage. Bring the idiot to me.'

When Roberto showed up, he already had the revolver in his belt, a long-barrelled .38.

'Happy now?' I asked. 'Got yourself a little toy?'

'Listen, Juan Carlos, it's not just a whim. If Dave and I are going to stay up there alone, the piece could be useful. You know, if all goes well, we're going to have a fair amount of gold with us. And, in any case, some of the dough in our kitty is mine – just deduct the cost of this gun from my share.'

I didn't want to waste any time over this business. I was sick and tired of having to explain everything to them.

'OK, you've got it. It's done. But it's your responsibility. Don't come running to me if there's a problem. And it has to stay in the pulperia. I don't want it seen around here, and I don't want to have to repeat this.'

Luckily, they'd be gone in a month.

The next morning we began loading up for Cerro de Oro. I'd rented nine horses, but it took a lot of time. The bottles of liquor would never survive a fall, and to limit the possible damage we loaded the animals with no more than seventy pounds. It took us several days to transport everything. Roberto stayed up there while I directed the coming and going. Our guide, who usually supplied Cartago's pulperia, also took up some merchandise. We were clearly going to ruin Cartago's business, and he looked as sore as hell.

At Cerro de Oro the arrival of this caravan of nine horses loaded down with alcohol was quite an event. It looked as though I'd carried out my promises.

Despite my precautions, we had some losses because of all our tumbles: basically, a few bottles were broken, and a couple of toothpaste-tubes took on some strange shapes. All our supplies had a distinct smell of guaro, even the picture magazines. So much the better – it would attract more clients. When the booze ran out, they could distil the cakes of soap.

I stayed up there that first day to get things started. My prices were 25 per cent lower than Cartago's, but the profits were still enormous: more than four times the price of what we'd paid in San José, even counting the cost of transportation. People could pay for the goods in either gold or colones, and from the very first day the customers came flocking.

Now that the pulperia was launched, I could leave Dave and Roberto to run it and take care of the other part of the business with Sancho. Using a survey map, we marked out a two-mile area along the Rincón.

My plan was simple. I knew that if the river had gold upstream, it also had it downstream. But the gold was in the form of small particles that could only be exploited with machines, so my idea was to buy all the land below and work it with machines or trade it later. We scouted the land and made endless trips back and forth to meet with the proprietors scattered along the river.

My method of buying depended on several factors. To begin with, the proprietors weren't gold prospectors but small farmers who survived by planting a few bananas and a few beans and never gave a thought to exploiting the gold potential of their plots of land. In addition, those playones, as they were called, were barely farmable: because they were at the edge of the river, they were constantly flooded, so they had little value; I could snap them up for almost nothing.

Second – and this was the most important factor – the whole operation was based on the collapse of the local money in relation to the dollar. In three months, the rate per dollar had gone from eight to twenty-five colones – and the end was nowhere in sight. A devaluation of such magnitude was bound to take on speed, and that would suit me fine since I'd be selling gold in Panama in exchange for dollars.

I immediately paid each proprietor 2 or 3 per cent of the total price, and in exchange he signed a receipt which, though it had no legal value, would prevent him from selling the land. I agreed to pay the rest of the money within a year, with no interest; by that time, what with the increase in the cost of living and the fall of the colon, the price of the land per acre would amount to about the price of a pound of rice. . . .

Obviously, it was a little crude, but the local peasants found it too complicated to figure out. Completely hypnotized by Sancho, they understood only that some madman wanted to give them money for worthless land – and was also promising each of them work for at least one member of his family, because there's always someone who's already seen a tractor or has a vague idea of how to use a shovel.

That way everyone was happy. They were unloading useless acreage, and I – for less than nothing – became the owner of a two-mile stretch that contained gold.

Once all the owners had been contacted, I planned to take them in a group to a local lawyer and have our transactions legalized. Meanwhile these preliminaries were exhausting; Sancho and I would get back to Las Palmas very late at night and leave again before dawn. I didn't do much gold-buying, because I was counting on the pulperia to keep us in funds.

Unfortunately, things over there weren't going as well as I'd hoped. Dave and Roberto were constantly stoned, and I had to keep an eye on them. When I'd get there in the morning, there were always Ticos sprawled dead drunk on the floor. It was messy, and I like things to look neat. The Ticos were given special treatment – I fired a bullet

74

into the floor about two inches from their ears. As loaded as they were, they usually jumped to their feet and beat it to the door without waiting for any explanations. It was amusing, but I'd have preferred the clean-up to be done before I arrived.

In addition, Dave told me proudly that he raised the prices at the end of the evening when the customers were loaded to the gills.

'That's dumb. It makes no sense. We're not going to get rich by cheating them out of ten or fifteen colones here and there. We're not out for a quick small profit. I've got bigger plans but, first, we have to settle in and make them trust us.'

'Oh, we're not talking about a lot of money. . . .'

'No, but you're ruining the image I want to establish. Sancho and I go around talking about co-operation and association, and you, – just to turn a quick buck – are making the same error Cartago's made. Your stupid little profits amount to less than the tips I leave the peasants when I drink a cup of coffee in their houses.'

'But nobody even knows. . . .'

'There's always some idiot who notices. And, besides, I don't like this shopkeeper mentality. To sell them guaro at five or six times the normal price – fine! If they want to get drunk, they've got to pay; they've got to reimburse us for the risks we take by selling the alcohol without a licence. But to cheat them out of three or four colones on stuff they really need. . . .'

'OK, OK. I didn't think you had anything against a small rip-off.'

'It's not the rip-off I mind; it's that it's a nasty small-minded rip-off – it's too easy.'

And, in any case, the profits were already pretty high. Our supply of gold was growing because almost everyone bought at our place.

At the end of a week, the alcohol had run out. Four hundred litres in six days, and no need to worry about spoilage! I was happy to have introduced the blessings of civilization into that backward mountain area.

As we were getting ready to renew our supplies, Roberto and Dave told me they no longer wanted to stay up there.

'We're going out of our skulls. During the day they work, and there's no one here. At night they're all here, but soaked to the gills, and we have to put up with all their crap.'

'All you have to do is keep your distance.'

'Even so, it's a drag being stuck up here.'

I really couldn't blame them.

'What do you suggest? Close the pulperia?'

'No. We discussed it with Andres' grandson, and he's agreed to look after it. He's honest and, besides, it's easy enough to check on him. We could go with you now.'

I knew the kid, and I figured we could trust him. In any case, he couldn't do any worse than those two clowns.

And so there we all were back in Las Palmas. It got a little sticky sometimes, especially with Roberto, who had no manners and behaved like a pig. Diane put him down a few times, but it was uncomfortable. On the other hand, I got to like Dave. Completely irresponsible, he did a lot of trivial dumb things, but he brought a sense of fun into our group. Always absentminded, he broke a lot of stuff, and once he even accidentally managed to start a fire in the café.

Our presence created some excitement. The small village had been a sleepy little place before our arrival and had never experienced such an uproar. Sometimes we'd spend several days just relaxing and farting around. There as a lot of shooting because – with the excuse of having to keep in training – we had target practice every evening in the back yard, behind which was a path. Once it was dark, nobody would use that path. We must have been a pain in the arse but, thanks to their vision of me as a generous and slightly nutty millionaire, nobody dared complain. We'd annexed the café and were getting better-known all the time.

The rumour that Don Juan Carlos was buying land had spread, and in the morning I often found several people quietly waiting for me. Some had come about their land, others with all kinds of propositions. Sancho, perfect in his role as secretary, sent them to me one at a time; I listened while I had my breakfast, then made my decision. Most of the men had only come to tell me stupid stories, and I sent them packing.

I was in the process of getting control of the area, and we didn't miss a trick for reinforcing our position.

One day the village organized a turno, a kind of carnival with a band. Essentially it was an excuse to get drunk. As a local bigwig, I had to show up.

At one point, a farmer put a little roast pig up for auction and things became interesting. To save time, I made a bid that was three times the last offer and, to my great surprise, someone topped me. It was my old friend Cartago, who'd come to attend the celebration and score a point off me. Just wait, you old bastard, I thought. I'll have your hide yet!

The bids rose in a dizzying fashion, reaching incredible prices. It was a fight for prestige, one that Cartago couldn't help but lose. The arsehole was stubborn. I was almost tempted to let him win so I could have the pleasure of seeing him pay up. But I had a reputation to maintain and, for the Ticos, whoever carried off the pig would have proven himself the stronger man. Every bid was greeted with exclamations of joy. My adversary finally gave up, and was hooted by the crowd; the pig had cost me the insane price of $250.

The farmer couldn't have been happier. At that price he was ready to sell his herd, his farm and his wife. Gambling had always amused me, and I sent Sancho to the microphone to announce that the company was giving a case of beer to the crowd. They went crazy.

I kept repeating this little routine all night long. A signal to the singer, and he'd coo into the microphone: 'And another case from the company!'

There'd be a rush towards the bar, with a lot of pushing and shoving and cries of 'Long live the company! Long live Don Juan Carlos!' The band usually stopped at midnight, but I paid them to keep playing until four in the morning – on condition they shouted 'Long live the company!' between each number. The cry was taken up by the entire crowd.

We weren't drinking, but all night long we quietly puffed away at enormous joints, enjoying the spectacle.

By dawn the meadow in front of the band had been churned up into an enormous field of mud that covered everybody, and in which more than a dozen drunks had collapsed. After a celebration like that, there wasn't anyone for miles around who didn't know about the company.

I continued to buy up land, but now the peasants came looking for *me*, asking me to go out to see their places. We went to all of them, and while I was there I'd do a little testing to check on the grade of gold.

One day we went to examine a site about an hour and a half from Las Palmas, and Carlito came along. As we were about to set out for home again, Dave suggested we go down-river by way of 'trunk-mobile' – in other words, by grabbing on to some of the floating tree-trunks and letting ourselves be carried along by the current. The idea was insane, because the current was very strong, but all of us except Sancho got very enthusiastic about it. I gave my weapons and money to Diane, who returned with Carlito and the horses, and then we all dived into the water.

With one man or several clinging to a trunk, it was very fast; Sancho was scared stiff, and we amused ourselves by pushing him. Often the tree would run into the bank or get caught in some branches, and sometimes the current was so swift that we were thrown on to the rocks. Though we got knocked around a little, it was fantastic. The only really dangerous stretches were the whirlpools: when the branches formed a barrier, the water went under it and literally sucked us in. It was a little scary, because if you were pulled down too deep you could be stuck at the bottom and maybe never surface again. The first to have this happen to him was Sancho, who disappeared completely under the water and showed up, half-drowned, some twenty feet farther downstream. The same thing happened to each of us, but it was all part of the fun.

We were frozen stiff when we got back. Our river escapade had lasted three hours.

I'd contacted practically all the landowners, and between visits I managed to return to the camp to buy gold. The pulperia was still bringing in money. Andres' grandson was on the level, and once a week I'd stop by to pick up the take. We'd already renewed our alcohol stock – which we brought from Golfito by boat – twice.

When we were buying gold, Sancho couldn't keep himself from cheating; between the scales and his calculator he always managed to shave off a few colones per gram. I didn't approve, but I never interfered, because it was obviously part of his somewhat petty nature. Cheating those illiterate prospectors, who didn't make very much to begin with, was really nothing to boast about. Once they caught him at it and got furious. I let them push him around a little so he'd learn his lesson, but when they threatened to slice him up I got out my guns. I couldn't let them do any real damage because I still needed him.

He complained to me about not having come to his aid sooner, and I explained: 'If you cheat, you have to take your chances. I don't like your methods, but I wouldn't have let you down; I just wanted you to understand a few things.'

Except for this little failing, he was great to work with. His contacts with the peasants, his way of introducing me to the Ticos and of receiving them at Las Palmas, had speeded up the purchase of land. I had two kilos of gold, but I wanted to keep buying as much as possible because the colon was falling rapidly.

One morning I took stock. We'd been on the peninsula about a month, I had more than two kilos of gold – about $24,000 – and I still had $3000 in cash; it was time to take the next step. Roberto and Sancho would go to Panama to sell the gold for dollars, while Diane, Dave and I would wait for them in San José. Then Sancho and I would go to see his mother and discuss our 'machine' project.

78

We left early in the morning. After a smooth crossing, we reached the Golfito dock, where Sancho's brother was waiting. He'd been phoned the evening before, and had driven all night to Panama. After some fast introductions he left for the airport in a great hurry. Once we'd turned the boat over to Wayne we all headed for Villa Nelly, a small city about twelve miles from the Panamanian border. In order to make sure that everything went well, I'd decided not to leave Sancho and Roberto until the last moment.

There was one little risk – crossing the border with the gold. Costa Rica paid for gold at less than the international market price, and exporting it was forbidden. If you were caught, the gold would be confiscated and there'd be a big fine – and maybe even a prison sentence as well. That would be too stupid after all our work. I hid the two kilos of gold in the back-rest of the driver's seat – it was unlikely that they'd methodically search a Costa Rican vehicle – then I gave them some final instructions.

'Sancho, you're in charge of the gold. Keep it with you even when you're sleeping or taking a shit. Roberto, you protect Sancho, but leave the gold alone. Understand?'

The big Basque was a little ticked off but he agreed. I continued.

'Here's the address of Aldo, an Italian friend of mine who lives in Panama. He'll take you to Nat Mendez, an important jeweller who pays well. Another thing – come back to San José as soon as the gold is sold; I'll be waiting there. Don't spend too much, and good luck.'

But at the Villa Nelly airport we had a nasty surprise. The plane had already left, and there wouldn't be another until the next day. Since Villa Nelly is too crummy to spend even a night in, we decided to return to Golfito in a taxi. Sancho and Roberto pushed on.

In the afternoon Diane and I were taking a siesta in the Hotel Delfina when Dave knocked at our door.

'Come in.'

'I'm bored out of my skull, and it would help if I had some dope.'

'You really want some?'

'Well, I'm alone, you know, and I'm about to go out of my mind.'

'OK, wait for me in your room. I'll meet you there.'

Irritated, Diane said: 'You're too nice to him. We're leaving tomorrow, and it wouldn't kill him to do without pot for a day.'

'You're right, darling, but in a few days I'll have enough money to pay them both off and get rid of them. I'm just as eager as you are for the two of us finally to be alone.'

I telephoned Fernando, my usual dealer. We agreed to meet an hour later at Las Cabinas Tortugas, a quiet little place just outside Golfito.

He was waiting when Diane and I got there, and had half a key of

Mango-Rosa. It was too much, but I bought it because Fernando doesn't make penny-ante deals. He's a wholesaler who looks after several plantations scattered around the Osa jungle, and he had come as a favour to me.

The plane was scheduled to leave at nine in the morning, and the arsehole at the desk never woke us. While Diane was getting our stuff together, I ran to wake Dave.

'Get a move on, we're late. Bury this,' I said, handing him the grass. 'I've kept a little out and stowed it in my underwear.'

'Don't bother, I'll take it with me. I've got the gun, so I might as well have the dope, too.'

'What do you mean, you've got the gun?'

'Roberto's .38. He told me to keep it just in case we don't go back to the peninsula.'

'You stupid shitheads! Sancho and I left our guns in Las Palmas, and I don't want to run any risk with yours.'

'Don't worry, Juan Carlos. I'll take care of it.'

'We're late, and there's no time to argue. Do what you want!'

I was tired of giving advice, and I was tired of playing the nervous papa. If he got caught, fuck him!

When we got to the airport, the plane was already there. The taxi left us about a hundred yards from a kind of shed that served as a waiting-room on the other side of the runway. It wasn't until we were crossing, luggage in hand, that I became aware of the number of uniforms. There's usually a cop there, but that day I counted six of them, Commando Sur types – half cops, half soldiers. As I went to sit on one of the benches, I noticed there was an unusual amount of activity for this rural airport.

On my left a small stone wall about three feet high marked off the waiting-room; in front of me was the window where they checked tickets; alongside to the right was a table on which the cops were searching baggage. It wasn't being done systematically, but three Europeans were sure to get a careful going over; I could smell trouble.

Turning to Dave, who was sitting next to me, I said casually: 'You'll have to dump the dope because we're going to be searched. The best thing would be to toss it over the wall without attracting any attention. Afterwards, we'll go on board separately. Don't get up when I do.'

'But the grass is packed with the gun!'

'Dump it all!'

Masked by Diane, I threw my little stash of grass behind the wall.

An intimate body-search is rare in these Latin American countries, but I decided not to take a chance. While Dave was getting up, Diane and I walked over to the baggage-search table. As I'd foreseen, they gave us a careful going-over. While they were checking my knapsack, I looked around discreetly and saw that Dave wasn't in the room. As we were walking to the plane, I spotted him: about fifty yards from the shed and being escorted towards the runway by two cops.

'Shit! The dumb arsehole!'

I realized that the idiot hadn't wanted simply to ditch the rod and had gone off to hide it – as if a guy leaving the airport and setting off across a field wouldn't draw attention! The local cops were dumb, but not that dumb.

He was shitting bricks. I only had to look at him to know that he hadn't had time to dump anything. Only a miracle could save him. Standing among the passengers observing the scene from about ten yards away, I watched trouble drawing close. The cops were unpacking his stuff, and after unrolling a pair of trousers they found first the gun, then the grass. They surrounded him, rifles at the ready.

He'd been nabbed. What a bad break! There wasn't a thing I could do for him – certainly not intervene in any way. I was just thinking about what lawyer I could get when that idiot, that moron, did the stupidest and most unprofessional thing possible: he waved his hand in my direction.

Arsehole! Triple arsehole! It was just the sort of thing a panicky kid would do. But what did he expect me to do now? The cops, surprised, looked my way, and one of them signalled me to come over. I quietly told Diane to stay put and went over to them.

On the way I tried to get a grip on my boiling anger, but I couldn't keep myself from saying to Dave: 'Well, you've done it!'

'Do you know this man?' asked the cop in charge, a swarthy nasty-looking type.

'A little.'

'Are you travelling together?'

'No, we met here.'

A miracle! They seemed to accept what I said and, satisfied with their prey, paid no more attention to me. They were all riled up, and stopped the loading of the passengers. Then they put Dave in a jeep and drove away, their guns still pointed at him; only one of them – a man in civilian clothes and wearing dark glasses – remained behind. That kind of blunder is unusual and can only happen in banana republics, but I'd had experience with such situations and knew the reprieve wouldn't last: there was sure to be one who'd be smarter than the others and start wondering if Dave was really alone.

I took advantage of those few minutes to give all my cash to Diane.

'They're going to search me, so we've got to separate. If you get through, take the plane as though nothing's wrong. Don't worry. I'll get in touch with you through Jean-Paul.'

'Are you sure they'll be back?'

'Unless the plane leaves in the next two minutes, I'm in for it.'

And five minutes later the jeep returned in a hurry. The guys got out and trained their rifles on me. They must have got quite a roasting, because they were in a nasty mood. I was careful not to make any sudden moves, because I could see they were nervous and ready to fire. While one of them gave me a quick frisk, I saw the cop in civvies signal them to take Diane along, too. The cocksucker! It was just what I was afraid of!

In the jeep I managed to reassure Diane.

'Everything will be all right. You don't know a thing, and that's all there is to it.'

When we got to the police station, they searched me again and took me to the cell Dave was in – their second mistake. Diane was sitting in the office, and I had just enough time to signal that all was well.

But I was far from sure that all was well, and I was furious when I entered the cell. I've rarely felt so much like killing someone. I tried to cool off so that I wouldn't immediately explode and splatter Dave against the wall. That he had put me in the shit was what could be expected, but that he'd got Diane in trouble was something else again. It wasn't the first time I had been in this kind of mess, but it was the first time one of my women had been dragged in. Generally, when I feel there's any danger I separate myself from the people I like and face it on my own, but Dave's reaction had been too stupid for me to be able to foresee. The whole succession of idiocies – the gun, the dope, and that wave in my direction – was what had led to Diane being in this jam. It was driving me crazy, because I was familiar with Latin American gaols and I knew there was reason to worry.

When the door closed behind me, there was complete silence. If Dave had so much as opened his mouth, I wouldn't have been able to restrain myself. He must have felt it, because he kept quiet. I looked at him sitting there, prostrate, tears in his eyes. He was spineless, a kid lost in a situation that was too much for him. I almost felt sorry for him, and that saved his arse.

After a while he broke the silence.

'I'm sorry,' he said, without raising his head.

'You should be. But what's done is done, and we have to figure a way out.'

'You're not too mad at me?'

'I'm furious, but we'll settle scores later. For the time being, I want to limit the damage. We've got to take advantage of the unbelievable error they made when they put us in here together. Open your ears, little boy, so I can prepare you for what's coming.'

I talked to him for two hours, trying to instil all the experience of a lifetime of adventure and many arrests. Above all, he mustn't crack. He had to accept his responsibilities. I was used to violence, and I knew by then that he wasn't.

'If you feel the interrogation is going to turn nasty, if it begins with a beating, don't hesitate – take a swing at them. Your only chance is to be knocked out as fast as possible so that you won't feel it when they hit you. After two or three times, they end by respecting you.'

'You think it might really get that rough?'

'Frankly, I don't know. I've never been arrested in this country. At first glance they don't look all that tough, but the cops on this continent are generally cocksuckers. It's just as well to be prepared for anything and everything. We'll make up a story that holds water. To begin with, I'm going to deny any dealings with you. I'm going to say we barely know each other, and that's all. If I'm going to help, I've got to be on the outside with Diane. Now, pay attention and get this through your skull. If you listen to me and do what I say, I give you my word of honour that I'll get you out of here one way or another, no matter how much it costs or what I have to do. You can trust me, understand?'

'I understand.'

'But if you buckle under, if you let me down or pull another dumb trick like the last one, I'll see to it that you get at least twenty years. And you can trust me about that, too. OK?'

'OK, Juan Carlos.'

'Good. Now, let this sink in. You're not to give anybody away, and especially not the guy who sold me the dope. If our story gets too complicated, we'll never get out of the mess, so we've got to make as few waves as possible. Now, make up a description of the character who supposedly sold you the dope. The best thing is to describe one of your buddies; that way, you won't get balled up in your description. But don't be too exact, either. Think up a good story: how he approached you, where you bought the stuff, et cetera. And be sure you insist it was for your own personal use. That's crucial, because they're very tough when it comes to dealing.'

'What about the piece?'

'The piece isn't so important. Make up somebody for that, too – a tourist, for example, who sold it to you before he left.'

83

I built a whole story for him, and I made him repeat it several times to be sure he'd got it straight. I also did everything I could to reassure him. He was only a kid, who might collapse under the pressure, and everything depended on how he'd behave. We were lucky that they'd put us in the same cell.

Two hours later a cop opened the door.

'You,' he said, pointing a finger at me. 'Follow me!'

I gave a last bit of advice to Dave.

'And, whatever you do, don't fall for the classic nice-guy approach and the promises. Never forget that they're all bastards. Good luck, kid!'

While the guard was locking the cell door, I asked him: 'Where's my wife?'

'She's fine. Don't worry.'

He didn't seem too bright, and I pumped him for information.

'Where are you taking me?'

'Just changing your cell. We got hell for putting you two together.'

'Who from?'

'From the narcotics people. We told them what happened, and two of them are coming down today by plane. Are you terrorists?'

'No, why?'

'Because a Liberian plane was hijacked last week. That's why they're searching everybody now.'

What a break – to get nailed because of what was probably the only hijacking ever to take place in Costa Rica! Of course, up there in the mountains, I'd never seen a newspaper.

The guard put me in a cell right next to Dave's. The guy's were real pros. . . . In any case, I didn't have anything else to tell him, and I was beginning to be seriously worried about Diane. I'd been arrested several times in Third World countries, and I knew just what those cops were capable of. Knowing she was at their mercy, I paced restlessly around my cell, almost crazy with helplessness. I knew there was something about her that would make these guys think twice, but even so. . . .

Time was passing, and somehow I had to relax. I stretched out on a piece of cardboard and tried to wind down. It was maddening that this should happen now, just when I was doing great and things were going well. I might lose everything, including my freedom, and all because of some dumb kid! That son of a bitch Roberto – he was the one who was really responsible for what happened.

It was night when the sound of the cell door opening brought me to full consciousness. This time I was taken to the office and handcuffed. On the way I saw Diane, sitting alone in a room. She seemed completely relaxed and gave me the thumbs-up sign – all was well.

I felt an enormous sense of relief. That Diane! She must have been leading them around by the nose. I was feeling absolutely great when I got to the office, where two narcs were waiting. The look of them surprised me. They were young and had long hair – Starsky and Hutch, Latino-style. But obviously these two clowns weren't there to fool around, because they started in right away, using a classic method.

'We know everything, so there's no point in lying. If you tell us the truth and co-operate, we'll see to it that nothing happens. You're already up to your neck in shit, so don't go any deeper! All right?'

'All right.'

'Who sold you the grass?'

'The grass wasn't mine. I have nothing to do with all that.'

'You didn't know your buddy had it on him?'

'Absolutely not. I don't know him very well, and it was only by chance that we ran into each other in Golfito.'

'But you smoke dope, don't you?'

'No. I never touch the stuff.'

'Then, what's this?' one of them asked, showing me a roller and a packet of cigarette-papers for making joints.

Damn, I'd forgotten the roller in Diane's knapsack. I never use it – it was just a souvenir. But I had to clear Diane.

The cop could see that I'd been shaken and he pressed me.

'So you do smoke?'

'Yes, a lot, and I always have. I was born in Morocco, and it's more or less legal there. Everyone in my family smokes – my father, my grandfather – and I've been smoking since I was fourteen. I don't consider it a crime.'

I saw they were surprised by my reply. They didn't look really nasty, and I knew that the first five minutes were crucial: if I could get them to forget their official roles and start talking man to man, I'd be able to sell them a story. So I went on.

'Try to understand. I live in Osa. I'm a gold prospector, and if you know the area you know it's not exactly a resort – it's full of snakes, mosquitoes, and lots of other slimy critters. The pot helps me fall asleep.'

'You're in Osa? We've been there a few times to check for marijuana plantations. You're right, it's a hellhole. Where exactly are you?'

'Cerro de Oro.'

'I know where that is – on the Rincón, right?'

They'd completely forgotten why we were there and were gabbing about the peninsula and the places they knew. I could tell that there was no problem, that everything would work out. They were city softies; Osa seemed like a tough place to them, and they respected the kind of guy who lived there. They saw it as a sign of prowess – imagine a European surviving up there! The atmosphere was completely relaxed, and there was even a certain amount of sympathy between us. Occasionally they asked me a question about dope, but it was nothing more than a professional reflex. They had Dave, and that was enough for them.

For form's sake they made a last attempt.

'You didn't intend to sell the grass in San José?'

'On my honour, no! That's not my thing – my bag is gold. I've sunk low, but I've never sold drugs.'

It was true enough; I'd never slipped into drug traffic, nor had I ever urged anyone to use drugs.

'OK, you're free. Your wife, too! We won't press any charges against you!'

I thanked them, feeling a lot happier.

There was a little trouble when it came to removing the handcuffs – in their haste to leave San José, they'd forgotten the keys. If the damn things hadn't been cutting off my circulation, the situation would have been funny.

'Look, just saw them off, and I'll pay for them.'

'It's not that easy. We'll get hell from headquarters.'

'So what do we do? They're too tight, and they hurt.'

'Be a pal and wait for tomorrow. We'll work something out with a locksmith. Meanwhile, we'll tell your wife to get you something to eat, and then we'll settle you comfortably for the night.'

The situation had flipflopped: now they were the ones to be thanking me for being a nice guy. It was funny all right, but I'd rather have been somewhere else. I took advantage of my new position to see what I could do for Dave.

'Don't give the kid too hard a time. He's not a bad guy.'

'Don't worry, we'll just work him over a little. Wait in the refectory, and we'll bring him to you later on.'

Another hour of suspense. If Dave had learned his lesson well, everything would be fine. I was confident, because Dave was a sympathetic type, and those guys weren't really bastards.

I was already feeling considerably more relaxed when a gargantuan meal – five roasted chickens bought by Diane – was delivered. Just as I was working on the second, they brought Dave in, all smiles and looking in great shape.

'No problems?'

'None. I said exactly what you told me to say, and it all went off without a hitch. They weren't as tough as you said,' he added.

'Don't make me laugh! Remember that I went first and softened them up before they got to you. Now, eat!'

'Yes, I know. They told me they'd been scared shitless of you. That's why they put the cuffs on. Considering how big they are, you must have thrown the fear of God into them.'

By now he was completely reassured, and I even made him laugh by describing how sick he'd looked at the airport. I invited the two narcs to eat, but they refused because of the other cops. While we were drinking our coffee, a big sergeant came over and said he could get the cuffs off. For half an hour, while he worked away in vain at them, he gave a eulogy of Señor Monge, the favoured candidate in the coming presidential elections. I had no idea why he was chewing my ears off with all this, but I agreed with everything he said.

Dave had already returned to his cell when, exhausted, I asked if I could go to sleep. Luis, one of the two narcotics agents, prepared a somewhat primitive but comfortable bed for me. He was a nice guy, not the usual inspector type; a blond, with curly shoulder-length hair, he looked more like a hippie. He liked Dave and was embarrassed by the whole business.

'What are you going to do now?' I asked.

'We have to send a report to San José. We'll try to water down the charges against Dave, but that's about all we can do. All this has caused a big fuss over there, and we can't just hush it up. . . . Well, good night, Juan Carlos.'

' 'Night, Luis, and thanks.'

In the morning, after a very uncomfortable night, I was finally freed of the handcuffs: Luis had got a key from a buddy in another squad. After a round of handshaking, I left the police station. The big sergeant who'd worked on the cuffs drove me to the Golfito Hotel, where Diane had taken a room. Before leaving, he took my hand for the third time and made me promise never to forget him. I didn't understand, but I promised.

After all that anxiety, the joy of my reunion with Diane was indescribable. While I took a shower, she told me everything.

'From the beginning to the end, they couldn't have behaved better. They're probably not used to European women.'

'I was pretty worried about you.'

'I was lucky. There was a television set in the room I was in, and Monge was making a speech. For no particular reason, I said: 'Oh, it's Monge.' The cop looked at me strangely and asked if I knew Monge. I

87

grabbed at the opening and said that my husband knew him a little and had done some business with the Partido del Pueblo Unido. The guy's attitude changed completely. He suddenly became very obliging and spread the word that I wasn't to be bothered.'

'Good work, baby. You certainly know how to handle yourself. And now I understand why that dumb sergeant kept yammering away about Monge – he was doing a little boot-licking. If he only knew the truth!'

After a well-earned rest, I went to see Dave. They had transferred him to the Golfito prison, which was minute – a waiting-room with a desk, a door opening on to a patio surrounded by cells, a shed in the rear, and all of two guards.

Dave didn't seem quite as high as he had the day before.

'Everything all right? You look as if something's wrong.'

'It's really cruddy here. You see those cells back there? They're flooded, so we've been piled into the shed.'

'I'll buy you whatever you need. Sheets? blankets?'

'Yeah, and a foam-rubber mattress if you can get one. There's nothing to sleep on.'

'OK, I'll take care of it. Anything else?'

'Some money. A few guys on the outside are peddling joints. They shove them through the intersections in the planks.'

'All right, but be careful. This is serious. So far you've done fine. The real danger is over. You have my word that I'll get you out, and I will. Just hang in there.'

'Thanks. I've got confidence in you.'

'Incidentally, any problems with the other prisoners?'

'No, everything's all right. There are just two arseholes who want to play tough guy.'

'Call them over so I can talk to them.'

I knew that there were always some bullies in any slammer, and that the important thing is to stand up to them. The two wise guys Dave pointed out were about twenty, twenty-five years old – not very dangerous but pretty stupid. I offered them each a cigarette.

'Look, Dave here is my kid brother. He won't be here long, but if you give him a hard time I'll make sure that you get yours. Got it?'

'Got it.'

The guards were there, and they enjoyed my little demonstration. One of them let me know that there'd be no more problems.

Late that night somebody knocked at our door. It was Fernando the dope-dealer. He'd heard about our problems and had probably been sleeping badly since our arrest. He didn't quite know how to approach the topic, so I immediately supplied the answer to the question burning on his lips.

'Don't worry, your name was never mentioned. You're free and clear. But don't ever again do anything as stupid as coming to see me at the hotel, even late at night.'

'I know, but I couldn't get in touch with you and I had to be certain. You're sure I'm not in for trouble?'

'Why would you be? Nobody gave you away.'

'Thanks.'

'No reason to thank me – but now I have to get the kid out of clink before they transfer him somewhere else. Who's the best lawyer in Golfito?'

'José Araya. He's the best, but he's expensive, and he's got me out of this kind of trouble before because he's got good contacts with all the important people in town. His office is right here; if you like, we can meet there tomorrow morning at nine o'clock. Since he's my lawyer, nobody will think anything of our being seen together.'

'Good. And now I think you'd better disappear.'

Just before leaving, he turned to me.

'There aren't many people around here who know how to hold their tongues, so if you need any dough for the lawyer, or any kind of help, just ask. I owe you that.'

'I've got enough money. If I need anything else, I'll ask you, don't worry. Good night.'

'Good night. See you tomorrow.'

The next day at precisely nine o'clock I was in the lawyer's office. Fernando was waiting for me as agreed. He must have already spoken to the lawyer about me, but he introduced me anyway.

'He's a good guy, and he deserves all the help you can give him.'

The lawyer was a big pudgy man with the face of a vulture. His beady eyes studied me from behind large glasses. He struck me as pretty shady – just what I was looking for. In this country an honest lawyer doesn't make a cent. The more corrupt he is the more chance there is that he'll do what you want – if he's well paid. Those guys have a gift for sniffing out money, and Señor Araya was no exception.

'This business of yours is serious – it's more than a misdemeanour. Did you see *La Cronica* this morning?'

He handed me the local newspaper. Inside there was an article about the capture of three dangerous European terrorists arrested on a charge of possession of weapons and drugs. Though it was badly written, it might have made an impression on people. It wasn't very long: I'd got better coverage in other countries.

Handing it back to him, I said: 'It's not that bad. People forget this sort of thing very quickly.'

'People do, but not the courts. Once they get a grip on someone, they don't let go. The case will be a difficult one to defend.'

It was the usual technique: to present as black a picture as possible. To save time I asked: 'What do you suggest?'

'The best thing would be to get the charges dismissed, and then to make the file disappear. The judge is an old friend of mine, but it won't be easy because he's very fond of money. . . . I don't know if you'll be able to pay. . . .'

I interrupted the old chiseller.

'Look, let's not waste time. I want this man free within a week. If you can manage it, there's twenty thousand dollars in it for you.'

The size of the figure startled him; it was a fortune in Costa Rica. I was aware of this, but you don't bargain where freedom is concerned. I had given Dave my word, and I wasn't about to try to save pennies at the expense of someone who had complete faith in me.

'At that price there won't be any problem.'

I thought: There'd better not be, you old bastard.

'I'll let you have two thousand dollars right now. You can have the rest in four or five days.'

'You realize I can't give you a receipt. . . .'

'I don't need one. I don't believe in useless pieces of paper. But let's be clear about something: the minute you take this money, you're committed to getting the kid out within a week. Once you agree to this, I won't accept any excuses or tolerate any cute tricks. I haven't collected any lawyers' ears yet, but it's not too late to begin.'

'I understand completely. He'll be free within a week.'

As I left the office, I knew I'd played poker. If the lawyer didn't keep his word, I'd have to keep mine, and in that case I'd have to put a bullet in his brain and try to escape with Dave.

That afternoon and the next morning we went to see Dave. The guards were used to our visits and to my tips, so we could speak to him without being watched. They even let us talk on the steps outside the prison.

The morning of my third day there, the two Canadians I'd met several weeks earlier in San José showed up. They'd read the story in the papers and came to the rescue – they talked about taking the prison by storm. Two idiots playing tough guys. Great help they'd be! Feeling a little ridiculous about being trailed around everywhere by those two would-be avengers, I got rid of them by sending them off to wait for me in Puerto Jiménez.

I figured that by this time Sancho and Roberto must be in San José. When I phoned them, they already knew about Dave, but I quickly assured them that all was well; I couldn't allow them to panic, because if Sancho even suspected what I was going to do with his dough he'd never come down to Golfito. We agreed to meet the next morning at the Miramar restaurant, a quiet spot right outside Golfito.

The next morning everyone was there. When I saw the big Basque who was responsible for this mess, I got angry all over again. Cutting short everybody's questions about what would happen to Dave, I said: 'Everything's fine here. How did it go in Panama?'

'Everything went fine for us, too,' Roberto said, laughing.

Just wait, you lard-arse, I thought. You've got a surprise coming to you.

'I had to keep a close watch on Roberto,' said Sancho. 'I think he tried to steal the gold.'

'Are you out of your mind?' exclaimed Roberto.

The two of them began to argue. They obviously couldn't bear the sight of each other, and my gut feeling was that Sancho was telling the truth.

'OK,' I broke in. 'We'll settle all that later. Exactly how much money is there?'

Sancho handed me a stack of dollars and a receipt. 'Here it is: $21,775.'

I did a rapid recount and shoved it all into my pocket. Now that I had the money on me, I'd be able to settle accounts.

'We've got to take care of Dave. I can get him out of the cooler, but the lawyer is greedy. I'm going to pay him with Dave's share and with yours, Roberto.'

'Hey, easy now! Why my share? He's the one who fucked up, so let him take the consequences! I'm not about to give up my dough to get him out.'

The bastard was ready to sacrifice his friend for the dough. I'd known he was rotten, but not that rotten. I stood up and slammed my fist into his face.

'You little cocksucker! You're the one who got everybody in deep shit, and you're ready to walk out on your buddy!'

The big son of a bitch, his face a bloody mess, sat there on the ground, passive and contemptible. That just made me more disgusted, and I continued my little lesson with some kicks to his face and body: there was no point in soiling my hands on the prick. Crawling on all fours, he made it to the road with a little help from my foot.

'Beat it, shithead. Don't let me ever see you around here again.'

A last kick started him off in the right direction, and I watched him disappear down the road, his tail between his legs.

Sancho didn't open his trap, but I could see he was happy. His worst enemy was finally out of the picture.

A few minutes later I was in José Araya's office. I counted out $18,000 in hundred-dollar bills, and it made a nice little pile on the table. The rat was so excited that his hands shook as he re-counted the bills. Until then, I don't think he had really believed I'd come through.

'Let me remind you of our agreement. You've got four days, and don't forget it.'

'It's a question of hours now. Things are going to move very quickly.'

'I hope so. Just remember that if you don't keep your word I'll keep mine.'

Dripping with servility, he saw me to the door. If I'd asked, he'd have let me fuck him in the arse.

As I left, I came to a decision. If Dave wasn't free by the end of the week, I'd try a faster method.

I already had a notion in the back of my mind and, though I wasn't ready to discuss it with anyone, I knew I needed a free hand. I didn't want Diane mixed up in this, so when she mentioned a toothache I jumped at the opportunity.

'You might as well take advantage of the fact that we're stuck here and go see the dentist in San José.'

Here feminine intuition, plus the experience of having lived with me, told her something was up.

'I don't want to go up to San José now. The dentist can wait.'

My displeasure must have been clear, because she added: 'Out with it – you've got some sort of scheme!'

'Look, baby, don't force me to lie. I need to be alone, to have some elbow room. Take the plane tomorrow. I'll call you every day.'

Now I had to perfect my plan. I went to see Wayne because I needed his help, and he knew how to keep a secret. In addition, I thought my idea might appeal to the former Marine.

He was in his usual spot, with his usual bottle in his hand.

'Hello, Wayne.'

'Hello, Juan Carlos. What's new? Still in the shit?'

'Yeah, that's why I've come to see you. Do you have any guns right now?'

'Not many. Everything's moving to Nicaragua.'

'Then, I'll need dynamite. Do you have any?'

'A few sticks. Say, you must have something serious in the works! Are you going to blow up Golfito?'

'No, just a lawyer – and maybe the prison.'

'Great! Want some help?'

'No, thanks.'

Old Wayne was really a great guy. He got up, bustled around the place, and handed me some boxes.

'I've got eight sticks of dynamite, five caps and plenty of fuse. How long a piece do you want?'

'Enough for about fifteen minutes will do.'

'I've also got a bulletproof vest if you want, and I can let you have a .45 automatic.'

'No, I don't trust automatics. They jam too easily.'

'Do you need anything else? What's your plan?'

'To blow up the lawyer, then take advantage of the excitement to free Dave. I'll go see him at three o'clock – there's only one guard on duty during siesta time, and as soon as he brings Dave to me I'll tap him on the head with my gun. At his age, he ought to go out like a light. He kind of likes me – it'll be the surprise of his life. I'll have a car parked outside, and we'll make for the port. From there I'll head our boat towards Punta Burica, and after a few hours of hiking through the jungle we'll be in Panama.'

'Sounds all right. You're sure there'll only be one guard at the prison?'

'One or two, it won't matter. I can handle it.'

'You're sure I can't help? I could see to the lawyer for you.'

'No, he's mine. I promised I'd take care of him. I'm going to tie him down in a chair, with dynamite in his mouth and his pockets, then light a fifteen-minute fuse. That should give me enough time to take care of everything else.'

'If it were me, I'd shove the dynamite up his arse,' said Wayne dreamily. 'Makes me think of the good old days. By the way, I've got two Swiss passports if you want.'

'Sure. How much do I owe you? I'll leave all this here and take delivery just before going into action.'

'You can pay me if you get to Panama. Just let me know what time the curtain's going up. We'll snort some coke, and my wife and I will drink a beer while we watch the show. It's not every day that something interesting happens in Golfito.'

'OK, Wayne. I'll let you know.'

The next morning I took Diane to the airport. I could see that she was worried, and I did all I could to reassure her. I gave her enough money to cover any eventuality, and when the plane left I went back to the hotel, where Sancho was still asleep. I woke him up.

'We're going to Las Palmas, and then to Puerto Jiménez, where two Canadians are waiting for me. We'll give them the "bomb" and take them to Carate. I know a little lode there, and we can build up some capital. We'll have to because that lawyer has made a serious dent in our finances.'

Before leaving, we went to see Dave, and just the sight of his unhappy face was enough to tell me that he'd had it.

'Courage, kid. You'll soon be out of here!'

In Las Palmas I picked up my Magnum, and with the help of Alfredo and his son Carlito we loaded the motor and the tubing for the 'bomb' in the land-rover. Two hours later we were in Puerto Jiménez, where I found my two Canadians at the Rancho de Oro bar. They were enthusiastic about my notion and got along very well with Sancho.

Though he was leery of foreigners, Sancho could see that those two empty-headed kids weren't very dangerous, and that if they were well directed they might even do some good work.

'It's a chance for you to get in on something exciting. I'll take you and all your equipment to Carate by taxi-plane, then when we get there you can stay with a friend of mine, Saltarana. He'll show you a good place to work and how to get started.'

Twenty minutes later, the taxi-plane was there, still with the same pilot. This time he complained when we loaded the motor and the tubing, and with good reason: the motor was black with grease, and the mud-clogged tubes took up so much room that some of the passenger-seats had to be removed. Suddenly his nice little plane looked old and tired, and he wasn't happy about it. I had to force him down in front of the controls and strongly suggest he take off. . . . With tubing everywhere, he barely had room to manoeuvre. Laughing like maniacs, we pushed it aside as best we could so he could fly the plane but, even so, a section of the tubing managed to get him in the neck.

When we landed in Carate, Saltarana was waiting. A few quick explanations while the plane was being unloaded, and then we immediately took off again, because it was growing dark. The two Canadians were a little surprised by the speed with which everything happened, but it was just as well that they fell into step right away.

We slept at Puerto Jiménez. At dawn, when we left in our boat for Golfito, Sancho asked the question that had been eating at him for some time.

'How much did you give the lawyer?'
'Twenty thousand dollars.'

'Twenty thousand dollars! Why so much? We could have done it with a lot less!'

'I couldn't play games with the kid's freedom. You wouldn't have wanted to let him rot in gaol the way Roberto did, would you?'

'No, of course not. But that was our entire capital!'

'Get off my back. It's done, and I'm not sorry, so just drop it. I've got other things to think about.'

I decided to go into action two days later. I couldn't wait any longer, because if they transferred Dave to another prison or to San José we were fucked. I planned to ask Fernando, the dealer, to let me have his car, which he could always say had been stolen. He'd offered to help me, so I was pretty sure he'd agree.

Though I'd made armed visits to public buildings before, this time I was a little excited. It would be the first time I'd ever attacked a prison – but there's a first time for everything. The only thing that really bothered me was that we'd have to leave everything behind. All that work for nothing! But a promise is a promise, and with the kind of life I'd laid out for myself I'd never be able to look in a mirror again if I didn't respect that promise.

All that was going through my mind as I returned to the hotel. When I opened the door to my room, a surprise was waiting for me: Dave, spread out on my bed and sleeping like a baby. The lawyer had kept his word. Wayne would be disappointed.

We went up to San José that same day, since I didn't want to hang around Golfito. In any case, we had to settle accounts, and Sancho's mother was waiting to hear about the rest of the operation. Our plans would have to be revised: of the $24,000 we had started with, only $3000 remained.

In addition, after the tension of the past few days we wanted to relax a bit. Diane was glad to see me, and everyone except Dave, who'd gone off to San Pedro with a girlfriend to celebrate his freedom, went to visit Sancho's mother.

As a businesswoman, Señora Riviera was a pain in the arse. The projects didn't interest her; only the results counted. Our meeting was reasonably frosty since she gagged on the amount of the laywer's fee.

'What I don't understand is your helping your friend by using common funds without consulting anyone,' she began.

'Señora, I'm the one who makes the decisions, and I do what seems best to me. If I had to do it over again, I'd do the same thing. Just tell yourself that, if it had been your son, I would have behaved the same way. It's not a question of friendship but of loyalty.'

'All right, what's done is done, and there's no point in discussing it. On the other hand, Sancho, was it a good idea to hire a plane to drop the motor off near Carate, where there's no one to guard it?'

'Mama, you know that it's Juan Carlos who directs the. . . .'

Poor little Sancho trembled in front of his mummy like a guilty schoolboy. Diane and I could hardly keep from laughing. I'd known he was a coward, but not that much of one!

The old lady continued. 'Now, please explain why this association is based on a 45–55 per cent split when we're the ones contributing almost all the capital.'

I was beginning to have a bellyful of this old witch. From the time I was able to outrun my father, no one in the whole world had given me orders. I couldn't let her confuse politeness with weakness. Despite her age, she was in for some surprises if she kept on in that tone. I decided to make short work of it.

'Listen. Money can be got anywhere, and it's not that hard to find people who want to make an investment. Me, I know gold and I know the jungle – not everyone can say that much. Your son was the one who asked for this partnership, not me; but, if you're not satisfied, we can call it off here and now.'

'No, I didn't mean that. In any case, we're in too deep to back out at this point. We'll continue on the same basis, but I'd like to make one condition: I don't want Dave to be part of the deal. He's too irresponsible.'

'No. I didn't get the kid out of prison just to toss him into the street without a cent. I intend to keep him with me until I can give him a few hundred dollars. Don't worry – I refuse to drop him right now but, believe me, I have no intention of keeping him for ever. It'll all be over in a few weeks.'

So we finally decided to go on together. We had to block out a fairly large area and go to work. But by the time I left this meeting I'd lost some of my faith in the deal. The old lady had got on my nerves – I don't like to make any concessions – and I had lost all respect for Sancho, who was just too spineless.

We stayed in San José a few days to take advantage of the good restaurants and the movies, and then we went south to Las Palmas.

Everyone there knew about the arrest, and with their usual tendency to exaggerate the Ticos had considerably embroidered the incident. We decided to remain to choose our site, but the atmosphere wasn't the same. We didn't have as much fun – it was impossible to make a big splash since we had no money – and there was absolutely no team spirit. I was getting along with Dave pretty well, but Sancho was beginning to disgust me.

We'd been there two days when one of the Canadians I'd left in Carate showed up. He'd lost weight and could barely walk. Nothing was going right down there, he told me.

'You dumped us as if we were some kind of shit! We thought you'd be coming back soon. We don't know anything about gold, and your friend Saltarana is worthless – he's a jack-off who never even lifted a finger to help us. We haven't collected a gram!'

I could hardly keep a straight face. It was true that I had kind of dropped them. I'd thought up that scheme just in case the lawyer kept his word, but I was so sure I'd have to choose the other solution and then leave Costa Rica that I hadn't attached much importance to the plan. Once the enthusiasm of the plane ride had faded away, they must have felt a little lost there on the beach, with that hydraulic pump on their hands.

'Never mind, it's not that important. In any case, I need the "bomb" for some work here. Go back and tell Claude that I'll come for it in a few days.'

'I'm not going back – I've had it! I've already made the trip between here and there once, and my feet are killing me. Osa and I are finished. I'm going back to San José.'

His yen for adventure hadn't lasted very long.

One day I went up to inspect some land: an old peasant wanted to sell his property and take off with his son. Surrounded by jungle, adjacent to the park, and some three a half hours on foot from Las Palmas, the property was about two thousand acres and not expensive. Our money was running out, so I had no choice but to be interested. I went to Golfito the next day for the papers.

Sancho wasn't very enthusiastic. He was irritated with Dave, who'd bounced him around in the car, but I ignored his mood and forced him to make a choice.

'Sancho, we have to fish or cut bait. We've got the land, and we have to get some tractors here before we run out of cash.'

'But it's too early – there's no road. A tractor can't get through everywhere, and we might ruin everything.'

'We've got to get it here, even if it means dismantling it and bringing it up piece by piece.'

'That's crazy! I've had enough of all this. Why don't we just buy a pulperia here and do some peaceful trading in gold?'

'It doesn't bring in enough, and it's too late to back down. You're not going to quit on us now, are you?'

'OK. I'll go along with it if you drop Dave. He thinks everything's a game, and there's no way of making him take things seriously. He almost lost the car in the river today. God knows what he'll do tomorrow!'

Ever since Roberto had been dealt out, Sancho had got his hopes up. Unfortunately for him, he was beginning to annoy me – even the way he looked was bugging me. Meanwhile, the more pissed off everybody got at Dave, the more I liked him. It's true he was irresponsible, but I've got a soft spot for lunatics.

'Sancho, I've already told you I won't agree to any conditions, and especially not that one. If you want to go on with me, it's with Dave or not at all. And that's my last word on the subject – take it or leave it.'

'Well, then, I think I'll leave it. I'm tired of these crazy goings-on. Let me have my dough back.'

'It's probably better this way after all. We don't have the same values, and we don't like the same things. I suggest we divide the money that's left. Take back the jeep and the boat, my friend, but I'm afraid I'll have to keep the "bomb" because there's not much I can do without it. I'll return it later.'

He wasn't very happy to be separated from his motor, but he was surprised to get off so easily: he'd thought he'd lost everything. I gave him $1200 and one day to clear out.

I knew it was crazy to get rid of Sancho, who was the one contributing everything, and keep Dave, who was contributing only trouble – but I'd had enough of the Tico, and it wasn't the first time I'd chosen friendship over a good deal. What a sentimental bastard I am! You can always get me by sounding the right note.

With Sancho gone, I went to Golfito with the landowner to register my new property. I paid an advance of ten thousand colones, a fraction of its worth; I was still using the same old methods. When I got back, I found Claude, the other Canadian, who'd come by truck from Jiménez. He told me the motor was safe with Saltarana. His buddy had left the peninsula for good, but he wanted to work with me. This decision to go on after the Carate fiasco proved he was a fighter. He was strong and had the right attitude; that made him a good recruit.

We remained in Jiménez another three days, just long enough for the former owner to put up a shack on my new jungle property; he assured me that that would be enough time. After that, we flew to Carate to pick up the 'bomb', in the same plane and with the same pilot as before. Next we rented a truck and brought the motor to Las Palmas, where I hired a few Ticos to help at the site. We stayed there two days, then went back into the jungle.

And the shit began all over again.

It took a whole day to walk a stretch that usually took three and a half hours. The motor unbalanced the horses, and they fell several times. It was a heavy compact unit, and there was no way to distribute the load equally over a nag's back. In addition, we'd attached several hundred yards of tubing to their rear, and the damn stuff got all tangled up, caught in the trees and slowed us down. And finally there were our supplies, all the stuff we needed to settle in for a long stay – we even had a hen, a gift from the pulperia-owner's wife.

The expedition looked a little like a convoy of refugees, but I was glad to leave Las Palmas: after having lived there in style, I couldn't stand watching the pennies.

When we arrived that evening, soaked and muddy, we found that the shelter the owner had promised didn't exist. There was nothing but the basic frame and about a quarter of a roof. We had to make do with hammocks, and the next day we went to work seriously.

It took us a week of backbreaking labour to set up something halfway decent in this jungle – it was thicker than anything I'd seen so far. Up at four in the morning, we slaved away until nightfall with only short breaks for food. The place was really foul, and unbelievably damp – the river was only about thirty yards away – so the vegetation grew almost as you watched. For days on end, we used our machetes to clear away a fifty-yard area around the house, but the stuff grew almost faster than we could cut it – about two inches a day; I'd never seen anything like it. The ground was red and sticky mud that clung to you, and there were snakes everywhere. Dave, Claude and I worked on the roof under Diane's watchful eyes.

I decided to make a road from the river to the house. There was a drop of more than nine feet, so it meant three steps, a platform, three steps, etc. It was an insane undertaking, because I was determined to cover it all with gravel, which meant endless trips from the river carrying sacks of gravel that were then dumped and spread into a wooden framework. It was hard and exhausting work, and shortly after returning to the jungle my body was weakening again and I had dysentery. I did my share, but it made things even harder. Luckily, Dave really pitched in; and Claude, built like an athlete, was very efficient. The road took form and was a pleasure to look at. When you live in such a rotten hole you need to see something beautiful, something that's not really useful but that keeps you from degenerating into an animal. Not a single Tico saw the point of this Japanese-style road, and I have to admit it was certainly odd, right there in the middle of the jungle.

Diane's contribution was to see to the house. She began by isolating a corner for the two of us in order to create the privacy of a bedroom; the rest of the building was a latticework common room and bedroom for the others. She put it all together tastefully and efficiently, did some decent cooking, and kept the place as though it were an apartment in Paris.

Even though we still had no walls and the forest invaded the kitchen, no one was allowed inside wearing his muddy boots; we both wanted to create something clean in the midst of all the rot.

We ate a lot, but badly: spiced rice, spiced beans, stalks of bananas. We ate so many bananas that they never had time to ripen. A stalk lasted three days. Dave ate like a monster and would cut the stalks down singlehanded; it was the first time in his life that he'd done such hard physical labour. We all wanted to eat the hen, but she stayed out of sight. Though she was still quite young, we kept hoping for the miracle of an egg.

I marked off the boundaries of my territory and used my pistol to enforce them; I was determined to teach any Ticos who ventured into the jungle to keep their distance. They were used to crossing the property, so I'd fire over the heads of all those who came near, because if you let them they'd come right up to the dinner-table and draw up a chair. I got a kick out of seeing them jump and take to their heels. There was a path that went right in front of the house; I didn't allow anyone to use it after nightfall, and whoever tried to, was treated to a good scare. More than one Tico dropped his load so as to be able to run faster. I'd put up a large sign – PRIVATE PROPERTY, KEEP OUT – and they all had to follow an all-but-impossible detour along the other side of the river. I couldn't have cared less; this was my place, and I didn't want to see any of those bastards on it.

I was used to travelling just about everywhere with only a pair of jeans, a shirt, and some boots. I don't own much, but I have a strong sense of property about what I do own. The news of what I'd done got around quickly, and nobody came that way without first calling out 'Don Juan Carlos'. In addition to everything else, the Ticos have no respect for beautiful things, and one of them even went so far as to ride his horse up our gravel walk. Diane, furious, fired at him, and horse and rider went racing off in different directions.

Evenings were the only time we could relax. After the spiced rice, we would smoke some enormous joints and listen to Radio Golfito on Diane's small transistor. The station's slogan always gave us a laugh: 'Radio Golfito, the biggest station in the world.' I'd seen it once, and everything was jammed into a ten-by-twenty room!

There was something special about the atmosphere of those evenings coming after a day of hard work. Dave was as crazy as ever, but he'd at least learned to respect certain rules of social behaviour

100

and didn't just come barging into my room whenever he felt like it. As for Claude, he was cool and collected, but he also liked to horse around. We did a lot of dope, and in the evenings, when we were stoned, almost anything amused us. For example, we'd watch for Ticos trying to slip along the path, and laugh like crazy at the way they jumped as our bullets went whistling past their ears. All four of us were good shots, and when we were doped up we'd aim as close to those guys as possible; if you hit him, you lost!

I was soon minus the men who were helping to build the house because they'd been rude to Diane. I bawled them out and threatened to string one of them up by the balls – which was just a way of talking, but he took it seriously, and they left without even waiting for their pay.

My big problem was the recurrence of my malaria. The unhealthy climate and bad food had undermined my strength, and the illness got the better of me. I suffered from permanent dysentery, and spent sleepless nights shivering and perspiring; Diane was constantly changing the sweat-soaked sheets. In the morning I'd be exhausted and want to go on sleeping, but I'd have to get moving: I was supposed to be the leader and, if I didn't pitch in, no one would lift a finger.

One night I went to sleep in a hammock. I couldn't bear the bed any more, and I wanted Diane to get a few hours of undisturbed rest. The hammock was rotten and reached practically down to the ground. At dawn I was awakened from a drowse: a few inches from my hand, which was touching the ground, the hen was pecking away at the neck of a tercio pelo about a yard long. I'd almost, in my agitated sleep, brushed my hand against it! Good work, bird! She'd saved my life – and her own, too, because from then on she was under my protection.

A lot of people came to sell me gold now that I didn't have a dime to buy it with. I told them that I was just settling in, that I'd consider it later. Since I had a little more time to talk to them, I discovered something new about Osa: many of the men were Nicaraguan refugees who had fought with the anti-Sandinista forces; others were Cubans who'd asked for sanctuary in the Venezuelan embassy in Havana a few years earlier.

One guy gave Diane a reddish monkey he'd captured in the jungle, and we named it Arturo. He was a regular devil, a total catastrophe. We'd find him – or signs that he'd passed that way – in the bed, in the overturned and half-emptied sacks, on the roof, whose leaves he stripped off, on the table while we were eating, and even on our plates. He'd got into the habit of lifting the covers of the pots and would regularly scorch himself, after which there'd be endless cries and gesticulations while he ran around and overturned everything. He also became attached to the hen and would run after her trying to remove a few souvenir feathers; they'd race through the shack, turning over everything in their way.

Considering the lack of meat and the uproar they caused, I was seriously tempted to eat both of them, but they were sacred. It did no good to discipline Arturo: if I hit him or tied him up, his screams were unbearable. I often wanted to strangle him, but Diane always came to his defence, and after every dumb trick he'd seek shelter at her side. He knew very well when he'd gone too far, but we were really fond of him and had fun in the evening when we'd get him high. He loved it when we blew smoke up his nose, and he'd get even crazier. The best thing about that was that afterwards he'd fall asleep.

An old man named Tonio often came to see me. He'd been living at the edge of the national park for quite a while, but now the government wanted to pay him to leave. To collect the money he would have to go up to San José, and since he'd always been an orero and had left the peninsula only twice in fifty-six years he wanted me to go with him: he was afraid of cities. It was with him that I checked on the grade of the gold on the land.

Four men working hard for four days opened a trench along the entire length of the property, and we found gold almost everywhere about three feet down. The concentration was excellent, but there was no way to work it by hand. We needed machines, and I didn't have a nickel to rent any. I had to make a few thousand dollars very quickly so I could begin exploiting my land.

Tonio told me of a dried-up river-bed from which he could come up with five grams of gold a day by loading a sack with shovelfuls of auriferous gravel that he washed in a river some fifty yards away. That was just right for me, because with the 'bomb' I could bring water from the river directly to the site and increase the yield. The only problem was that the site was an hour and a half away, and right in the middle of the national park. It was against the law to go in there, much less work there with a motor. I went with him to see the place and verify his story. The area was rich, but hard to get to: the hill was too steep for horses, and getting the equipment up would be no picnic.

I went back down to our camp, excited by the prospect of action.

'Dave, take the horses and go to Las Palmas to buy two jerrycans of gasoline.'

'You're not planning to take the motor up there?'

'I am. We're going to be working there.'

'But didn't you see that incline? The horses will never make it!'

'Who said anything about horses? We'll bring it all up on our backs. Don't tell me a little jaunt like that bothers you?'

'Well, sure. It's hard enough if you're not carrying anything. You have to be a maniac to do this!'

'No problem. Maniacs are all we've got here. Hurry, you have to leave now if you expect to be back before midnight. I want to do some of the climb under cover of darkness – I don't want anyone to know about this, or the rangers will be on our backs. OK, move it!'

Like conspirators, we left in the night, the motor loaded on one horse, the gasoline on the other. The horses, exhausted by the trip back and forth to Las Palmas, had trouble getting as far as the cliff. From there we had to carry the motor, and that's when the real fun began. It was even harder than I'd thought. The slope was terrible; even with our hands free, we kept slipping back. The fucking motor was really heavy, and there was no way to get a grip on it. We had to take turns carrying it on our backs, and even though it had been wrapped in jute sacks some corner of it always managed to jab you. Built like matchsticks, Dave and Tonio could hardly lift it, so I sent each of them up carrying a jerrycan and dragging along behind them yards of tubing attached to their belts, because you needed a free hand to grab the trees. Claude and I traded off with each other. With my dysentery, my lack of sleep, and the shortage of food, I was very weak and had a hell of a time climbing. I gave the baby back to him every ten yards. Luckily, Claude was used to mountains and he worked miracles. He did thirty-yard stretches – slowly but surely; neither of us could afford to fall because the weight of the motor would crush us – or, worse yet, it might roll all the way back down.

While one was carrying, the other cleared the way and kept an eye out for snakes. When we got to the river, there were stars dancing in my head, and I was so dizzy I had to lie down. I'd have liked to spend the night that way, but I couldn't; I had to get back on to my rubbery legs.

The next morning we were at the site bright and early. While I set up the canoa, Claude and Dave got the 'bomb' running. It started suddenly, and Dave, terrified by the noise that echoed through the silent forest, cut the motor – after which it was impossible to start again. We tried everything we knew, pulling on that fucking cord as though it were a mortal enemy. I felt like smashing it and scattering the parts in every direction. We swore at it, but that didn't help: the inertness of that block of scrap metal seemed to mock us. Nobody knew a thing about mechanics and, in any case, we didn't even have a screwdriver! Everybody was depressed, and I could feel them brooding about what was awaiting them.

After a few minutes' silence, I spoke the fateful words: 'OK, back we go.'

It may seem insane, but I'm a stubborn man and I'm used to seeing through whatever I start. Even if you die in the attempt, you go on to the end. This was the only thing we could do, and that fucking pump wasn't going to make the decisions: I was the one in charge!

We half-slid, half-carried it down, each of us tempted to give it a small shove that would send it tumbling down till it smashed against the rocks.

When we got to the house, it was still daylight. Everyone was worn out, but I didn't want things to end on a note of demoralization and defeat.

'Dave and Claude, load up the horses. If you go now, you can catch the boat that leaves Playa Blanca for Golfito at four in the morning. Find a mechanic there, get this piece of shit repaired, and come back.'

'But we're exhausted! It's a long way to Las Palmas, and we'll sweat bullets before we get there.'

'We'll all sweat bullets and we'll go on sweating bullets. Just look at the state I'm in! This isn't a resort – a deal like this takes some doing! Now, get a move on. You can be back by tomorrow evening. And buy some pot while you're there – we're almost out.'

With nothing to eat, we could still make it; but with nothing to smoke – forget it.

The next day, after a night spent suffering from malaria, just as I was stretched out on the bed and smoking my first joint of the day, the house was suddenly swarming with uniforms. They came from everywhere – through the door, through the windows – pointing their rifles at us.

'Don't move! Hands up!'

Christ! Where did they all come from? Were they starting their routine all over again? It was becoming a habit! I'd casually swallowed the joint, and my stash was safe under my balls, my usual hiding-place. The tension was high, and the cops were nervous – I'd barely moved my hand when I was told not to budge. Once again they were Commando Sur cops, but this time from Jiménez. They frisked me quickly, then began searching the entire house, making us leave the room while they looked everywhere, emptying all the sacks. One of them got up on a chair and methodically inspected each beam and poked his hand into the leaves of the roof; it looked as though they were going to turn over the stones and tree-trunks around the house, and even inspect the adjacent parts of the jungle. I had no idea why they'd come or what they were searching for, and I was trying to figure it out. Diane, completely cool, watched to make sure they didn't steal anything.

I asked them what they wanted.

'Keep your mouth shut and don't try anything funny,' said one of them, turning his rifle on me.

'What's the complaint against me?'

'Where's your gun? Where's the dope?'

'I lost the gun crossing the river, and I don't have any dope here.'

The guy began to laugh.

'Save it, Frenchie, we know you're a wise guy. We also know all about what happened in Golfito, so don't play the innocent! Where's your gun?'

'I swear I lost it. Search everything – you'll see for yourself.'

'That's exactly what we intend to do. And it'll be your arse if we find it.'

I knew exactly where my gun was: inches away from his feet, crammed into my boots. It never occurred to them to look; if they had, I don't know how I would have explained it. The same went for the grass if one of them started to stare at my crotch. I was wearing shorts, and it made me look like I had an enormous pair of balls.

'And where have you hidden the money?'

This was something new! I didn't understand. They certainly weren't interested in a few thousand colones and, even if I had the reputation for being rich, there was nothing illegal about that. . . .

After having interrogated and searched in vain, they relaxed a little. I suggested some coffee, and they accepted. While I had my back to them, I quickly tossed my bag of grass into the fire and had just enough time to breathe in a noseful. The smell of the burning plastic covered the odour of the dope, and the place was too open for them to have smelt anything. I came back with the coffee. Outside, with the cops, I saw Sancho; he looked frightened and ill at ease.

'Sorry, Juan Carlos, I'm a prisoner, too. I had to tell them about what went on in Panama.'

He looked scared shitless, and I couldn't figure out if it was because he'd betrayed me or because he'd been arrested.

Then Diane nodded towards a bump in his shirt – obviously made by his gun. Furious, I pointed at it, telling him: 'You son of a bitch! Are you trying to make me believe they let you keep your revolver after they arrested you?'

I jabbed towards him with my index finger, and he jumped.

Suddenly I understood the aggressiveness of the cops and all their questions – he must have told them that I was dangerous, that the best thing would be to shoot first. Dave, to shake him up a little, had told him I was a former mercenary who got a bit kick out of cutting people's heads off. . . . I also realized that Sancho had never believed I really gave the lawyer all that money. He must have made a deal with the cops to split whatever they found, his bait being the prospect of confiscating my gun: they could never treat themselves to a chrome .357 Magnum on their salaries.

Then I spotted the one-eyed man – the guy who sold me the land – and Carlito, Alfredo's son, who must have been the ones to lead them here since Sancho hadn't known where I was. All of them were accusing me of the worst things: rats deserting a sinking ship. It had been a long time since they'd seen any money, so they figured they might as well turn nasty. . . . The cops took our passports, and the officer in charge turned to me.

'I'm going to keep these passports. You're expelled from the peninsula. Pack your things. We'll go with you. We don't want you around here any more – you've made too much trouble. You're charged with threatening the life of one of your employees, carrying arms, shooting at people, using drugs, trafficking in gold and, on top of everything else, building a house on government land! I want you out of here immediately.'

I sat down. I was feeling a little dizzy.

'I can't. I'm too sick to move today.'

'What's wrong with you?'

'Malaria and dysentery. I can hardly stand up.'

'It's true you don't look too good.'

And then the same thing that always happened whenever I'd been arrested happened again. After the first rough moments, I'd win the others over to sympathy and respect. A kind of relationship develops: something man to man.

Lieutenant Nogales was no exception to the general rule. He was a tough guy, but he could recognize someone just like himself. We talked for an hour. He was more intelligent and made of better stuff than most, and I could tell that he was more than a little disgusted by the servility of my accusers. He was willing to help me if he could.

'OK, I'll give you a few days to get on your feet again. But I have to take your hydraulic pump.'

'Why? It's mine. It belonged to the company that I formed with Sancho.'

'No, no,' called Sancho from behind Nogales, where he'd been listening. 'It's mine! I've got papers to prove it.'

Poor little turd who could only protect himself with legal papers! I'd see to him when there were fewer people around. For now, I spat in his face.

'Easy now,' said Nogales. 'I want to be understanding, but don't push it. Sancho is perfectly within his rights.'

'OK, but I've sent the pump to Golfito for repairs, and that's where you'll have to pick it up.'

'We'll go there now. Come by and see me when you're feeling better, and we can talk.'

They'd been exhausted when they arrived because they'd come the long way round. I liked Nogales, so I pointed out the short way down for them.

Two hours later, while Diane and I were talking about what had happened, Dave and Claude showed up.

They both looked kind of funny, and I soon found out why. By chance, they'd met the cops right in the middle of the jungle. True, I'd told Claude to hurry, but I hadn't thought they would move so quickly! The mechanic had given them a ride in his truck, so they didn't have to take the boat, and that saved a hell of a lot of time; but, unfortunately, the cops had taken the pump and found some grass attached to a saddle. Luckily, Claude had assumed full responsibility for it, because since Dave had a record it might have gone hard with him. Nogales had given them a break – and only picked up their passports; but, still, that made a lot of recent run-ins with the cops!

I decided to settle it all as quickly as possible, and the next morning Diane and I left for Jiménez.

At the station in Puerto Jiménez, I was very well received. After one glance at my sick-looking face, Nogales even offered me lunch in his office. We got along fine, and he apologized for his heavy-handed arrival the day before.

'You understand that with your reputation and the nature of the complaints against you I had to take every precaution. I don't mind telling you that everybody was afraid, and we were expecting a fight. . . . What do you plan to do now? You can't stay up there – this business has caused too much of a fuss.'

'I can't go anywhere else, either. I haven't got a nickel and I've got to scare up some money.'

'Listen. I'm leaving to spend Christmas in San José. I'll be back on January fifth. Promise me that you'll be gone by the time I return. This is only the fifteenth, so you've got twenty days. It's the best I can do, and I'll arrange things with my superiors. But if you're still up there when I get back I'll put you under arrest. . . . Give me your word, and you can have the passports back.'

'It's a deal.'

While we were in Jiménez we bought some supplies – rice and beans, which was about all we could afford – plus half a key of weed. We could only hope we'd have time to smoke it. I also treated myself to a plate of meat, because every time I ate well my fever would go down. Then we went to Rancho de Oro, where I ran into a German called Hans and a buddy of his, Faulker – another German – married to a nineteen-year-old Tica. He hadn't been on the peninsula long and he was still in good shape. His boots, his stetson and his healthy face all made him look like the Marlboro man.

I told them my story, and they were both interested – especially Faulker, who already had a 'bomb' working on the Tigre.

'Everything should have been all right because it was a good lode, but I don't have a pump any more.'

'Mine's only turning out ten grams a day. How much were you getting up there?'

'Practically two hundred grams a day when there weren't any problems.'

It was a big lie, but I had to work something out. His saloon swagger was really too cute, but I needed his pump.

He took the bait. 'Maybe we could team up and use the "bomb" together. When can I come around?'

'Whenever you want – the sooner the better.'

They took me to Las Palmas in their car, and while we drove I managed completely to convince them. I had to have that pump! I was finally able to persuade them to bring it to Las Palmas the next day and then hire someone to guide them to my place.

Soon Faulker, his wife and a Tico employee showed up. Faulker had dealt Hans out because he sensed he was on to a good thing and didn't want to share. Underneath that operetta-cowboy get-up beat the heart of a pirate – one of the nasty kind who can make friends walk the plank even when they've done them a favour, as was the case here: Hans had taught him everything about the peninsula. I saw no reason to treat Faulker with kid gloves.

When they showed up, muddy and exhausted, they seemed to think they'd accomplished a great feat. I didn't unload the horse because I wanted to take the pump right to the hill. Faulker was terrified of snakes and scared out of his skull when he saw us kill them. We exaggerated a little, saying we'd seen an enormous one close by, but I had to put a muzzle on Dave, who was getting ready to invent one more than thirty feet long.

Faulker's pump was even heavier than ours, but the four of us managed to get it in place before nightfall. The effort, the mud and the snakes had completely demoralized 'Viele Schlange' ('Many Snakes'), as we'd already nicknamed him. We all disliked him from the very beginning. He hated animals and couldn't understand what a hen and a monkey – that kept pulling his hair – were doing in the house. He tried to win over Arturo, but the latter gave him a bite that drew blood. As Diane put it: 'He can't be a nice guy if Arturo doesn't like him.'

The monkey's reaction to him sealed his doom. In the evening Faulker couldn't eat the food we prepared because he found it too spicy – we'd purposely added even more spices than usual, and it was almost too much even for us – so he took from his knapsack a whole stack of supplies: powdered milk, bouillon cubes and canned stuff. His wife opened a can, and the two of them ate off in a corner without offering to share. You just don't do that kind of thing.

When the time came to turn in, he looked around uneasily. We'd rapidly set up a double bed for him right in the middle of the common room. Dave, Claude and the Tico had their hammocks on either side and kept sneaking looks at his wife. Standing there in pyjamas, they both looked kind of silly. The cowboy image had quickly faded.

I felt a little hungry and went to the kitchen, where I found Dave, Claude and Arturo already seated in front of Faulker's food-supplies. We had a little nocturnal orgy, even eating heaped spoonfuls of his powdered milk. Arturo was enjoying the joke and silently stuffing himself with everything that came to hand. By the time we left the kitchen, we'd done away with half of Faulker's provisions.

At breakfast he looked kind of unhappy, but since Arturo's face was covered with powdered milk the finger of suspicion seemed to point that way.

'Why did you eat Viele Schlange's provisions?' Diane scolded the monkey. 'It was very, very, naughty of you.'

Faulker was wise to us, but he was afraid to say anything.

We went back up to work. An enormous amount of time was spent installing the tubing, and when we returned in the evening after having hidden the pump we had only eight grams of gold. Viele Schlange was very unhappy. His employee, who could see the way the wind was blowing, immediately quit and headed for home, preferring to leave in the dark rather than spend the night with us. Faulker found Arturo (who was really getting into bad habits) in his bed and wrapped in his sheets. At Faulker's cry, the monkey took off shrieking, but not before leaving a turd on the pillow.

No sooner had our little couple bedded down than we scooted to the kitchen and began the previous night's routine. This time we gave Arturo the bouillon cubes so that he'd let us eat the other stuff in peace. As long as he was busy unwrapping them, everything was fine. It seemed like such a good joke that we just kept stuffing ourselves, and in the end we left only a single bouillon cube. Even Arturo seemed full.

In the morning, as though on purpose, Diane killed two snakes in the kitchen. Viele Schlange looked a little pale and left for work on an empty stomach: a bouillon cube isn't much of a breakfast.

Faulker got on our nerves. He was always interfering, always complaining, always giving advice. I have to admit that if he was expecting two hundred grams a day he was badly disappointed. It wasn't a bad spot, but nobody had his heart in his work – and, besides, I was tired of the arsehole. Suddenly I motioned to Dave and Claude; we gathered up our stuff and left without another word – without even turning off the pump.

Faulker was dumbfounded and began to yell in German. He ran towards us like a madman, then ran back to try to hide his pump. But he was terrified of staying on by himself and returned with us, shouting and complaining every step of the way. We paid no attention to him and treated it all like a big joke. To get him to calm down, I threatened him with a miner's bar and he shut up.

Back at the house, the situation really came apart. We all made fun of him, and the stickier things got the funnier we thought it all was. Claude began making faces and singing German songs. . . .

I might have been able to work seriously with him, but he had behaved too badly with Hans and things had got off to a bad start. He'd completely lost his sporty look, and his wife hated us for making him seem ridiculous. He asked me to help bring his pump down, and I told him to fuck off; then he asked the others, and got the finger for an answer. In any case, I wouldn't let the horses be used, since they were looking rather seedy. . . .

Eventually, Faulker lost control and began to yell. In the beginning it was funny, but we'd soon had enough. I was feeling fairly weak that day, and I turned to Claude.

'Do me a favour, buddy, and let the gentleman have the back of your hand.'

Claude got up, and Faulker, who didn't understand French, thought he was going to lend him a hand. He was surprised to get a fist in his snout. Claude was six foot six inches, and Faulker was only five feet eight, so he decided not to hit back. But we could see that he hadn't liked it.

I told myself that, if he left his pump up there, I could always make use of it. I could also have confiscated it, but there'd recently been too much ado with the cops.

By scurrying here and there, he eventually found three Ticos who were willing to go for the pump and the canoa. They went off with a rented horse, and brought only the pump down.

The adventure was drawing to a close, and the end was in sight. I went to Golfito to sell the gold we'd got those last two days and to buy something that might help us celebrate Christmas. Wayne offered me a little coke; we spent Christmas Eve as high as kites. We had a great time, and there was a sense that everything was over and we'd soon be going our own ways.

Before leaving, we called in the peasants and sold them everything – the horses, the pots and pans, the shovels, and even Faulker's canoa. We ended up with a few thousand colones, just enough to get back to civilization with. Then Dave couldn't resist the temptation to set the house on fire, so that we sat on a tree-trunk, passed around a big joint and watched the place go up in flames. We turned the hen out into the jungle because we didn't want to leave anything behind.

We returned to Las Palmas on foot, with me carrying Arturo in my arms. That was 3 January 1982. So far I'd had no luck on the peninsula: the first time, I had crawled out half-dead; the second time, I'd been kicked out by the cops.

Part Three

THREE

FOLLOWING MY EXPULSION FROM OSA, Diane and I spent our three last months together. It was the sweet end of a beautiful love that had begun five years earlier on a Caribbean island, when I arrived flat-broke from the Amazon forest. Her father was the last of the Caribbean adventurers, the mayor of a neighbouring island. Married to a woman who descended from one of the old white families, he had three superb daughters. Diane was the most beautiful.

I'd put together a deal that had brought in a lot of money, and for a year and a half we lived like royalty, depriving ourselves of nothing. Then racism, and the many enemies I'd made, forced me to leave the island when Diane became pregnant. We settled first in Turkey, next in Egypt, and then in the Indian Ocean.

The tragedy that started my long slide down occurred while we were on our way to Spain, where I was involved in a show-business deal. In a matter of seconds, Cizia, our year-old son, died in my arms of some unknown sickness. Drugs and gambling had always been part of my life; but after that, in an effort to numb our depression, Diane and I plumbed the depths. Asia, Hong Kong and Macao were the steps down the ladder to Osa.

After the recent series of misfortunes that had plagued me, I needed to be on my own in order to begin all over again.

On leaving Osa, I went to see Wayne and left him my .357 Magnum in exchange for five hundred dollars, which I used to buy some authentic pre-Columbian artefacts that I gave Dave to sell in France. This was my way of respecting our contract. Later, as agreed, he returned my five hundred dollars and kept the profit. The money reached me just as Monge, the candidate of the Partido del Pueblo

115

Unido, was elected to replace Carazo, who had ruined the country.

Alone with Diane, I was free to devote our last moments to her.

A daughter of the sun and the sea, raised on an island, she wanted to live on a beach somewhere. But it wasn't my style to leave Osa without having in some way made it pay, so we surreptitiously went back there by another route.

We crept back through the marshes of Sierpe, the other approach. My first stop was Isla Violin, where according to legend the treasure of the pirate Morgan was buried in a grotto at the edge of the water.

Like many adventurers who'd previously searched for it in vain, I, too, was disappointed. In a natural shift of terrain, the sea had piled up sand and alluvial deposits and was about twenty yards further out than in Morgan's time. As a result, I would have had to explore not just a fringe along the shore, but a band some twenty yards wide – an area too large to sift through.

From there I went off to Guerra, where the terrain was thick with pre-Columbian cemeteries; but the area was filled with colloradillas and mosquitoes, and I couldn't bear seeing Diane uncomfortable.

Eventually I did as she asked: after a twelve-hour march through the forest, we reached Drake Bay, a superb cove of clear calm water where the privateer Sir Francis Drake was supposed to have come to put in a provision of fresh water.

Our arrival at Drake was funny. I had only a few hundred dollars on me when I rented a room in the fishing village's only pulperia, but the pulpero immediately tried to sell me some land. That kind of thing has been happening to me all my life, and even more so now that a few grey hairs around the temples have given me an air of respectability. I might not have a cent in my pockets, but people think I'm rich, and lots of landowners, hotel proprietors and businessmen try to make deals with me.

Though the pulpero's property was fantastic, it certainly wasn't worth the astronomical price he asked for it: fifty thousand dollars – as much money as the average Tico makes in a lifetime! In my usual way, I agreed, but told him I'd first have to live there a while to see if the place suited me. He immediately cleared his family out of the house and rented it to me for two hundred colones a month – about four dollars.

From that day on, the pulpero – the most important man in the village – treated Diane and me with servility: he was counting on making a bundle from us. And it was there that I tranquilly spent my last three months with Diane.

We both knew we'd come to a parting of the ways. I didn't want her to continue being unhappy, and I needed to be alone to get back on my

116

feet. After a series of failures, I had to make a clean sweep of things so I could start fresh. We'd reached the end of the road, but I wanted us to part with some good memories.

The place was magnificent – a point of land with the sea on one side and a rio that separated us from the village and ensured a certain privacy on the other. There were long stretches of sandy beach, and the sea was calm.

The well-cared-for vegetation consisted mostly of fruit-trees, and there was a freshwater spring where the fishermen put in for supplies. In honour of Drake's memory, there was a commemorative plaque, set in cement, in the middle of the property.

We spent peaceful days there with Arturo, and since our needs were simple our expenses were low. The people in the village weren't infected with gold fever, but were mostly gentle and polite fishermen. The only baker on the peninsula had set up shop there, and his bread was wonderful. We wondered what the hell he was doing in that out-of-the way place.

The only dark spot in that paradise was the number of sharks seething in the superb sea; it was dangerous to swim at all, and madness to go more than a few yards from the shore. In the evening, we'd throw out long lines with enormous hooks, and in the morning we'd pull in little hammerhead sharks – unless they'd already been devoured by their relatives.

I took advantage of those peaceful days to build up my strength. I wasn't having fever attacks any more, but I wanted to harden my body against future crises, so I did a lot of swimming in the river, and when the sun wasn't too hot I ran for miles along the deserted beach. We enjoyed the intimacy of the first privacy we'd had in a long time – just the two of us together without any uneasiness and with nothing to think about but our own well-being.

To keep myself from complete inactivity, I'd occasionally go off with one of the local kids to dig around a pre-Columbian cemetery right off the beach some six or seven miles away. Again for conditioning I'd force myself to do the entire distance at a run.

The cemetery wasn't a very rich one, but I did find a few small gold artefacts that I sold to American tourists, which enabled me to treat Diane to a trip to San José so she could collect mail from her family.

Old Nizaro, a lively guy who knew what he was about, lived with his ten children – seven enormous daughters and three sons. His house was literally rotting away, and it seemed to me that if he chose to live in this crowded mosquito-infested hole there must be something murky in his past. He had told me that when he was twenty some-body had shot him in the head with a .22. The bullet had entered his cheek – where it left a clearly visible small pink scar – and lodged in his spinal column, where it remained. He hadn't thought it worth while to have it removed. Now seventy-three, the old man had spent his life digging around the pre-Columbian cemeteries and pros-pecting for gold. He knew the peninsula like the back of his hand, and the information he gave me was invaluable.

He told me he'd once found a 700-gram nugget at a place called Rancho Quemado – 'The Burned Ranch.' 'The site is very rich, prob-ably the finest on the peninsula, but I was kicked out of there about ten years ago by a son of a bitch named Barbaroja – a one-eyed thief and murderer who won't let anybody even come close to his territory! And up there he's the law.'

'I heard about that. An orero told me the story back in Carate, but I didn't know you were the one who'd discovered the site.'

'Of course it was me! It's even because of me that the place is called Rancho Quemado. I burned my house down trying to dry the meat of a wild pig. Who told you about it?'

'Gato, an orero I met in Carate.'

'Gato? I know him – we worked together. A slippery bastard who drinks a lot. Back then, his speciality was swallowing nuggets and retrieving them later. He took a lot of guys in that way – including me.'

Our stories were very much alike, but at least I had the satisfaction of knowing that I hadn't been one of Gato's dupes. The old man's tales interested me because I still hadn't completely given up the idea of going after gold.

As a matter of fact, with an eye to some future enterprise, I did a little work during those three months, carrying out some tests with the catiadora in all the nearby rivers. The results were encouraging: the peninsula was full of gold. Three times a week I'd go off into the jungle, and in a short time I'd checked just about everywhere, even around the Chocohuaco lagoon, not far from the spot old Nizaro had told me about. There were signs of gold all over, especially around the lagoon. I felt that this marsh in which a good part of the peninsula quebradas end up must be an enormous untapped source of gold – but that it would take hundreds of thousands of dollars' worth of machinery to exploit it.

Since the peasants kept coming to offer to sell me their land, at the end of three months I'd taken an option on almost the entire bay, or at least on the part that interested me. It was the same old story: even

118

more broke than usual, I'd paid everyone in promises, which seemed to do the trick. But what I really wanted to do was tackle Osa again.

I still didn't know how, but I knew I had to go back there. And I knew I had to do it alone.

That was the beginning of May, and Diane and I had been living an idyll for the past three months. Everything was going along fine, but I hadn't struggled all my life just so I could end up on a Pacific beach. Diane knew me – and she knew I wouldn't remain inactive very long. She, too, felt that the end of something was in the air. Our relationship relied less and less on words and more and more on a communion of minds. We would wake up in each other's arms and remain together all day long; the idea of separating from her was painful.

I have to say that, though I'm a man of no illusions, a man who's known from an early age women and the pleasures they could offer, Diane was the only woman I'd ever truly loved, the only woman worthy of being the mother of my children. For more than five years, she'd been my mate in all senses of the word; through good times and bad, she'd been supportive, sincere, loyal, and a full participant in my life. She had an unusual strength of character, and she was the only one who could claim a place alongside me. When other women might have weakened, she was there, fighting at my side, with never a sign of weariness, never a word of reproach for the situations into which I had dragged her. She was made for love, but love could never be the only thing in my life, and it was just because I loved her as I did that I no longer wanted to involve her in my insane adventures. There was no possible future with me. I might be a billionaire one day, then find myself a week later a penniless vagabond who'd gambled it all away.

Knowing our separation was inevitable, Diane nevertheless wanted to remain with me a while longer. I convinced her that it was best for us both to go back to San José and from there to phone her father – who immediately sent her a plane ticket home. I knew that the sound of a familiar voice would bring back wonderful memories that would help her through this bad time. I didn't feel guilty: after all, I wasn't abandoning her or leaving her alone in a strange city. She was going to rediscover the security of being with her family, the familiarity of places she'd been happy in before I'd entered her life.

She made one last attempt to talk me into going back to her island, where I knew I could have a luxurious and easy life, but I couldn't see myself returning flat-broke to a place I'd left as a conqueror.

We spent our last night without ever going to sleep – just looking, and talking to each other, each of us trying, one last time, to fill our eyes with the image of the other.

Our farewell at the airport was brief but intense. No tears, no useless words. Our pain was interior, and it was the same for both of us. There was no need to talk about it.

'Will I ever see you again?'

'Who knows, baby? In any case, I truly hope so. No, go – don't make it harder than it has to be!'

A last loving kiss and she was gone, without even turning around.

After she left I had no interest in remaining in the capital, and it was still too soon to return to Osa. I decided to go to Punta Burica. Thanks to my talks with dealers in pre-Columbian artefacts, I'd learned that the largest gold object ever found in the country came from that area, which was enough to make me want to go there even without any specific plans. I needed to sweep away five years of conjugal living and get used to the bachelor's life again. A few days after Diane left, Arturo had stopped eating and soon died – of sadness, I thought. So I was really on my own again.

Two days earlier I'd met a young Frenchman, Nicolas, who'd heard about me and come to seek me out. He'd left France several months earlier and wanted some excitement off the beaten track, so he asked to go with me. He was the same type as Dave – a Paris punk with dyed red hair and an earring; he seemed less irresponsible and more venal. Still, he wanted to have some fun, and so did I, which is why I accepted his proposal even though I was tired of getting involved with non-professionals. Besides, I'd never been able to refuse anyone the chance of adventure. . . . Since I'd decided to make an excursion to Punta Burica anyway, just for fun, someone I could talk to and kid around with on the road was welcome.

We were going to head directly south, and I arranged a meeting-point for us. He didn't look very strong, so to avoid having him be a burden on the road I first suggested he take as little as possible and ended up by advising he take nothing at all. After all my wanderings in the jungle, I'd come to think of it as no more than a garden. He seemed surprised.

'What should I prepare?' he asked. 'Do I need anything special?'

'No, nothing at all. Don't worry about it.'

'A hammock?'

'No. We're sure to find some idiot whose place we can sleep in.'

'Well, at least a machete for the snakes?'

'If you want – but they're heavy and not very aesthetic. And, besides,

120

everyone makes a fuss about snakes, but they're more afraid of you than you are of them.'

So at the appointed time we met empty-handed to trudge south along an endless beach. The route was really very simple. There was only one way to reach Punta Burica: you had to follow the beach, then climb a path used by smugglers to get herds over into Panama and cross the Indian reservation. After that, we'd see. No map, no baggage, just a stroll. We bought food on the way from local peasants. Everything went fine, except that when evening fell we still hadn't got to the smugglers' path. The tide came in, and we had to go up the first river we came to. At nightfall we were far from anywhere, and I decided to stop where we were.

'OK, we'll sleep here. We have to settle in before it gets completely dark.'

'Settle where?'

'I'll take this branch. Find another comfortable one for yourself.'

Nicolas was a little surprised, but since I seemed to find it very natural he accepted the situation.

'OK. The last one in bed puts out the light.'

I rolled a final joint before falling asleep. I noticed with some anxiety that I'd reached the end of the Old Testament, and in the fading rays of day I even took the time to read Nicolas a few lines of the Gospel According to Saint Matthew, while he looked at me in astonishment. Then, lulled by fatigue and grass, we quickly fell asleep.

The next day we were back on the path. There were traces of a recent passage of animals, and by following the tracks we came to an Indian camp.

Don't think they were bronzed Indians sporting feathers everywhere: they were more like a band of degenerates, turned into idiots by too much intermarriage. They were generous with their food, but the crap they ate was disgusting. The women remained hidden and watched us discreetly, but the men sat around us.

As we were getting ready to leave, the oldest of them asked me: 'How did you find your way here?'

'By following the animal-tracks down below.'

They seemed surprised, talked excitedly, then gathered their horses and carbines and galloped out of the village. I decided that they must have some agreement with the smugglers and that during the night the latter had passed that way without respecting the pact. In any case, it wasn't our problem.

I went looking for Nicolas, who was hanging around the kitchens.

121

'Come on, we're out of here. The idiots seem to have gone on the warpath.'

We wandered along for three days, sometimes on the Panamanian side of the border, sometimes on the Costa Rican. There were enough houses on the plateau to allow us to stop and have some coffee here, eat a snack there, buy cigarettes or sleep somewhere else. The rainy season was over, and the sun wasn't too hot.

Talking with a kid we met on the way, I learned that an old Dane named Lars had set himself up in Punta Burica at Penas Blancas several years ago, and I decided to go see him out of simple curiosity.

He didn't have many visitors and was pleased to have someone to talk to, so he immediately invited us to stay with him as long as it suited us. I soon saw that he was a man of real ability. After working in the country for a long time, he'd withdrawn to this nowhere spot at the edge of the beach because civilization no longer interested him; he preferred to remain here and raise his kid, a thirteen-year-old brat who drove him crazy.

Despite his sixty-eight years, Lars was a true natural force: very tall, blond-haired, powerfully built. He bought his supplies at Puerto Armuelles, on the Panamanian side, and walked for two days with his sixty or seventy pounds of provisions on his back. In Europe men of his age aren't even capable of crossing the street alone! He didn't want to do his shopping where he lived because the prices had tripled since the only supply-boat had crashed against the rocks.

His house was pretty basic, but he set a good table, which was just as well because we had monster appetites and the three weeks we spent with him made quite a dent in his supplies. Having gathered some thirty avocados, he assumed they would last a week, so he was pretty surprised to find them all gone the next morning; a nagging hunger had driven us to the kitchen during the night. He had generously told us to help ourselves to whatever we wanted: that may have been an error. I can put away a lot myself, but I was amazed by Nicolas' intake. The tall thin kid ate like four men – and I wondered where he put it all.

I decided to stay until 17 June, the date on which I wanted to return to civilization for the Mundial, the World Cup soccer matches.

Soon after my arrival, I'd discovered in the shack a catiadora and all sorts of gold-prospecting equipment, including a metal canoa and some tubing, and to my great surprise I learned that Lars was a geological engineer.

'I've worked for mining companies just about everywhere, but especially in Alaska,' he told us. 'Here in Costa Rica I spent twenty-five years managing a copper mine, but I can't stand the Ticos any more. They're absentminded and lazy, and they haven't got an ounce of professional conscience.'

'Does all this equipment belong to you?'

'Yes, I did a little prospecting around here out of curiosity. These rivers carry gold, but the density isn't high. In any case, I lost the gold fever a long time ago – I'm much more interested in other, more aesthetic minerals. There's a whole area on the beach covered with agates.'

'I've done some gold prospecting, too, and I wouldn't mind making a little tour with your equipment.'

'Help yourself; you're welcome to it. Ask my son to go with you – he's very familiar with the rivers.'

'Thanks. And do you happen to know if there are any pre-Columbian cemeteries around here?'

'I've heard that people in the area have found some things but, if you want, I'll introduce you to Pedro. He's an old Indian, about eighty-six, and not much of a climber any more, but he can give you some good tips.'

The very next day I began to work some of the rivers. There was gold all right, but it was impossible to get at it. It was what's known as 'microgold' – grains the size of half a pinhead – and it would only be profitable to work on a large scale.

Nicolas, who'd never seen gold, was fascinated, and couldn't understand my lack of interest. 'You're sure there isn't anything we can do with this? It *is* gold, isn't it?'

'Of course it is, but don't you see the size? You'd need a thousand of these dots to make up a gram. You can work it if you want – all you need is about a million dollars in machinery.'

'What rotten luck! This is the first time I've ever seen gold. Shit! In spite of everything, it's exciting.'

'It'll be even more exciting when you find nuggets weighing several grams, which is what happened to me in Osa.'

'I don't get it! You know the really good places, so why don't we go there? I don't understand.'

'Buddy, it would take too long to tell you the whole story. Let's just say I don't want to go back to the peninsula unless it's to do something really big this time.'

Except for those excursions, I didn't do anything that required much energy, and even when the kid took us to the presumed site of a cemetery the expedition wasn't exactly intense. One day we left with two dogs; we'd been walking for about an hour when they flushed out a pizote. We immediately dropped our equipment and lost all interest in the expedition. The cemetery, the gold, the jade – nothing seemed as important as the possibility of being able to fill up on fresh meat. The animal, very violent, almost did for the two dogs; but a machete blow over the head finished it, and the twenty pounds of meat lasted us a day and a half. Lars, who didn't much care for meat, couldn't get over it.

As for taking the kid's information seriously, he was too much of a mythmaker for us to spend time checking out his stories. He was a real pain in the arse, and I didn't like the way he took advantage of his father. One day he brought us to an Indian who he said had found some gravesites; it turned out the Indian didn't know anything about them but just wanted to chat with me. While we were there, he asked us to fix his radio, and Nicolas kindly agreed; but, knowing nothing about radios, he only managed to finish it off for good.

We'd been there a week when Pedro, alerted by Lars, came to see us. He walked with the aid of a cane, the end of which curled into an iron hook that he used to latch on to the trees on the uphill stretches. Finally, an Indian who climbed the mountains more slowly than I did! He led us into the hills till we came to a spot where he pointed out some *molejones de hule* – balls of natural rubber which the Indians used to mark off the boundaries of their cemeteries or their villages.

'What do you think of it?' he asked, proud of his discovery.

'The way I see it, it's a village. There are a few bits of pottery, but too widely scattered to be worth the trouble.'

So we headed back. On the way Nicolas asked me: 'So there's nothing? That old geezer made us bring all this crap along for nothing? Another waste of time?'

'No, not this time. There's a good chance that this is a cemetery, and we're going to look into it.'

'Then, why didn't you say so to the old man?'

'Because I don't want him to know or he'd become a pain in the arse and be on our backs all the time. He'd also blab about it everywhere, and there are sure to be some locals who'd come back and clean the place out. We'll just do a little quiet searching ourselves. See if you can find an iron rod about five feet long at Lars's place, and put aside a shovel without anybody noticing. You've got your nose into everything, so you should know where to find these things.'

'You don't want to say anything to Lars, either?'

'No, I'd rather not. His son would talk about it.'

'But he follows us everywhere. It won't be easy to get rid of him.'

'Play one of your tricks on him – make him angry for a day or so.'

Three days later we went back. The technique is simple: you probe the ground with a T-shaped iron rod. Even after a thousand years the soil doesn't completely pack down again, and when you've had a little experience you can tell the difference in consistency. After several tries, I struck a series of stones about a foot and a half down. It was a small cemetery, about twelve feet by eighteen feet, and marked off by a one-foot wall of perfectly set-in stones that hadn't budged in all that time despite upheavals in the ground. I counted five graves, and decided to begin with the most easily accessible one.

Nicolas was enthusiastic, ready to make the first physical effort of his life. I let him dig a foot and a half down, and took over as soon as the soil changed colour. You had to go easy, raking the ground gently with the machete so as not to lose or break anything; the pieces of pottery, softened by their long stay in the humid ground, are very fragile. An hour later, the first of them appeared – a tripod about a foot high, which I carefully broke loose. I went back to work, and by the end of the day I had four of them drying in the sun.

I took one in my hands and showed it to Nicolas, who was very excited. 'You see – it must be at least a thousand or fifteen hundred years old. Sometimes in places like Guanacaste, for example – you can still find designs on them. But it's too humid here, and the designs have disappeared.'

'Just finding it at all is wonderful. Does it have any value?'

'Not really. In this country, only gold counts.'

And suddenly I threw the pottery against a tree, where it shattered. Nicolas, whose father was an archaeologist, was dumbstruck, and then he started laughing.

'When I think of how many Sundays I spent as a kid being bored shitless, gathering bits of ceramic that weren't half as beautiful as this, it does me good to see you treat it like that! Can I have one of them to commit a sacrilege with?'

'No, my friend – the right to commit sacrilege is something that has to be earned.'

We went back five times during the next two weeks; I wanted to space our visits so as not to arouse suspicion. The fifth trip paid off. The piece I dug out wasn't beautiful but it was pure gold: a cacique, weighing about eighty grams, bent in half, with a broken arm and a misshapen hat. It was what was known as a 'sacrificed' piece: its owner had been a coward, and his jewels had been twisted out of shape before being buried with him.

'How much do you think it's worth?' asked Nicolas, whose eyes were full of dollar signs.

'About five thousand dollars.'

'As much as that? And so far we've only covered a third of the cemetery! With a little luck, there'll be more by the time we've finished clearing it out.'

'Well, it will have to be some other time! Don't forget that I want to go back for the Mundial, and that's in three days.'

'I know, but it's a shame to leave now that we've found this. Anyway, I don't get off on watching guys in shorts run after a ball. Why don't they each get one of their own and call it a day?'

'Hey, you're talking to someone who was the great hope of the Girondin team before he was expelled from the club! Every man has his own pleasures in life – and me, I like to watch a good game played by top teams. And don't forget – people in Central America do a lot of betting on the games, and I know enough about it to make a little cash.'

'Still, it's a shame. This is a sure thing here.'

'Maybe, but that's the way it is. This stuff hasn't budged for a thousand years, and it can wait a little longer. Look, I think the best thing to do is tell Lars about this spot – it's the least we can do after the way he's treated us. I don't know if you've noticed, but we've eaten up all his supplies. There's not one avocado left on the tree, and even the banana-trees are starting to look bare. He's beginning to give you funny looks, and it might be better to leave before he poisons you.'

'OK, OK. You're the one who's running the show.'

He thought I was crazy, but there were some things he couldn't understand. Since discovering the cacique, I'd been wondering if my luck hadn't turned, and I wanted to test it by betting on the matches. I'm a gambler, and it was too good an opportunity to pass up. I also knew that just because we'd found one piece didn't mean there were others – and I really wanted to see the Mundial.

I gave Lars ninety of the hundred dollars I still had left and told him where to find the cemetery. He let us have his son to guide us to a short cut through the mountain.

We left at four in the morning because I wanted to try to do in one day what had taken us three days on the way in. After three hours of walking through the jungle, and a steep descent, we reached the beach and said goodbye to the boy.

He'd had to go with us as far as the beach in order to get back the boots his father had lent me, since mine were unusable, and he looked unhappy about the climb back up; but it wouldn't kill him, and it might teach him to be more respectful to his father. A last joke and a final whack on the back of the neck, and off we went.

126

I hadn't taken the tide into consideration, and we had to hurry: best not to be caught by high tide with our backs against the cliffs because they were sheer, and there was no way to escape – once you started climbing you had to go all the way. We did the last twenty-five miles at a run. Luckily, the stay with Lars had put us in good shape. We just about made it, and as we climbed over the last rocks we were soaked by the waves lapping at the mountain. We slept where we were, and then in the morning a bus took us to Paso Canoas, on the border of Costa Rica and Panama.

The atmosphere was typical of border towns. The only people who lived there were small-time operators, smugglers who gambled on the fall of the Costa Rican colon in relation to the dollar. The frontier is like a Swiss cheese: the streets begin in Costa Rica and end up in Panama. The whole city was in a state of excitement, and the Mundial was all anybody talked about. Soccer plays a big role in Latin American countries, and this was a major event even if there was no Costa Rican team playing. The first match was between Belgium and Argentina. Belgium was an unknown country to most Ticos, but they knew Argentina, so it was naturally their favourite. A young Peruvian dealer I met in a bar confirmed this:

'Nobody wants to bet against Argentina. They're Latins like us, and they were the world champions in 1978.'

'We'll see. Where's the best bar for watching the TV?'

'The Chinaman's, across the street. That's where most people go.'

Apparently, I was the only one who knew that Belgium had been the runner-up for the 1980 European championship. That, and my change of luck – in which I firmly believed – made me want to do a little gambling; I had a hunch, and I wanted to bet on Belgium. But for that I needed some cash.

'Nicolas, you're going to lend me two hundred and fifty dollars. Go change your traveller's cheques on the Panama side and get one hundred-dollar bill and a hundred and fifty dollars in singles.'

'You're sure you know what you're doing?'

'Don't start worrying, or we won't grow old together. Here, keep the cacique as a guarantee. Fair enough?'

Three hours before the match I was in the Chinaman's bar and began my little act. Though I'm not a drinker, I bought a bottle of whiskey, and at the end of half an hour I pretended to be stinko. The bar was full, and the guys, overexcited by the approach of the match, began chanting: 'Argentina! Argentina!' After a couple of minutes, to everyone's surprise, I began bawling 'Belgium!'

The Ticos turned to me; I said it again even louder, then added:

'You don't seem to like Belgium. Me, I'm a Belgian, and I'll cover all bets for my country. I'll give three-to-one odds that Belgium wins. If it's a tie, I lose.'

They looked at me and laughed. Everyone thought I was a big-mouthed idiot. Then I took out my bundle with the hundred-dollar bill on top. 'I've got enough to pay up, and I believe in my country. Anyone ready to bet?'.

The men began to take me seriously and, excited by the prospective windfalls, drew near. Nicolas, uneasy, wrote down the names and sums on a large sheet of paper. He also must have thought I was crazy. I was careful not to accept any bet over a hundred dollars, because if, as I hoped, the Belgians won, I didn't want any welshers. I asked everyone to show me his money and to leave it on the table in front of him. Some of them even went back home to get their dough. Not one of them thought of asking to check my bundle of bills.

I made Nicolas responsible for publicity.

'If they ask questions, tell them I'm very rich but a little crazy. Tell them this won't be the first time, and that I often do dumb stuff like this when I'm bombed, but that I can pay up.'

'OK. From now on, you take the bets. I'll stand near the door.'

'Don't worry, everything will be all right. The Ticos aren't nasty.'

'Maybe not, but they outnumber us.'

That was true. They seemed to be coming out of the walls – I had the feeling that the entire village had decided to meet here. Luckily, the border was close.

By the time the match began, I'd made about thirty bets amounting to $2450; if I lost, I'd have to pay back $7350 that I didn't have. Too bad. I wanted to do something wild, and in any case I believed in my lucky star.

I called over the waiter. 'Drinks for everybody. The loser pays.'

At half-time, the stupid Belgians hadn't managed to score a goal and I was getting a little apprehensive.

I called out to Nicolas, who was still standing near the door. 'Let's eat. I'll order a chicken for each of us. We've got to build up our strength in case things go wrong. If that happens, we'll meet up in Panama.'

'I don't know how good you are with your fists, but I'm fast with my feet. How do you think things are going?'

'Relax. Sure, there are a lot of these Ticos, but if our Belgian arseholes score and keep the lead we're going to treat ourselves to a good time.'

'Yes, but if they don't make a goal it won't be a laughing matter.'

'Keep cool. Be confident. Have a drink!'

'No, thanks. Don't you think you ought to stop drinking? If things don't go well, it would be better if you were in shape.'

'No problem. My body is so used to strong drugs that alcohol has practically no effect on me.'

He bolted down his meal and went back to the door. And just then Belgium scored a goal.

Hurrah for the french-fry eaters! I loved them, I adored them. I shouted victory cries at the bar; and Nicolas, suddenly more confident, came to sit beside me, a big smile on his face. The others became anxious. Five minutes before the end, I got up.

'Come on, let's stand at the door and see they don't run out on us. I've pulled off my bluff, but we've got to work fast now.'

'The way I'm built, do you think anybody's going to be impressed?'

'That doesn't matter. Just look nasty!'

As soon as the match was over, I took the list of betters and called the names out one by one. When they didn't come forward, the others would give them a shove. The Ticos had the vague feeling of having been had, but a bet was a bet. Those who hadn't bet were having a fine time and were all on our side. The young Peruvian joined us and teased the men who came up to pay. When I got to the end of the list, I gave the signal to leave. The Ticos aren't violent, but I preferred not to linger, since a lot of people knew that I was walking around with a nice little bundle on me.

We headed for the Panamanian side, and the Peruvian, who came with us, pointed out a pool-hall that served as a nightclub and straddled the border with doors on each side. I was in a great mood and decided to have a big celebration, so I sent him off to buy ten grams of coke, and we settled into the nightclub. I gave Nicolas back his $250, plus another $250 in interest, and I reclaimed the gold cacique.

As night fell, the Ticos came pouring in, and the orchestra launched into a salsa. All the flora and fauna of dealers were there, and since they were making a quick buck they didn't hesitate to spend it; soon everyone was sky-high.

Our supply of coke didn't last long, and we spent the time kidding around. It was almost dawn when I decided to vary the pleasure. We had just spent three weeks in the jungle without even catching sight of a woman. I sent the Peruvian, who knew everybody, to scare up half a dozen whores so that we could make our choice. We decided to keep them all. Nicolas took one, I took four – when quality is lacking you might as well have quantity. Our Peruvian buddy also chose quantity, but in one package; for himself, he brought back an Amazon three times his size.

We returned to our hotel with our ladies on our heels. The porter looked as though he were going to make trouble, but a banknote brought him around.

Two hours later I went to look for Nicolas and the Peruvian. 'Have you paid anything?' I asked him.

'No, I said it was your treat.'

'What about you, Nicolas?'

'Same thing. I said you were very rich and you'd pay for everybody, as usual.'

'Fine. I'm not paying a dime – not one of my four was worth anything. Come on, let's get out of here.'

And we left the hotel under a storm of abuse from our lovelies. All work deserves to be paid for, but their lack of professionalism had to be penalized.

Coked to our eyeballs, we still hadn't slept. We got a taxi to Golfito, about fifty miles away, and we went to Wayne's place, where we found him still sleeping. Two lines of coke later his eyes were wide open, but he looked strange without a beer-can in his hand.

'What are your plans? Are you going back to Osa?'

'No, I'm going to the Mundial in San José. Do you still have my piece?'

'Yes, and I've kept it in shape. It's a real honey. If you ever decide to sell it, keep me in mind.'

'Will do. Here's your five hundred plus interest.'

'No, none of that between us. I enjoy helping you, and that's enough.'

'Thanks, that's decent of you. And now we've got to go. I want to take the morning plane.'

At the airport two cops were watching the loading. I'd forgotten about them. I had the revolver in my boots and coke in my underwear. One of the cops came up to me. It was that sergeant who'd talked to me about Monge when Dave was arrested.

'Hey there, Frenchie, did you see what happened? Monge was elected. Remember me when you're with your Pueblo Unido buddies, OK?'

'That's a promise. No problem.'

'Thanks. Do you have anything on you this time?'

'Not much. Just a revolver and some cocaine.'

He burst out laughing. I clapped him on the shoulder and we boarded without any trouble. It helps to have a friend in the force.

In the plane Nicolas, who'd been open-mouthed at my exchange with the cop, asked what was up. I told him the story as I prepared two lines of coke.

'Hey, stop! Not here. Everybody can see us.'

'What if they do? They'll assume it's medicine. Besides, this is the last of it.'

During the flight I started thinking. I no longer wanted to sell my gold cacique at what would probably be a loss; on the other hand, I really wanted to enjoy the Mundial in style, and to do that I'd have to produce. The simplest thing would be to go on betting. With a little luck, that should be enough. There was only one problem – my appearance, which might be off-putting. In action – in the jungle or in the country – my big physique was a point in my favour, but in the city it made people suspicious of me. That's why I decided to keep Nicolas: though you might quickly come to suspect he was crooked, at first glance he looked like a nice guy, and that made contacts easier.

In San José I went to the Hotel Balmoral and Nicolas went to the Amstel. The receptionist at my luxurious hotel was Vicky, an old girlfriend of Dave's – a nice chubby little thing. While I was filling in the registration form, I was surprised by the heading: *Balmoral, Hotel, Casino*. So there were casinos in this place! Vicky confirmed it. That was good news. During my first visits there, I hadn't checked it out very carefully. I was sure that Diane had been aware of the casinos, but knowing my weakness had kept the information to herself.

I'd agreed to meet Nicolas that evening at the Key Largo, an American bar, and after a few hours of sleep I headed there. The Key Largo is a luxurious place run by Americans and frequented by the rich gringos in the area. It was packed with little Ticas who'd come to look for a good catch. One of them, seduced by the sight of my pockets, immediately came to our table. As I was explaining to Nicolas how happy I was to have found a casino, she suggested taking me to one called the Torre Blanca. According to her, her brother was the croupier, or something like that; I was sure the Tico was just a drummer.

Nicolas, who'd run into a girlfriend at the hotel, quickly left us. For me, there's nothing more important than a casino table: I much prefer a serious game of poker to a night with the most beautiful girl in the world.

The Torre Blanca was a little house that served as a nightclub and a striptease joint. The gambling salon was on the first floor – a small casino with three blackjack-tables.

I was the only player, and from the eagerness of the croupiers I gathered there must never be much of a crowd. I sat down, and the struggle began. I played until five in the morning – closing time. My luck had come back, though no thanks to the casino, which had tried to fleece me. They'd taken me for a sucker from the very beginning.

Given the lack of clients, they couldn't allow themselves to lose too much, and I was the only player that night. It was really a battle, because all the unoccupied croupiers were gathered around me, and I could feel the tension mount every time I won.

I say it was a fight because in blackjack there's always an adversary relationship between the croupier and the player. In Macao the croupier would curse at us in Chinese. Here, alone at the table, I could feel them all against me. The manager signalled to the waitress to keep my glass filled, but that was fine with me because alcohol had never made me lose my head. And it was in this warm family-like atmosphere that I picked up $1300.

I was euphoric when I got back to the hotel. My conquest had hooked on to my arm and followed me. In the elevator, to put her affection to the test, I blocked the doors and quickly sodomized her. Her protests convinced me that her love, alas, was far from sincere, and while she was putting herself together I hightailed it to my room and locked the door. She kept banging at it, but I remained calm. I knew one should never overdo a good thing, and my mamma had warned me against women who are too forward.

When Nicolas came to wake me at four in the afternoon, I told him about my victory the previous night. Since my luck had turned, I was sure the Mundial was going to be great.

'Come with me tonight,' I said. 'We'll have a ball together at the casino.'

'I'd love to. I've never been in that kind of place before.'

When we got there, a minute after opening time, there was a warm welcome. After my clean-up the night before, they'd been afraid I might not return, and now they thought they'd be able to get their own back. But they were wrong. I began well and went on winning. As the chips piled up in front of me, I explained the game to Nicolas, who was sitting next to me. They were still treating us well, and it did my heart good to see their forced smiles. Keep paying and keep smiling, I thought. At about midnight I gathered my chips.

'Are you leaving already?' the manager asked stiffly.

'No, we're just going to scout around downstairs.'

The floor below was where the shows were put on. The show on stage was less than nothing: non-professional dancers stripping as they swayed to more or less modern music. In the back, two or three rooms were available for the customer lucky enough to be able to treat himself to a dancer. It was nothing but a whorehouse for the rich, since the cost of a room and a girl was fifty dollars, whereas out on the street the hookers cost only five.

I'd noticed a cute little dancer who ended the show with nothing on but a pair of white socks. Since I'd always had a weakness for young girls, I sent the waiter to get her, and before going to the back I said to Nicolas: 'I'll be gone for a few minutes. Choose one for yourself, if you want, and put it on my bill.'

'When you say "all expenses paid" you really mean all expenses, don't you?'

'All, buddy. Have fun!'

I wasn't disappointed with Eva's looks under ordinary lighting, as often happens with girls you first see on stage. She suggested we light up a joint, but I preferred a line of coke. When I took off my shirt, the gun fell on the ground. She seemed a little surprised, but didn't say anything. She was sweet, young, not at all disagreeable.

I went back upstairs immediately, and Nicolas soon joined me. I was still the only player in the room. My brief hygienic interlude had cost me a hundred dollars that I wanted to make back. When I'd won five hundred, I decided to leave. The manager looked unhappy; a big bear of a man, covered with gold chains, he'd lost all his joviality.

'Leaving already?' he asked me.

'Yes, why? That makes you unhappy?'

'No, but why don't you stay a while?'

'You want me to go back to playing?'

Their rapacious insistence on trying to fleece me was getting on my nerves. I wasn't coming there to lose my money, but to get some of theirs, and they might just as well get used to the idea.

'Look, highest card takes double or nothing on all I've won. OK?'

I spread everything on the table, chose a card, and turned it over. My heart gave me a little stab because it was only a seven. Well, you can't win them all. Too bad; I'd been on a good roll. Like me, the manager was sure of the result; he turned his card over and gave a great sigh: it was a three. I picked up my thousand dollars and left, saying I'd be back the next day. Since they insisted, I'd go back; they seemed to consider it a personal challenge, and that amused me.

Nicolas was happy because he felt that at this rate our future was assured.

'The funny thing about it,' I told him, 'is that I must be the only customer at the casino. Every time I win I feel that I'm taking it out of their pockets – and that's fine! I'll keep going back every night until they have to eat their own nuts!'

'Let's hope you go on winning.'

'Don't worry – it's all going to work out fine. I'm on a roll, I tell you.'

I went back fourteen times. I won fourteen times. It was getting to

133

be a habit. Every day at three o'clock I was awakened by a famished Nicolas; we ate, then visited the barber and the bootblack, who knew us quite well by then. I had my own taxi-cab driver – Roberto, a big happy-go-lucky fellow with a moustache – who supplied me with coke, bringing me five grams every day for my use during the night. From four o'clock on, he reserved his time for me and waited wherever I went. After we had our shoes shined, we had another big feed, did a few lines, and by then it was the impatiently awaited time for the casinos to open.

Out of politeness, I always began with a visit to the Torre Blanca, which continued to pay me royally. I'd discovered other casinos that were classier, but I would have felt disloyal if I had abandoned my friend the manager. I think he'd have been disappointed if I hadn't come to take a little of his money every evening. He was like an old girlfriend you fuck out of politeness. Besides, I really felt at home there by now.

After I'd given them their daily draining, I'd have a quick and stimulating session with Eva, and then Roberto would take me on a tour of the casinos: the Irazu, the Cagliari, the Balmoral. Not all of them paid up as voluntarily, and some even got a little of my money; but in general my daily take was more than sufficient. Even though I denied myself nothing and our style of life cost me plenty, I somehow never managed to spend everything, and my capital kept growing.

In the morning, after the gaming-tables closed down – which always made me feel a little sad – we went to the Soda Palace, the only place open at that hour, to eat a paella or do a last line. It was also where we could find a fine way of finishing the night.

In that crisis-ridden country, prostitution was the surest means of survival, and the faster the colon fell, the more crowded the sidewalks became. But eventually supply exceeded demand, and at six in the morning the Soda Palace was filled with surplus girls. For the most part, they were the really young ones. As minors, they couldn't exercise their trade freely – a heavy handicap when it came to making pick-ups. A cup of coffee and the prospect of sleeping in a bed were generally enough to decide them to come with us.

At about ten o'clock, after a last meal, each of us went back to his own hotel to gather strength for the evening ahead.

One morning when my studies had kept me up a little longer than usual, the narcs raided the hotel. We were in the lobby when I recognized Luis, who was directing the operation. He recognized me, too, came over, and we went for some coffee. We were like old friends at this point and had a good laugh when we thought of that business in Golfito.

134

He mistook Nicolas for Dave, and I had to set him straight. I sensed that he was preoccupied; he explained that he had some problems.

'My fiancée is pregnant, but I don't want to marry now. The best thing would be for her to have an abortion, only it's against the law here and they're real butchers. She should go to Panama, but it costs too much.'

'You behaved like a sport with me the last time – now it's my turn.'

I gave him six hundred dollars.

'Thanks, that's nice of you. But I can't accept because I'd have no way of ever paying you back.'

'I know that, so take it as a gift. I've had a streak of good luck.'

'OK, Juan Carlos. Maybe I'll be able to do something for you some day.'

Even though I honestly liked him, my gesture wasn't completely disinterested. Considering the amount of drugs I use, I thought it might be useful to have a friend on the right side of the law.

I hadn't forgotten the Mundial, and every time there was an interesting match I'd wake up a little earlier, or cut back my researches, and we'd go to see it at the Escurial, a café-restaurant run by some Spaniards who'd installed a giant video-screen for this special occasion. Many foreigners, mostly Europeans, gathered there, and the bets varied according to which countries were playing. It had become harder to win big because the spectators weren't as naïve as my Ticos in Paso Canoas.

One day at the Escurial I met a Spanish North African who'd become a naturalized Frenchman and was working for a Belgian company. He was a union delegate who after a strike had wound up as the Latin American representative for a company that made refrigerator cars. He became interested in my stories about Osa and, like all those who have had no contact with gold, he was fascinated by the mines and asked a lot of questions. I replied out of politeness, but without giving the matter much thought. He was, however, the first link in my return to Osa.

For the moment I was much too preoccupied with the pleasures of the city. I had no serious worries, so gambling, coke and the available schoolgirls were enough to fill my time. The bachelor life has much to recommend it, and I could allow myself to live tranquilly from day to day.

I continued my daily rounds, and my visits to Torre Blanca were mainly excuses for kidding around. In the back rooms I spent part of the money I won upstairs. They were beginning to know us very well there. One dealer even asked if I had a special method for winning,

135

and Nicolas told him that I had a super memory – since I could remember all the cards that had been dealt, I could predict what was to come. Considering that they used 250 cards in playing blackjack, this explanation was preposterous, but it contributed to my growing reputation.

One evening, returning from a lesson in natural science with Eva, I met two Europeans sitting at my usual blackjack-table. The first was a Belgian wearing a white dinner-jacket like Humphrey Bogart in *Casablanca*, though the fact that he was dumpy, bald and short ruined the effect he wanted to create. The other was French – taller, older, and with a face like Judas. He'd dressed with care, but the red jacket with its exaggeratedly nipped-in waist and the tartan trousers that stopped short over the ankles lacked seriousness. He kept flashing a ring large enough for a pimp, and his Marseillaise accent added to the image of a petty crook.

The duo thought they had class, but they only managed to look like Laurel and Hardy. They played for small sums and complained every time they lost. The Belgian had something agreeable about him; he was a small-time gambler who won you over with amusing chatter, making us laugh by talking about the problems he'd run into in his country. But he played very badly, and several times his chatter made me lose. I decided to try for something big before leaving, so I took over the entire table by putting down seven hundred-dollar bills, one at each spot. As I hoped, the dealer busted. The big arsehole was flabbergasted, and the Belgian made fun of the croupier. I liked his attitude and invited him and his friend to my suite at the Balmoral.

After an hour or so, the fat guy was loaded and began dozing in a corner; the tall one asked me for a line. Coke has a tendency to loosen tongues, and it really got him going. Driven by some dumb need to impress me, he painted himself as a professional con man and told me about his last 'sting'.

He got all balled up in his explanations, and I understood only that he had robbed an old buddy by taking advantage of his friendship. Worse yet, he'd got nervous about possible reprisals and turned his friend over to the cops.

'As long as he's in the slammer in Europe, I'll be all right,' he told me smugly.

How could this cocksucker have told me that? And on top of everything else he was proud of his story! It wasn't a sting, it was an ignominy! I couldn't bear the sight of him a minute longer and was sorry I'd ever invited him. I woke the fat fellow by giving him a friendly pull on the ear and, saying I was tired, I got everyone out of there fast.

Before they left, I casually said to Nicolas: 'Come see me early in the morning. We've got a big day ahead of us.'

From his smile I could see that he'd understood. He knew the turd had had it.

At ten the next morning he was there. I'd already worked it all out in my head.

'This guy is a complete son of a bitch, a bastard of the worst kind. I want to teach him a lesson he'll never forget. He thinks he's a con man, but he's only a small-time nothing. You wanted to see how a sting works – this is a good chance to show you. If you do exactly what I say, we'll clean him out in a few days.'

'I'm willing. He really turned my stomach!'

'Then, listen closely. The guy's turned on, very turned on. Ever since that business with the seven hundred dollars yesterday, he's convinced that I'm very rich. He's the tight-fisted kind who really doesn't understand gambling. First let's find him.'

'He told me he often went to the Key Largo in the afternoon.'

'Good. You head over there. If you find him, pretend you've just run into him by accident, be cool, join his table. If he's not there, settle down and he'll show up sooner or later. He should come looking for you as a way of keeping in touch with me. After my coldness yester-day, he won't have the courage to phone me directly. But he's got a whiff of money and he's sure to ask you just what it is I do. Don't be afraid to embroider. Tell him I'm enormously wealthy, that I'm into big deals in pre-Columbian art. Talk up the gigantic profits to be made by selling the stuff in England – four or five times the original investment. You can bet that he'll want in. Don't seem to agree too quickly. Tell him I'm very busy and that I don't like dealing with strangers, that I've got a nasty temper or something else like that. If he feels it's too easy, he'll be suspicious – do him a favour, tell him you'll see what you can do for him. One last thing, but it's important – find out just how much money he has. We have to know that for what's to come.'

'Suppose he's not interested?'

'Don't worry, he'll dive right in. If he asks for a meeting with me, tell him it's hard to arrange. When he insists, tell him you'll be eating with me tomorrow afternoon at the Balmoral and he can just sort of happen by. The important thing is for him to be the one to ask, for him to feel I'm doing him a favour. At that point he'll be ripe, and I'll take care of the rest.'

'I have a feeling this is going to be fun.'

'And, above all, remember – don't seem too interested. Let him ask the questions, and never make him feel he's being manipulated.'

That evening Nicolas came to report.

'It all went smoothly, just as you said it would. He jumped at the chance. He's really impressed with you, and tomorrow he'll pass by while we're having lunch. Do you know what the son of a bitch had the nerve to tell me? That it was just as well, because he'd been planning to eat at the Balmoral. The hell he was—a tight-fisted bastard like him! He was just a little nervous about having talked too much yesterday.'

'Did you manage to find out how much he's got?'

'Yes, that was the hardest thing I had to do. He's got exactly ten thousand six hundred dollars. And, with all that, the bastard didn't reach for the bill! I had to pick it up myself.'

'Don't worry. In a few days he won't have a cent.'

Everything was ready for the next day's show. When the Frenchman arrived, we were both at a table and Eva had been rented for the occasion. He greeted us and began moving towards another table, but he was relieved when I signalled him to join us. At first I said nothing, merely ordered the best on the menu and watched while he mentally added up the price of the French wines. Towards the end of the meal he took the plunge.

'I've heard you do business in pre-Columbian art. Is it really profitable?'

I pretended to be surprised.

'I'm the one who told him,' said Nicolas, looking embarrassed.

'No problem. It's not really a secret. It brings in enough to let me live without worrying about the future.'

'I mention it because I'd be interested in doing business with you. I've got some money I'd like to invest.'

'We could probably work something out. How much do you want to put up?'

'I'd thought of about five or six thousand dollars.'

'Sorry, I never do business for less than ten thousand. I can't afford to get involved in penny-ante operations.'

'But ten thousand is too much for me!'

'Don't worry, there are plenty of other opportunities. But I've had to establish certain rules for my business dealings.'

I let a silence fall, then paid the bill—twelve thousand colones—and got up to leave.

'Well, gentlemen, I've got some pressing business with Madame. Nicolas, I'll see you this evening.'

As arranged, Nicolas remained at the table. The conversation that followed had been prepared in advance, and I could pretty well imagine it.

'Your friend's got a heart of stone.'

'I know. Like all rich men, he's not interested in little deals. He's used to juggling big sums.'

'But five thousand dollars is nothing to sneeze at. If I shelled out ten, I'd only have enough left to pay my air fare to London. Once I was there, I'd be high and dry, and I wouldn't even know where to sell the stuff.'

'If that's the problem, I can probably help you out. I look after his business, and I can give you the addresses of galleries that specialize in the sale of pre-Columbian art.'

'That would take time, wouldn't it? Don't you have the addresses of some collectors?'

'I can't give them to you – they're Juan Carlos' special contacts. But it should be easy enough to get to them through the galleries.'

'I'll have to think it over. Will you be here for a while?'

'No idea. Normally, I'd say yes, but with Juan Carlos you never know.'

Since I'd been sure he was going to ask those questions, I'd been able to work out the answers in advance. When Nicolas came upstairs, he could hardly contain himself.

'Everything go OK?'

'Like on wheels. He's scared shitless he may miss out on a deal, but he's nervous about putting up all his cash. He completely swallowed the part about you. Did you see him squinting at the bill?'

'Perfect. We'll leave him alone and let him stew a while. Does he know where to get in touch with you?'

'Yes, I gave him the address of my hotel.'

'If he shows up, throw in everything you've got. Tell him that I thought he was a nice guy and that I might be willing to give him a good address.'

It was Nicolas' first sting, and he was afraid the sucker might get away.

'Don't worry. He'll be back. Let him ripen!'

In the afternoon I had a visit from Ureba, the North African I'd met at the Escurial. He'd spoken to some clients who wanted to do business with me since they were interested in gold.

'These aren't just anybody. They're important people. Do you know the Caracas family? They're the ones who manage the country behind the scenes. The old man founded the Partido del Pueblo Unido, which is currently in power.'

'I'm not overly fond of politicians. They're all thieves. Every time I've had dealings with them it's always led to grief, and it's no different here than it is in Africa.'

'These people are different. They deserve your confidence and they love their country; they're not corrupt. I'd like you to meet their spokesman, Herman Weinberg.'

'Are you sure?'

'Certain. I told them you were the most important prospector in the area. Don't let me down – if you don't come, I'll look like a liar and an arsehole. If you reach an agreement, it would help me because I'm involved in a big deal with them, and this little service would come at just the right time.'

'OK, I'll go see them as a favour to you.'

'Now?'

'No. Come see me tomorrow at the same time.'

I went to the offices of the Malessa company to meet Herman Weinberg. He was the kind of businessman who tries to make you forget his dumpy greasy body by a flow of flattering talk. He always had a smile and a joke on his lips. At first you liked him, then you soon realized that he was an excellent negotiator. He was wearing a suit and a tie, and as usual I was wearing a T-shirt, jeans and a pair of boots. You have to decide on the image you want to project and then keep to it – either a salon adventurer or a jungle explorer.

After the usual polite exchanges, Herman came to the point. 'Ureba tells me you know a lot about gold, and that's something we're interested in. You're probably aware that the country is going through a serious economic crisis and that gold might help us find a way out. We've got a lot of machines at Malessa that we can't sell because of inflation. They could be used in a mining operation.'

He had carefully thought out what he wanted to say, and I felt he'd been on the watch for someone like me. He took me to the showroom of his factory, where machines of all sorts and sizes were on display. While he was explaining their advantages, I began wondering why he was wasting his time with somebody like me who could barely tell the difference between an automobile and an aeroplane. I didn't feel really involved in those technical explanations – all I know is they never give you a machine without a technician to go with it, and I knew all about how to run a technician. After half an hour, seeing my lack of interest in his equipment, Herman brought me back to his office.

'You know the peninsula, and we have the machines. It's a good beginning. Politically, we're in power for the next four years, so it wouldn't be very difficult for us to obtain a mining concession or any necessary permits. I know you had a few problems on the peninsula, but so far as we're concerned those problems don't exist. Whether it's a question of a residence permit, a gun permit, or what have you, we take care of it immediately. Is there any reason we shouldn't become partners?'

'It sounds interesting, but I can't give you an answer right now. To tell you the truth, I want to see the end of the Mundial before coming to a decision, and that won't be for another two weeks. You might think it's crazy, but I've always put my pleasures first.'

'You're interested in soccer? So am I.'

His interest sounded phoney, and I quickly decided that he knew no more about soccer than I did about machines. Since he'd gone to so much trouble to be pleasant to me, I must have represented something he needed. I decided to say goodbye, and we more or less agreed to meet after the Mundial.

In the car taking me back to the city Ureba asked: 'What did you think of my friend?'

'A hypocrite.'

'Right, but so are all businessmen. I was talking about his propositions. Interesting, aren't they?'

'Yes, of course. He could be a good ally. . . . But, you know, I don't really like the idea of a partnership, of having to share the right to make decisions with someone. . . .'

'I understand, but you really ought to think it over.'

'Maybe. . . . We'll see. In any case, there's no hurry.'

When I got back, Nicolas let me know that the other turkey wanted to see me and was ready to go ahead. They'd set up a meeting for that evening.

During the day I went to the Esmeralda, where I hadn't so much as set foot for a long time. I ran into Carlos Finca and asked him for his cheapest and lousiest stuff. I bought thirty-seven dollars' worth of reproductions in light green and dark green stone parading as jade; for good measure, I threw in two little gold-plated brass bells and a sculpted bone that was supposed to be two thousand years old but that had probably been found in a meadow with the rest of the cow six months earlier.

That evening we all got together.

'I've brought you a few sample specimens. You can decide what you can get for them. Let me just say that the darker jade pieces are the most expensive because they're rare and in great demand. The sculpted bone is also worth a lot. It's hard to find anything like this in such good condition – time and humidity destroy organic material. This piece is so well preserved because it comes from the Guanacaste desert, where the climate is dry.'

141

Luckily, he didn't smell the bleach used on the bone!

'The gold things can be sold easily – they're pure gold. Here, feel the weight for yourself.'

He hefted them with the air of a connoisseur. If he'd really known anything about gold, he would have been surprised, because the bells should have weighed four times what they did. I was having a ball.

'Well, obviously it's good stuff, but can't I buy less than ten thousand dollars' worth?'

'I thought that you and Nicolas had settled all that – but, if not no sweat. Forget it. We've already lost enough time.'

I began to pack up my treasures. Nicolas, who thought the deal was slipping away, was uneasy. As for me, I knew he was going to fall for it, and anyhow I had my secret weapon. A few lines of coke later, he was completely won over. I pocketed his bundle, generously leaving him a phoney address and some small change. Even an amateur would spot my fakes after a thirty-second examination, but presented in a box lined with black cloth my collection looked elegant: it was more than convincing for a neophyte.

Eventually, the stuff might serve as toys for his kids – if he had any, which seemed unlikely because I couldn't imagine a woman who would put up with an arsehole like that. At least my baubles weren't likely to get him into trouble with the Customs people.

When Nicolas came to wake me the next morning, he was laughing fit to burst, but eventually he got out the story.

'At the beginning, everything went fine. He was all excited and wanted to celebrate. At about three in the morning, when the coke had worn off, he began wondering if he hadn't done something really dumb. I had to slip him a little more coke so that he'd get off my back. As soon as the agency opened, we went to Air Florida to buy his ticket, and then things really got funny. Since he didn't speak any English, I took care of the reservations. No problem as far as Miami, but there were no seats on a Miami–London flight for three days, so I put him on standby and told him everything would be all right. I don't know how he's going to manage over there, but there's a surprise waiting for him! He doesn't have a dime, so I had to give him enough money for the airport tax, but I refused when it came to the cab. I gave him fifteen colones for the bus – no point in being too generous.'

'Are you sure he's gone?'

'Yeah, I'm sure. I took a taxi out so I could watch him take off. He looked happy as a clam. Let's hope it lasts.'

'You were right not to share the taxi out with him. If he's got no money, he can't expect to live like a rich man. Here's your share – five hundred bucks.'

'I never made money so fast! And we also did something that needed doing. This will teach him to be dishonest!'

'Let's celebrate. I'm inviting you to a lobster dinner in Golfito. We'll stop by and say hello to Wayne.'

I was a little tired of the casino and of celebrating. We'd been going at it hot and heavy for several weeks, and between our late nights and too much coke our health was beginning to suffer. Two days on the beach seemed just the right thing. Thanks to our 'friend', I was able to treat myself to a small plane to Golfito. When we got there, Wayne was getting ready to leave for Jiménez to do his weekly gold-buying, and he invited us to join him and do a little partying. I hesitated, and Nicolas, who didn't know the problems I'd had there, was surprised by my reluctance. Wayne was sure that after all those months they must have forgotten me, but as a precaution I left my revolver at his place.

In Jiménez, while Wayne went off to see his contacts, we went to the Rancho de Oro for a lobster feast. We hadn't been there an hour before five cops surrounded us, rifles at the ready. They gave us a quick search without finding the money hidden in my boots, and then the usual discussion began. Someone had recognized me and told the cops. Nicolas had again been taken for Dave, and they thought the old crew had come back.

While they were radioing San José for verification, the chief of the detachment gave me a lecture, repeating that you couldn't just go around shooting at people in his country. When I asked him if I looked like the sort of guy who'd do something like that, he said no, but I could see that he didn't really believe it.

Three hours later, we were released and told to return to Golfito. It was my third arrest in the country. Since I was getting such a poor welcome in the south, I decided to go north to San José.

To my great regret, the Mundial was coming to an end. The semi-final between Germany and France had been a hard blow for me. Counting on a surprise French breakthrough, I'd bet $3500 on them, and until the last penalty I thought I'd made the right choice; but the Krauts took my money. On the day of the final game I hoped to get my own back. The atmosphere of the Escurial was different from what it had been previously. The Germans were on one side of the room, the Italians on the other. My sympathy was more with the Eyties, who like good Latins were yelling and turning the café into a souk; they'd come with their wives and children, and the restaurant looked like a Neapolitan café.

On the other side, the Krauts remained calm and serious. I'd bet almost everything I had left on the Italians, and I hoped the macaronis weren't going to let me down. If I lost, there was no way of getting out of it, because the big bets had been turned over to the proprietor of the restaurant, who acted as bookmaker.

The match took place amid an unbelievable racket. Before long, the Italians had the lead, and after every goal there were big hugs and a finger for the Krauts. When the Eyties won, I raked in $9800, taking my revenge over the previous day's winners. The entire Italian colony turned out into the street for a spontaneous parade, blocking traffic and turning the place into a madhouse with their shouts of 'Italia! Italia!'

Seated in the rear of a Mercedes that went by blowing its horn, we joined in the shouting. It wasn't patriotic pride but a very financial joy that overwhelmed me. I had good reason to cheer them – after all, thanks to them, I'd won almost ten thousand dollars. That evening the celebration ended up in the house of a rich Italian; and, while the Italians, loaded to the gills, told one another that they were the best soccer players in the world, with the help of some coke we tried to demonstrate to their daughters that the French weren't too bad in another domain. When the celebration came to a halt in the early hours of the morning, the women of the Italian colony held no secrets for us.

Two days after the Mundial was over, I was beginning to wonder what the future would bring when Ureba dropped into the hotel on a mission from Herman Weinberg. I'd actually forgotten all about him.

'You know, you really oughtn't to let such a great opportunity slide. A lot of people wouldn't mind being associated with them. You should take advantage of the fact that Herman thinks so well of you.'

'You're sure it's not just the possibility of some new deal that dazzles him?'

'Stop kidding around. Phone him. His business associates want to meet you. Tino Caracas will be there, and so will his cousin, Orlando, who went to West Point.'

And so I went back to Malessa. When I entered the office, a man I didn't know was in Herman's seat, and Herman himself was in the corner. There were also four other men waiting for me, and I was welcome – to say the least.

We started on the introductions. Tino Caracas, son of Juan, the founder of Costa Rican democracy; Orlando, Juan's nephew; Oscar Trous; and Mario Terrino.

144

The man behind Herman's desk was Tino. At first sight he looked like a timid provincial schoolteacher: he wore sandals, and he was unkempt, tall and awkward. Though his face was inexpressive, I sensed that he was as cold and dangerous as a snake.

Orlando Caracas, the nephew, was the very opposite: small and fat, he had the face of a bull and no doubt the brains to match.

The two others were nondescript and looked like typical businessmen. They formed a semicircle, and sitting in the middle I felt as though I were in front of a court. They pulled the old trick of giving me a chair lower than the others, and they were obviously trying to impress me.

They asked me questions about Osa. Orlando made it clear that he didn't think I knew all that much.

'I've been told you're familiar with the entire peninsula. Is that right?'

'Yeah.'

'You've tried several times to exploit its resources and failed.'

'Yes, I imagine you know all about that.'

'And you'd like to try again with our help, if we agree to invest some money.'

I could see him coming a mile off. Did they really think they could beat me that easily? To begin with, to destroy their staging, I got up and stood with my back against the wall.

'Hold it a minute – you've got it all wrong. Who said anything about money? I haven't gone looking for anybody. Let's not get things backward – you're the ones who need *me*. I do very well on my own.'

Tino immediately took over. He was clearly the psychologist in the group.

'You're absolutely right. Orlando is sometimes a little crude – that's the way he is. But we're all here to see how a mutual association might profit everybody. I think we can supply one another with what we need. We know that your other attempts didn't work out. Maybe we can help you.'

'If my other attempts didn't work out, it wasn't for lack of gold, money or experience but because of problems with the police. As I'm sure you know. That's the only reason I'm willing to consider your proposition.'

'Understood. Tell me, is it true the peninsula is dangerous?'

'Maybe. Let's say it's inhabited by people who can be dangerous. And that's why you have to use the same methods they do – or even worse. That explains the problems I had in the past.'

'That's where I think our association can be advantageous. We can help you in so far as papers and protection are concerned – and, as for

145

us, we've got the machines but nobody familiar with the peninsula. We think your European know-how can help us work off our deficit.'

'All right, but you're going to have to meet certain conditions.'

We spelled out the details of our arrangement. I would have complete freedom of action, and I'd contribute both my knowledge and my capital; on their side they'd be responsible for all the paperwork and red tape – including my residence permit and an authorization to carry a gun. Above all, they'd agree to back me up in everything I did. I wasn't going looking for trouble, but the search for gold isn't exactly a Sunday-school picnic.

The entire discussion was carried on by three people: Tino, Herman and me. Orlando, irritated by my first reaction, brooded in his corner. The two others, obviously lesser members of the association, merely asked a few questions and then gave their consent.

'Juan Carlos,' concluded Tino, 'Herman is our spokesman. You can contact us through him. He'll take care of all the red tape. When do you think you'll leave?'

'Probably in about a week. I'm going to spend a month there scouting around, reconnoitring some areas in depth. I've already got an idea of where we can work – unlike other companies, we're going to set ourselves up high in the mountains. It'll be harder, but more profitable.'

'Fine. When you return, we can take care of the paperwork concerning our partnership and legalize our company. We've got the best lawyers in town working for us.'

They left, and I found myself once again alone with Herman. With his habitual smile on his lips, he offered me a Cognac.

'You've got class,' he said, 'but don't forget that these people are very important in this country.'

'That doesn't make a bit of difference to me. I make no concessions, and I've got my own way of doing things. You may have to bow and scrape, but I don't owe anybody anything.'

'It's not a matter of bowing and scraping – these happen to be childhood friends. What do you plan to do this week before you leave?'

'Get everything ready for the expedition, and go to the offices of the Ministry of Geology and Mines to look for maps of those areas already being worked as concessions so that I don't lose any time.'

'Do you need anything right away?'

'A jeep, if you've got one.'

'I'll arrange for one, and for a local permit. I'll even supply a chauffeur who may come in handy in the mountains. He's a mestizo' – a half breed – 'and as a child he used to travel everywhere in the jungle with his father.'

146

'Thanks, but I'm used to being alone.'

'Oh, he won't get in your way. He knows his stuff.'

I suspected he was really interested in planting a spy with me, but I wasn't going to worry about it.

'OK. Where can I get in touch with this guy?'

'Stop by before you leave, and I'll introduce you. Meanwhile, welcome to Malessa. You can be a great help to us. The company has an eight-hundred-thousand-dollar deficit which this project may help eliminate. You're a gift from the Gods.'

I wanted to leave before there was a new gush of oil.

Jimmy was a small slim half-breed with an open face. I quickly sized him up during the meal we ate together. He was the kind of man you could rely on – useful without being subservient, good-natured and likeable; but, though he seemed calm, he was capable of violent explosions: I learned later that during a fight he'd bitten off his adversary's finger. He was a childhood friend of Herman, who depended on him for a variety of jobs, and he knew the Caracas family. In the final analysis he was clever without being tricky, and I saw him more as an auxiliary than as a spy.

We went together to the Geology and Mines offices. What had to be done wasn't all that difficult and we did it by greasing a few palms. I got the information I wanted: there was no concession around Chocohuaco – the area I had checked out during my last days with Diane. That was good news, and I was eager to get back to the peninsula. When I was at Drake, I'd gone through practically the entire area.

Once a few details were settled, I was ready to leave by the end of the week. Herman was going to send me some topographers, but they wouldn't be free for a few days. I decided not to wait for them and to leave after the last weekend of the celebration. The pleasures of city life had lost some of their savour once I knew that a new adventure was in the offing.

Jimmy, Nicolas, Jairo and I left on Monday. Jairo was one of those little street dealers I occasionally used for small jobs. He'd take care of my personal stuff; since I was being given the opportunity to return to the peninsula in style I might just as well make a good first impression by having a valet.

Herman had understood my taste for unusual methods, and he cautioned me. 'Don't stir up a fuss. We can protect you, but it would be better to avoid attracting attention.'

'Don't worry. I plan to go through Sierpe and Guerra – that's a more discreet way to begin. We'll be on the site before news reaches Jiménez.'

147

'You already know where you're heading for?'

'I've got a pretty good idea. But the place I'm thinking about is occupied by a son of a bitch named Barbaroja – I might have to strong-arm him.'

'Go easy. Don't start a vendetta, and don't use too much violence.'

'Only as much as necessary. I'll do what's best for us.'

We left at night to make it easier to slip past the different checkpoints along the Pan-American Highway: despite Herman's testimonial, you never knew. I had a .357 Magnum with the number filed off; Nicolas had a .38 bought on the black market; and Jimmy had an unauthorized .22 carbine: if we ran into a serious search, that was enough to make us lose a few hours. Jimmy, a former presidential chauffeur, drove very well, but the jeep was a lemon. Except for the Cerro de la Muerte pass, where it was bitter cold, it was a good trip but a long one. We rolled along until Sierpe, where we left the vehicle because that's where the marshlands began, and Miguel, a man who often ferried Diane from Drake, took us in his boat, a simple hollowed-out tree-trunk.

Before reaching the peninsula, we spent three hours in those mosquito- and cayman-infested swamps from which only a few trees emerged here and there. Finally we got to Guerra, an unhealthy little village on the edge of the swamp, and the home of Nizaro.

The old man was glad to see me again and suggested we sleep in his house, but I refused because it was really too filthy. We hung our hammocks in a shed he used as a storeroom, but soon discovered that the pigs had chosen it as their own dormitory: they came during the night and settled under our hammocks. Every night they repeated this routine; no matter how hard we whacked them, they were too dumb to notice.

The days began with a little constitutional in the mud and rain to put us into the right spirit. Then we worked in a pre-Columbian cemetery about half a mile from the house. The site had been dug up time after time, so all we were really doing was getting into shape. In the evenings we talked and played cards, generally Nizaro and I against Jimmy and Jairo. Though he looked as kindly as could be, the old man cheated like a professional card sharp, and if we had stayed very long poor innocent Jairo would have gambled away all his pay. I have to admit that Nicolas, who sat beside Jairo, gave some help by calling out his cards in French.

Nizaro, who hated Barbaroja, was pleased to hear my destination, but too terrified to join us.

'You don't have to worry as long as you're with me. If you want to, you can wait for us some way off.'

148

'Yes, but he'll know that I was the one to bring you. You have only yourself to think about, Juan Carlos, but I've got to think about my family.'

And what a family. What with his wife and his seven enormous daughters, Nizaro and his son could barely see to it that everybody ate every day. They were skinny and spare. His wife, a large screaming shrew, urged him to accept my offer. She scented money and was ready to send him off to be killed – provided he'd been paid in advance. For the sake of peace, the old man ended by agreeing.

'Is Barbaroja as terrible as all that?'

'He's a thief and a murderer, with several deaths on his conscience – men who have just disappeared. He gets people to work for him by promising them a share, but he only uses them to prepare the site. After a week or so, he says they haven't produced any gold and sends them away without paying them a cent. If he gets any backtalk, he shoots them. Then all he has to do is work an already cleared site and keep everybody else away.'

'Does he own the land?'

'The hell he does! All he bought was a tiny patch for a few colones, a little bit of cleared meadow. The rest he stole, and he's even claimed the rivers. The last time I went there, he chased me off with rifle shots, even though I was the one to discover the place.'

'Don't worry. Just remember that you and your son will be working for the company.'

'If he gets nasty, you'll have to calm him down,' he said, pointing to my revolver. 'Shoot first, because he's dangerous.'

Too bad Barbaroja was in my way, because something about him appealed to me. The fact that he'd held out alone in the mountains for so long suggested he had more character than the arseholes who criticized him. I can appreciate a loner's courage. Nevertheless, I didn't plan to be sentimental, and if he got in my way I'd be merciless in getting rid of him. But if he behaved himself I'd leave him a way out.

When we'd been there four days, I decided the time had come to go up to the site. We left early in the morning so that we could make the round trip in one day. And the same shit began all over again: Osa seemed to be made of nothing but mud and mountains. It was the end of July, the height of the rainy season, and as usual the roads were unpassable. Half an hour of swamp in which the horses sank up to their bellies, then three hours of uninterrupted climbing to an altitude of almost two thousand feet. We had to follow a steep and slippery path hollowed in the mud by runoffs. Often we had to get off our horses and pull overselves and our reluctant nags along by catching on to the trees. Jairo, a city boy, had a hard time because we'd loaded him down with all the tools, and he took a fair number of tumbles. Jimmy, on the other hand, made it look easy. Small, light and adroit, he moved swiftly, without ever slipping, and scarcely left a mark in places where I sank up to my thighs. When we got to level ground, he was the only one who wasn't covered with mud.

Nizaro refused to go another step. 'It's right ahead of you. Barbaroja's house is about five hundred yards from here.'

'You're not coming with us?'

'No. Somebody's got to stay with the horses.'

Five minutes later we caught sight of Barbaroja's shack, right in the middle of a meadow. There were about a dozen pigs, a cow, some chickens, but no sign of a human being. The door and the windows were shut, and the house looked deserted. We advanced cautiously, and when we got there we saw that there actually was no one around.

'Jimmy, before we go to the rivers we have to know where he is. I don't want this cocksucker in our rear.'

He leapt up, climbed the wall, and with the agility of a cat slipped into an opening under the roof. Two minutes later he reappeared.

'There's warm coffee on the table. He must have left less than an hour ago.'

'We've got to find out where he is.'

'That's not hard. After all the rain this morning, there'll be fresh tracks. There are three of them over here,' he called after a moment.

He proudly showed me three different bootprints in the mud.

'Let's go.'

We followed him in silence, and after a quarter of an hour he signalled a halt. Three men were working in the river about ten yards away. Barbaroja, recognizable thanks to his red beard, was doing some panning. At his feet, two men, in the water up to their waists, worked with shovels and miner's bars. Leaving the shelter of the trees, we went towards him.

His first reaction on seeing us was to go for his carbine, which was a few yards away. I'd foreseen that and, pointing my revolver at him, made it clear he was not to move. When he hesitated, I fired a shot into the ground right next to his carbine. The report sounded like a cannon shot, and he stopped immediately, his face tense. The two workers had frozen and were leaning on their tools. I sent Jimmy for the rifle and motioned Barbaroja to come close. He was solidly built and had a bestial face; a pair of cheap sunglasses hid his eyes. He didn't know what was up, but he tried to put a good face on things.

'What are you doing here? This is my land.'

'You're mistaken, my friend – it's you who are on *my* land. As of

150

now, all these mountains are mine. I've put in for the concession and been made the legal owner.'

That wasn't quite true. But by announcing the irreversible I hoped to discourage any naïve notion that he could change the course of events by putting a bullet in my back. I showed him the safe-conduct Herman had written out for the authorities. I didn't know if he could read, but letterhead stationery is always impressive. As I talked about the company, the machines, the development of the country, he became less and less sure of himself.

'So you want to take my land away.'

'I didn't say anything about taking anything, did I? I just said that we had a concession on the mountains, that's all. If you want to stay here, you won't bother me. But you'll have to get used to having neighbours. In a little while, I'm coming back with engineers and workers, and you'll have to learn how to behave.'

I emptied the magazine of his carbine and gave the weapon back to him. The people around there rarely kept cartridges in their pockets: the rounds were so badly made that the humidity quickly rendered them unusable.

'I'm going to run a few tests. I'll be back at your place in a little while – make some coffee and we can talk.'

Once we were far enough away, we stopped behaving so seriously; we laughed as we talked about the look on Barbaroja's face. But I knew he couldn't be taken lightly – he might be just a peasant who could easily be confused, but the fact that he'd had things his own way for so long showed there was more to him, and I suspected he would soon take some sort of action. Before discussing the situation with him, I wanted to leave him a little time to think things over, but meanwhile every time we stopped to do some digging I put Jimmy out as a sentinel just in case he reacted more quickly than I expected. Once he got over his initial surprise, he was sure to do something.

Jairo, who'd been lugging the tools since morning, finally had the meagre satisfaction of using them: the poor guy was beginning to wonder just what he'd got himself into. As I expected, there were signs of gold just about everywhere. If we'd needed any confirmation, we had it.

On our return, Barbaroja was no longer down at the river. He must have gone back to his shack to think. When we emerged from the trees, one of his workers, who'd been on watch, alerted the others, and all three men were waiting for us at the door. Barbaroja, standing in the middle, motioned us to come on ahead.

We advanced cautiously, ready to react quickly in case of treachery.

151

Contrary to what I'd expected, Barbaroja seemed very calm and ready to talk. He invited us in for a discussion. The place was filthy, the home of a man who'd lived alone for years: a single room with a bed and some sawn-off tree-trunks for sitting on. On the table four glasses of milk had been prepared for us. I didn't know if he was crafty enough to plan a trap, but I remained on guard. Instead of drinking my milk, I spilled it on the ground. To Barbaroja's surprise, everybody did the same.

'Don't you like milk?'

'No, but I wouldn't mind a cup of coffee.'

Too bad if his offer had been made in good faith. He looked upset, but I didn't know if it was because of the waste or because he'd been plotting something. As he was getting up I said in French to Nicolas: 'Follow him and keep him in sight while he makes the coffee.'

'You think he's trying to poison us?'

'Poison us, no, but he'd probably try to piss in the water, just as he probably pissed in the milk.'

When our host came back he wasn't smiling quite so broadly. He told me that his real name was Gerardo, and he introduced the two others as his partners.

Partners my arse! From the way they'd been working I was convinced that my arrival had saved them from being conned. In the discussion that followed I explained to him that what was on the way wasn't simply a single orero but a whole company, and if he kept his wits about him he could profit from our arrival. It wasn't so much a conversation as a monologue, because he listened without responding except for some indistinct grunts. Either he hadn't understood, or he was playing for time. The atmosphere remained tense, and when we left him I had no idea what decision he'd come to. The fact that he didn't fire at our retreating backs seemed a good sign.

When we returned to Nizaro, he was all excited. 'So you killed the son of a bitch? I heard the shot. It's a good thing, because now I'll be able to work around here again.'

'No, I didn't kill him. But neither you nor anybody else is going to work over there – beginning today, that spot is mine.'

'But you won't forget that I'm the one who discovered it, will you?'

'That was thirty years ago. In any case, you'll have work enough with me once I'm ready. Right now, we're going back down.'

I wasn't too disturbed by Barbaroja's reactions. I knew people were scared of him, but he was living on his reputation – shored up by the natural cowardice of the Ticos. Perhaps they'd exaggerated the facts to excuse their fear.

152

Two days later I went to Sierpe to pick up the topographer, who'd come with his son – a tall gangling kid loaded down with equipment. Our expert was a smug little prick in the 'I've seen and heard everything' style, and I took an immediate dislike to him. On the boat trip back, he kept insisting that there were no alligators in the Río Sierpe – despite the fact that on the trip in I'd shot a twelve-foot specimen sunning itself on the river-bank.

He quickly irritated everyone. To avoid sleeping in a hammock, he'd brought a tent, so I generously pointed out a neighbouring meadow that I knew to be infested with colloradillas and suggested he set himself up there. In the morning, he and his son regretted their taste for luxury, and from then on he kept his trap shut when the talk turned to insects.

That day we went to settle in at the home of Nizaro's son-in-law at Rancho Quemado. It was a village much like every other one on the peninsula: five or six houses surrounding a dusty soccer-field.

Our host said that Barbaroja was telling everyone he'd never let us return. 'He said that if the Frenchman ever sets foot on his land again he'll shoot to kill. Be careful, because he'll do it.'

'I'm not going back there,' said Nizaro.

The topographer was a little surprised. 'What's all this about? I don't want to have anything to do with that. I'm here to take measurements, not to serve as someone's target.'

And the son of a bitch began to complain and talk about working conditions. He and Nizaro were really a pair; those two arseholes would demoralize my whole crew and panic the two boys I'd just hired.

'Listen, you gutless wonder, you're here to fulfil your contract and nothing else. If you refuse to work, you'll have to settle with me, so you can choose between a possible future danger and an immediate and certain danger. Anyhow, I can guarantee you that there'll be no problems.'

He wasn't reassured, but at least I'd shut him up.

The next day we went to Barbaroja's place. The topographer refused to take any measurements as long as there was a risk of being shot at in the woods. When we got to within two hundred yards of the shack Nizaro stopped, and the rest of the troop followed suit. I took my precautions before moving on ahead.

Like all Indians, Jimmy was an excellent shot. I posted him thirty yards away with instructions to keep Barbaroja from trying anything.

'If he makes so much as a threatening gesture, shoot him in the shoulder. The .22 shouldn't do too much damage. I only want to make him calm down.'

153

Nicolas, Jairo and I fanned out and advanced on the alert. Barbaroja appeared in his doorway, and luckily his hands were empty. I called out: 'I hear you intend to shoot me.'

'No, no. I never said anything like that – the people in the village don't like me, so they say just about anything.'

I didn't believe a word, and this kind of backing down only lowered him in my opinion.

'Look,' I said, pointing to the topographer and his son slowly bringing up the rear, 'these people are working for me. They're going to chart the rivers around here, so don't be surprised to see them passing your place.'

The topographer spent three weeks mapping the rivers and some three thousand acres of land. He was a jackass, but he knew his job, and with the help of two hired peasants who cleared a path with machetes he worked all day.

Every morning we left for the rios, an hour away on foot. The only problem was a river that had to be crossed on a thin and slippery tree-trunk. Every time, both coming and going, one of us was sure to fall in, and we saw to it that the topographer fell in more frequently than the others. I spent my days prospecting by doing some panning, and talking to Barbaroja. He was impressed by the power of my Magnum and by all the topography equipment, which struck him as symbols of knowledge and authority. He'd got used to the idea of having neighbours and tried to take advantage of it.

'So are you going to take over my land?'

'Of course not. I've got a concession on the mountains, and not having your half-dozen acres won't bother me at all. There'll be a few places you won't be able to go, that's all. I'm going to build my camp in this area, and if you're smart you can take advantage of that to make some money – by opening a pulperia, for instance.'

'You can set up here if you want. There are some cleared areas I don't use any more.'

'OK, that'll make things easier. How much gold do you get out every month?'

'Thirty, forty grams. My eyes are weak and I can't work for long stretches, but my mountains are rich.'

'*My* mountains, and don't you forget it! If you want – and if you promise to respect our agreements – I'll pay you twenty-five thousand colones a month as rent for the land you're offering me, and another fifteen thousand colones for any problems that might create. I can also bring in running water and electricity for you. If you work with me, there'll be advantages in it for you. Otherwise you're in for

154

trouble. If you choose violence, that's fine with me; I can take that road, too – and you'll be the one to lose, not me. You see, you have everything to gain by co-operating.'

The sum was enormous for the peninsula, and I knew he'd accept. If he refused, tough shit for him. The interests involved were too big to be resisted by a little local thug. Violence doesn't frighten me when it's necessary, but it can waste a lot of time.

As I'd foreseen, he agreed. My proposition represented more than double what he could make on his own, but he was irritated with himself for having accepted so quickly, and the whack he gave one of his men while I was looking was his way of re-establishing his prestige and reaffirming his shaky authority.

The topographer finished his work, and we got ready to leave for San José. I'd found a baby boa in the house and had broken its jaw by stamping down on it; I planned to take it back with me.

I went to see Barbaroja one last time.

'Well, are we agreed? You keep your promises, and I keep mine. In a few days I'll send some men to do some building here. I'll pay you for the trees they use to make planks. You don't have to help them, but don't try to get in their way, either. Here are twenty thousand colones on account.'

'Everything will be all right.'

It had better be, I thought.

I went back down to Guerra, where I had a lot of things to organize for my forthcoming installation. First, the house. I told Nizaro to hire people to do the construction under his supervision.

'How many men will you need?' I asked.

'Four, I think.'

'Take ten, but make sure it's all finished in two weeks. Try to round them up before I go – I'd like to talk to them. I'm going to leave you money to pay them and to buy whatever you can here. For the rest – saws, nails, everything you need for the bedrooms or the kitchen – you'll go to Palmar with me and do your buying before I leave for San José.'

'If you're going to San José, can you take me along? I'd like to stop in at the hospital for an examination – my heart's been giving me trouble, and I want to be in shape to work with you.'

Just what I needed.

'OK, we'll work something out. Another thing – I'm going to need two cooks up there. Can any of your daughters cook?'

'Sure. They'll handle it fine.'

155

'Choose the ones who eat least, just as a precaution. And put your son on the payroll for the construction work.'

It was a windfall for the family; those new salaries were going to make a real difference in their income.

Two days later, ten employees were gathered in his house. It hadn't been difficult to round them up, because in addition to his own family and the people nearby the inhabitants of Drake had learned that Juan Carlos was back and they'd come to look for work. Among the group were Max and Omar, two Drake fishermen; Miguel, a pure-blooded Indian who was a real force of nature despite the fact that he was only sixteen; Gabino, a toothless idiot from Guerra; Tonio and Jeremiah, Nizaro's son and son-in-law; and a few others whose faces meant nothing to me.

Taking his role seriously, the old man introduced them to me, and after circulating a bottle of rum I made a speech.

'I'm your boss. While I'm gone, Don Nizaro is in charge. I want my ranch finished as soon as possible, and I'll pay you three hundred colones a day. Do your work well and you won't have anything to complain about. When Don Nizaro isn't there, Tonio and Jeremiah will be in charge.'

I drew them a detailed plan of what I wanted.

I could now go to Palmar, but I had to do so quickly because I also wanted to go to Jiménez – via Golfito – where I had a few problems to settle. It was agreed that Nizaro would bring the equipment he bought to Guerra, then wait for me at Palmar so we could go up to San José together.

Jairo, who was completely exhausted and had already lost several pounds, left for San José on the bus with the topographer and his son, who were supposed to get busy preparing the map on which our application for a concession would be based.

As for me, I went to Jiménez with Nicolas and Jimmy: I was eager to meet Lieutenant Nogales so that I could make sure of the police. Jimmy knew him well, because he'd sold him a few pre-Columbian artefacts found by his father. We went straight to his house, and he seemed pleased to see me.

The first thing he said was by way of another apology for having arrested me in the mountains. 'I had my orders, and I didn't know you then. But all that's in the past, and we're going to celebrate your return.'

And he took out a package of grass and put it on the table.

'You know,' he told me with a smile, 'the grass we confiscated from Dave and Claude was great stuff. . . . It didn't last very long. But what brings you this way now?'

156

'I'm setting myself up in the mountains again, but this time much more seriously, and I need peace and quiet. The last time I passed through Jiménez, I was immediately arrested.'

'Yes, so I heard. But I didn't have anything to do with it, since I lost my job after the elections. When a president changes, all the police chiefs change. It was Jeremy, the boss of Rancho de Oro, who turned you in.'

'I'd like to keep that from happening again, and in addition I need dynamite for my work, and to get it I'll have to have the authorization of the local police chief.'

'That's no problem. I'll introduce you to Lieutenant Villanueva – he's thoroughly on the take. When I think that I was turned out in favour of a son of a bitch like that! The higher-ups among the cops all scheme to be assigned here because it's a good place to line your pockets,' he said bitterly.

'Since you can help me, I'll help you. I'm going to put you on to something.'

At that time the bank in charge of buying gold wasn't using the acid test.

'All you have to do is buy twelve-carat gold at a jeweller's, file it into grains, and sell it mixed in with twenty-four-carat river gold – and you can make yourself twenty-five hundred dollars a kilo.'

'What a great idea! I'd never have thought of that. Why don't you do it?'

'I'm on to something bigger.'

'Thanks for the lead. We'll have to celebrate that in style.'

With a gram of coke and a couple of girls, we spent a pleasant night.

The next day I met Villanueva, a white-haired veteran of the 1948 revolution who carried his .38 low on the hip with the butt outward, like a professional pistolero.

At least he didn't hide his game. Nogales had barely spoken to him before he said: 'No problem about the dynamite, but it will cost five thousand colones.'

I gave him five thousand plus an additional five thousand. 'Because I like you. You can expect the same every month.'

He swore eternal devotion, but that was more than I needed – I only wanted his devotion while he was in command at Jiménez.

While we were waiting for the Golfito boat, two guys latched on to me and kept asking for work. They'd come to try their luck at Osa, but things had gone badly and they were so broke they couldn't even pay their boat passage. One of them, Chita, lived near Palmar; the other, White, was a black from San José. I'd always found Caribbean blacks to be dumb and a pain in the arse, but this one was an exception

157

to the rule. They were both good guys, and they were on the ball. I took them with me and left them at Chita's place to wait for my return.

In Golfito I replayed my number with the cops. Nogales had told me the names of the newcomers and of the most corrupt officials, after which I had only to take care of the ones in Palmar. I knew, again from Nogales, that the police of that city were under a woman. I met her in a bar, and after a few glasses I sensed that she was not indifferent to my charm; however, since she was old, fat, and had a ghost of a moustache, I'll skip the description of our night of love. Suffice it to say that it's always nice to fuck the law up the arse, but I'd just as soon that this representative didn't call on me too often.

We picked up Nizaro and went north to San José.

During the trip I noticed that the old man really didn't look too well. I couldn't tell if it was age or the tension of the past few weeks, but he seemed even more dilapidated than before – which didn't suit me since I still needed him.

As soon as we got to San José, I went to see Weinberg, entering his office as though it were my own.

'Hello, Juan Carlos! I hear you've accomplished miracles. According to the topographers, you're not afraid of anything.'

Always trying to soft-soap me! Well, it was my turn to win *his* heart.

'Everything's gone well. I even brought back a little souvenir for you.'

And, taking the boa from my jacket pocket, I set it on his desk. I'd expected him to be surprised, but not that much: he literally jumped up, and his chair clattered to the floor. Pressed against the wall, he screamed: 'Please – get that out of here, fast!'

'It's only a boa – it's not poisonous.'

'I don't care – I can't stand snakes!'

Strange, considering the family resemblance, I thought. Too bad. I picked up my little friend, who was beginning to explore the drawers, and put him back in my pocket. It took Herman at least ten minutes to calm down. Looking quite pale and holding a hand to his heart, he sat in his chair and for once even forgot to smile. His face slowly regained its usual green colour, and we were able to get down to business.

'Well,' he began, 'fill me in. Is there any gold?'

'A lot. The area's very rich – for that matter, so are the other sides of the lagoon – and it shouldn't be too difficult to exploit it. The only problem is access – what with the boat across the swamp and then more than three hours of climbing, it's not as easy as the mines at the bottom of the mountain. Getting our equipment up will be hard.'

'Do you think you can manage?'

'Don't worry. I said it would be hard, not imposssible. It adds spice to the operation.'

Just as with the motor at Cerro de Oro, I liked this kind of crazy challenge.

'And who's this Barbaroja the topographer told me about?'

'A son of a bitch who could make trouble for us. I don't think he'll go in for open violence, but he might try stabbing us in the back. I told him he could keep on working the concession because his kind of puttering wouldn't get in my way – I wanted to leave him a way to save face. But if he tries anything I'll be down on him like a ton of bricks.'

'You're right. A company like ours can't afford to let one man hold us back.'

I stopped him before he could slip into a sermon.

'Speaking of things that could hold us back, I need a good cardiologist who can put Nizaro back together again. The old man's got a problem with his heart, and he's probably about to kick off. But, if he can be patched up so that he can hold out for a month or two, I can use him as a liaison with the peasants.'

'No problem. There must be a good sawbones in the family. I'm friends with all the directors of the different hospitals.'

'Fine. Another thing – the topographer probably told you that he surveyed three rivers that aren't shown on the map. I've baptized them Quebrada del Frances, Quebrada Rancho Quemado and – in your honour – Quebrada Herman.'

He flushed with pride. Nowadays it's not very often that you can give your name to an unknown river. When you're a 'great adventurer' like Herman, it's always flattering to see your name on an official map.

He turned to more practical matters.

'Do you know that a company can't have a concession larger than a thousand acres?'

'I thought of that. That's why I've included those three rivers. We can set up three different companies and name them after each of the rivers. They'll be run by a holding company directed by the corporation known as Quebrada del Frances.'

'Why that one?'

'Because it's mine, because it's the richest of the three, because I'm the president, and because that's the way it's going to be.'

'OK, OK. In any case, we'll have to get to work on the papers as soon as the topographers are finished.'

'I have no intention of going back before then – I have to buy some stuff.'

'Do you want any money? We can share in the expenses.'

'Thanks, but I can still cover everything.'

'Why are you so stubborn about refusing?'

'Because I don't want to be dependent on anybody and I want to have lots of elbow room. I refuse to give anyone an excuse for sticking his nose in my business. I went into partnership with you for one reason only, but in general I don't like the idea of partnerships. Let's just say that I'm making you a present in exchange for a service.'

'So you mean to manage things all on your own?'

'On the site, yes. It's important that we understand each other about this. You're the men in the city – you, Tino and the others. Just stay where you are and take care of the paperwork. To each his own. Me, I've got to be the only one to make decisions on the site. You have to understand that that's the only way I work.'

'It shouldn't be a problem.'

'It better not be, because that's the key to our partnership.'

The question was to come up time and time again.

I had to prepare the stuff we'd require, and it wasn't easy to plan for all the equipment some thirty men needed to survive in the mountains. I began by having a special twenty-foot canoa built, and it took me a week to round up all the other things on my list.

For the house I wanted:

– an electric motor and generating equipment
– pots, pans, and other kitchen utensils
– thirty plates, glasses, knives, forks, etc.
– food-supplies: rice, frijoles, etc.
– a cassette-player with the most powerful speakers I could find.

For the mining I wanted:

– fifteen shovels and the same number of miner's bars
– thirty machetes

For the comfort of Nicolas, Jimmy and myself I wanted:

– three pairs of sheets
– three foam rubber mattresses
– three pillows
– three mosquito-nets
– a rocking chair.

And, in addition, dozens of less important items: all in all, several tons of merchandise. While Jimmy was looking after these things, Nicolas recorded as many cassettes as possible. To give my employees a change from the salsa, I intended to have them work to the sound of The Clash, Nina Hagen, the Sex Pistols and other punk groups.

I still had my boa in my pocket in case I wanted to pull a practical joke. At the hotel he slept in a case into which I'd put a few chicks for him as snacks, but his jaw was in such bad shape that he couldn't eat, and the nasty little things kept pecking away at him. Poor boa. What a disgrace.

One evening Nicolas took me to the Tubo, a German-run bar frequented by tourists and San José's rich kids. There was a good selection of European women, and that's always nice after a month in the jungle. We ran into Curtis, the fat Belgian who'd been with the Frenchman I'd conned. To survive, Curtis had set up a little business that made paper coasters with the name of the café he sold them to. It was a good idea, and the owner of the Tubo was his first important customer. He'd had no news of his friend.

'He vanished without saying a word to me. He must have stumbled on to a good deal and been unwilling to share it.'

During the evening he noticed the boa. Not in the least afraid, he wound it around his neck and began to impress the peanut gallery. It really turned my stomach to see someone with his physique play the tough guy.

'Sell him to me,' he said when I wanted to take the boa back.

'No, you can't buy this sort of thing. You have to go to the jungle and get one yourself. Something like this has to be earned.'

'Come on, now, I've wanted one for a long time.'

'OK.' I laughed. 'Two hundred bucks.'

'That's much too much. Set a reasonable price, like ten dollars.'

This bargaining over pennies bothered me, but I could see he wasn't about to drop the matter. On the other hand, I couldn't take a snake that let itself be pecked by baby chicks very seriously.

'Here, take it. Just pay for a round of drinks.'

'Now, that's really great of you. Never mind a round – I'll pay for everything you drink this evening. The boss owes me for some coasters. I'll just let him know.'

He left to show off in some other bar, and I could imagine the tall tales he told about how he'd caught the boa.

As for us, by the time we left the bar early in the morning we'd run up a bill of six hundred dollars. I don't know if it was covered by what the boss owed him, but in any case it was the most expensive boa in the world. That at least was something he could boast about without lying.

* * *

161

The purchases for the mine came to a hefty sum, and to cover expenses I decided to sell the cacique I'd found in Burica – but not to Chocho or some other counterfeiter, because they all paid badly. From Carlos Finca I heard of a Peruvian who bought and sold to gringos, and who paid well. His name was René Sacaretta and he lived in Tibas. When I entered his place in the company of Carlos, who'd brought me, something about his light blue eyes and wrinkled Latin face looked familiar.

He recognized me immediately and called to his wife: 'Mamma, Mamma, come see who's here!'

When they were side by side. I recognized them immediately as a couple of old swindlers whose necks I'd saved in Colombia a few years earlier, when they'd been smugglers dealing in emeralds and had been caught cheating; my intervention had saved them from getting a bullet in the head, but they'd had to leave the country.

There were great cries of joy and an equally great round of hugs.

'The last time I saw you,' I said, 'you had another name.'

'Well, you know, a man has to change with the times. Here I'm known as René Sacaretta, elsewhere I've got another name.'

'You live in Costa Rica now?'

'More or less. Let's say that I've chosen the place as a kind of quiet retreat. Mamma has a little business that brings in something, and I do some trading outside the country – but never here.'

'I suppose your dealings are as honest as ever?'

'Well, everybody has his own definition of honesty. Mine is broad enough to suit my needs.'

To look at the old couple, you'd never know they were swindlers. His wife seemed like a nice old granny, easier to imagine knitting alongside a fire than carrying a handbag full of weapons or cocaine. That's what made them so good at their work.

When René heard that I was associated with the Caracases in a venture involving gold, he put me on my guard. 'Watch it, they're crooks and killers. Which branch of the family are you connected with?'

'Tino and Orlando.'

'They're the worst. Especially Tino, who looks as though butter wouldn't melt in his mouth. He's wild, and he's been mixed up in a lot of shady business.'

'I imagine he has, but I've taken a few precautions. It's all a poker game – but, if you win, you win big.'

'Maybe, but it's dangerous.'

I introduced Nicolas as the son of a famous housebreaker whose father had put him in my hands so I could complete his education.

The idea struck René as very funny, and we spent the afternoon with the couple. The little man had an enormous amount of vitality; he never stayed put but kept getting up, moving around, and doing a lot of talking emphasized by gestures and facial expressions. More than seventy years old, he had two great passions in his life: little girls and the alcohol with which he washed down the chilli pepper he was constantly chewing on.

'I'll see you back to your car,' he said when I got up to leave. 'Mamma and the children have to run some errands in town.'

On the way he stopped to pick up two young girls of about fifteen.

'Are they your daughters?' I asked. 'They're attractive.'

'Not exactly. I'll explain later. When do you plan to leave?'

'In a week or two. As soon as my papers are ready.'

'I'll phone you before then. We'll do a little celebrating.'

A few days later Nicolas came down with the same sort of malaria I had caught in Osa. He was skinny to begin with, and by the end of the week he was transparent. They wanted to hospitalize him, but I took him to the beach and put him in the sun; thanks to the Juan Carlos method, he was on his feet in three days.

At the hotel, when I got back from the beach two days before leaving for the south, I found a message from René asking me to phone.

'Before you shut yourself away in the jungle, I want you to attend a special celebration organized by Mamma. I'll pick you up.'

He took me to a house close to his, and when he rang the bell his wife opened the door.

'This is Mamma's domain,' he said, 'and I'm not allowed to go any farther.'

I was surprised by the interior decoration. Everything was mauve and white, the furnishings were nice, and there was a peaceful atmosphere in the place. Mamma took me to a dimly lit, windowless room, where the large hangings on the walls emphasized the sense of tranquillity.

'We've often thought of you over the years, and I'm finally going to be able to thank you for the great favour you did us. You're my guest,' she said, opening a door at the end of the room.

There, in a smaller room decorated in the same way, were six girls no more than fifteen years old. They weren't dressed as women but as little children; one of them even wore a schoolgirl's uniform.

'There are women in this country who are willing to pay very heavily for a moment of sweetness that the men here don't know how to provide. All my protégées are Bogotá orphans and, rather than let them prostitute themselves on the street, I try to give them a good education that will help them in life. You're one of the few men who's been allowed to enter here. Make your choice.'

Choosing was no easy matter! Each one was more beautiful than the others. Seeing me hesitate, Mamma took my hand and put it into that of a very young girl dressed in nothing but white veils.

I will say no more. But rest assured that when I left my companion was well armed for life and ready for a great future.

The company contracts were ready. I went to sign them in the Rosenberg law office, the best in the city and the one used by the Caracas family. The waltz of documents began. I don't know how many pieces of paper the lawyer read to me in his monotone: I was bored to tears and had trouble hiding my lack of interest. I've never liked contracts; they're weapons for the weak and, as far as I'm concerned, respecting a contract means respecting your word, not a sheet of paper. Down there, men had no respect for their word, but a contract was far from being a guarantee. My own weapon was my determination.

'Cut it short,' I said. 'Where do you want me to sign?'

I put my name at the bottom of a pile of papers, one more pointless than the other. The only thing that mattered was that I be president of the Quebrada del Frances company, which owned a thousand acres along the richest river. I couldn't have cared less about everything else: I had no desire to spend the rest of my life digging in the mountains. In a year or two I hoped to be free of it all – Jimmy could be named manager and take my place.

That same evening, at Malessa, where I had stored my equipment, we loaded everything into a truck – an old rattletrap that left with three men; the others went in the jeep with me. I'd recruited a few men in the city. Since they were strangers to the peninsula, when we got down there they'd be dependent on me – and therefore more loyal. There was Chiche, a long-haired hoodlum covered with tattoos and scars from fights; Eduardo, a tough young fellow who spent his time going in and out of gaol; Jimmy's brother and a friend, two guys who'd come from Guanacaste in the north and been recommended by Herman. One of them was called Barbas, had a Judas head, and did a lot of talking and even more farting; Nicolas had immediately nicknamed him 'The Bumblebee', and the name stuck. Unlike him, Jimmy's brother seldom opened his mouth – probably because, in spite of the fact that he was only eighteen years old, he didn't have a single front tooth. There was even a broken-voiced crooner.

At about midnight, when everything was loaded and we were all ready to go, I went to Herman's office for a last cup of coffee. We agreed that I'd spend three months in the mountains and come down at Christmas time. I was to keep in touch by telephone.

'I'm thinking of paying you a visit once you're settled,' he said.

'Come down in a week, so you can bring along the boat I bought. It should be ready by then.'

'No, I'll get it to you some other way. I prefer to come later.'

Of course – when things would be more comfortable and less dangerous; adventure, sure, but only when it was safe.

'My wife is proud to tell everyone that I'm the vice-president of a gold company. It sounds very respectable.'

It was certainly less contemptible than being a puppet behind a desk and polishing things up for Tino and the others.

'Before you go, I've got a present for you.'

He put a cardboard box on the desk. Inside, there were ten or fifteen pounds of Mango-Rosa.

'I know you smoke a lot, but there's enough here for you and your men.'

That was a guarantee against boredom, particularly when added to the five pounds of hallucinogenic mushrooms Chiche and Eduardo had brought from Monte de la Cruz, where I'd sent them for a few days.

'And I've got something else, especially for you,' he said, handing me what looked like a big box of matches.

It was filled with coke – about 150 grams. At this point I was almost getting to like the fat man.

'It's almost pure – a shipment direct from Colombia that was seized by Customs.'

I did a quick line. The trip promised to be a good one.

'Thanks. I've got to go now. I want to pass some checkpoints at dawn, when the cops are careless and I'm paying attention. . . . See you in three months.'

After some backslapping and a series of handshakes – all the Latin effusions I generally tried to avoid – we parted.

I sat up front in the jeep, and Nicolas and Jimmy took turns driving; the hired men piled in the back made themselves as comfortable as possible. The truck brought up the rear. It was slow, and on the uphill stretches we often had to wait for it.

Going through the Cerro de la Muerte pass in the rain was hell. In the middle of the night the cold was numbing, and the jeep was open. The hired men, wearing only shorts and T-shirts, were blue with cold; they didn't complain, but their enthusiasm was at a low point. A few enormous joints helped them get through the difficult time.

165

We finally got to Sierpe at three in the afternoon, and I found White, Chita, Omar and Max, who'd been waiting for me for several days. Some other guys were there, too, asking for work, and I hired a few of them – notably a Tico who said he was a carpenter, and a former cop who looked like a crook.

It was too late to go to Guerra, so I had the truck unloaded while I set about looking for a boat. One guy offered to help, and I explained: 'I need some boats to take all this stuff and all my men to Guerra.'

'I've got two boats with fifty-horsepower engines. They can each take on a ton, and I can get the job done in two days.'

'You're sure?'

'Positive. I'm expensive, but I guarantee the safe delivery of your merchandise.'

'OK. Be there tomorrow at four in the morning.'

All the equipment was piled on the ground, and the truck took off.

'Barbas and Garret, you take first turn at guard duty. I don't want the stuff left alone for a minute, understand? I'll send you something to eat, and someone will relieve you at midnight.'

After passing round an enormous joint, I led the others off to eat.

The men still didn't know one another, and the crew lacked a sense of unity. When the meal was over, I took them to a cantina and stood them all drinks. As I expected, after half an hour Eduardo began to fight with a guy from Sierpe. I urged my men on, and the situation soon became a general brawl – there's nothing like it to create team spirit. Then I called a halt to the massacre before too many people were badly hurt, and I paid for all the damage.

I'd been able to judge them. They all had heart, but they weren't in great shape. That would change in the mountains, and meanwhile they'd got to know one another.

I reassembled them near our stuff.

'You're going to sleep here. Because at least two people have to be awake at all times, I'll make up a guard-duty roster.'

Somewhat astonished, they looked at their bedroom, the village square.

'Where exactly do we set up?'

'Wherever you want – there's room enough and to spare. But get some sleep, because we begin early tomorrow.'

After some hesitation, they stretched out on the sacks as best they could.

Jimmy and I went to our two filthy little rooms off the bar.

When the boatman came at four o'clock, everyone was awakened. The uncomfortable night coming on the heels of an uncomfortable

166

trip had left the men slow and dispirited. I got into the act and began shouting, and ten minutes later the transfer of our equipment to the boat was proceeding at a rapid pace. I piled incredible amounts of weight on the men's backs, and they discovered unknown reserves of strength. In half an hour the boats were completely loaded.

'Jimmy, you're going to make the first trip with the men. Only White and Chita will stay here with me. Have the boats unloaded and sent back here as quickly as possible. If we work fast, we can do another round trip before nightfall. Afterwards, go up to Rancho Quemado and, if they're not finished, give them a hand with the construction. Have the men start bringing the stuff up!'

At noon the two boats came back, the first pulling the second. The motor of the second had given out, and from then on only one of them could make the trip. It left with White and one of the boatman's employees, whose excuses collapsed when I chewed him out. But by seven that evening they still hadn't returned, and I began to lose my temper. They must have been afraid to make the trip at night and were waiting for morning before leaving. I didn't care for hitches like that, and I was ready to break somebody's jaw.

In the morning I was at the bar with the boatman when my two clods, looking exhausted, showed up in a fishing-smack belonging to Mario, the owner of Guerra's general store.

'Well, arseholes, what's happened? Where's the boat?'

'It sank,' said White.

'What do you mean "sank"?'

'Last night, while we were on our way to Guerra, the motor suddenly conked out, and a wave tipped the boat over. It disappeared in a few seconds, and we couldn't save a thing. I even dropped my boots so that I could swim faster because of the caymans. We spent the night hanging on to a branch. When we saw Mario come by, we yelled out to him and he picked us up.'

I could imagine the night they must have spent in the tree, right in the middle of the swamp, with thousands of mosquitoes buzzing around them and caymans snapping at their heels. But I exploded anyway because I needed a scapegoat.

'Idiots! You'd have done better to stay there! As for you, you cocksucker,' I said to the boatman, 'you guaranteed delivery of the stuff, so you're going to pay for it all!'

'But I'm broke just now!'

'Tough shit, arsehole. I'll buy you a wig, some high heels and a miniskirt, and you can peddle your arse at ten colones a throw!'

'Hold it a minute! Maybe we can work something out.'

167

'I hope so, for your sake. White, what was in the boat?'

'All the food-supplies, the generator and the motor.'

'OK. Go along with Chita and tell Mario that I'm renting his boat. I'll be with you as soon as I make a phone call.'

From the pulperia, which had the only telephone in Sierpe, I called Herman. 'A boat sank with the food-supplies and equipment aboard. I'll see what I can do, but in the meantime buy some grub and send it as soon as possible.'

I gave him a list.

'But what happened?'

'I don't have time to explain. Get busy buying supplies. I'll call back this evening when I know about the motor.'

I hung up before he had time to ask any more dumb questions.

When I got back to the landing-dock the fucking boatman was gone. He'd been scared, and had preferred to do a vanishing act. But Sierpe wasn't that big; I'd find him – and when I did. . . .

We started along the river and soon reached the spot. Spunky Chita plunged in first, but after a quarter of an hour of useless searching he wanted to get back into the boat. To encourage him and play for time I dived in. The icy water was muddy, and I couldn't see a thing: ten or twelve feet down you had to feel around in the mud. I preferred not to think about the alligators and the big groupers that frequented those swamps, swallowing everything they came across. . . . At the end of an hour, all we'd found was a sack of obviously unusable sugar.

Finally, we found the motor. Using a rope, we attached it to the gunwale, since the boat was too unstable to allow us to bring it on board. It was impossible to find the sunken boat – the current must have already carried it away – so we returned to Sierpe. I phoned Herman and told him we needed more food-supplies, a generator, and a mechanic to clean up the motor – as quickly as possible.

That episode began to gum up the works. The men at Rancho Quemado hadn't eaten for two days and must have been in a foul mood – and when things begin to go wrong like that they just keep going on that way.

Chita introduced me to a girlfriend named Marcella, who cooked for the camps; I had a good feeling when I hired her. Tough, used to living in the forest with her seven-year-old daughter, she always kept a kitchen knife in her blouse.

While White and Chita went looking for the boatman, I waited in the bar, and to my amazement a blonde appeared from nowhere and came up to me. It was Sophie, a Swedish girl I'd met at the beginning of the San José celebration. I'd spent a weekend with her, and she'd serviced me well; then she'd gone home, and I'd heard no more about her.

'What are you doing here? How come you're not in Europe?'

'I'm on vacation. I've been in Costa Rica two days now. When I heard you were around here, I decided to look for you.'

As women went, she was only so-so, though her blondeness attracted attention around there. It was nice to see her, but I didn't want her on my hands. However, since she'd come all this way to suck me off she deserved a reward, and I decided to go to Palmar so we could at least have clean sheets.

In the mean time, White showed up. 'I found the boatman. He's in his shed, dead drunk.'

'OK, he won't go anywhere tonight. I'm going to Palmar. We'll meet here tomorrow and talk about it. Meanwhile, look after things.'

Sophie gave me the full treatment, but once the first moments of pleasure were over I wondered what I was going to do with her. The only thing that interested me was the project in hand, and I didn't want a woman hanging around. But she must have gone to a lot of effort to come there, so I had to make allowances.

'What do you plan to do now?'

'Well, I thought I'd stay with you, if that's OK.'

'It's OK for a few days, but you'd better get this straight – there'll be only men up there, and it's no place for a woman. You'll have to keep your nose clean, your eyes straight ahead, do what you're told, and stay where you're put. I don't want any more problems than I have already, and I won't have much time for you – so behave yourself!'

In the morning I went back to Sierpe, where my little buddy the boatman was waiting for me. He was still out cold when I got there.

'Chita, White, drag this son of a bitch outside!'

They each delicately took a leg. When his head hit first the ground and then three steps and the pebbles on the path, he woke up and struggled painfully to his feet – which was when they grabbed him by the ears and tossed him into a boat.

The mechanic had arrived that morning and already repaired the motor. We loaded it into another boat along with a new generator and some other stuff. Sophie, Nicolas, Chita, White, the cook and her daughter got into the boat with my prey; by the time we got to the spot we'd been searching, he'd fallen asleep. I shoved him into the water.

'Dive! Make yourself useful!'

He dived several times but had no luck. When he tried to climb back into the boat, I brought the flat of the oar down on his head.

'Keep at it. You've got to find my stuff.'

I was acting more out of bloody-mindedness than out of hope, because the current must have long since carried everything off. When he was exhausted and could barely stay afloat, I decided the joke had gone far enough and, pulling him by the hair, I dragged him to the foot of a tree.

'You're going to stay here and enjoy the pleasure of a night in the swamp, since I don't have time to take you back now. Mario, pick him up tomorrow, on your way.'

'You can't leave him here!' said Sophie, horrified.

'Shut up. I'll do as I please, and I don't want any nagging from you.'

If she'd said another word, I'd have left her with the other piece of scum. We left, reaching Guerra without further incident.

It was raining. Nizaro's house, where I'd stored all our stuff, was about eight hundred yards away from where the boat had hit water too shallow to navigate. We got out and had to do about four hundred yards in mud up to our knees before we reached solid ground.

'We'll go look for horses so we can unload, but take something with you – no point in going empty-handed.'

Everyone grabbed a hundred-pound sack of rice or frijoles. White, not quite recovered from his night in the marshes, struggled and walked barefoot in the mud because he no longer had any boots. It would teach him to look after his things! Nicolas was also carrying a hundred-pound sack and, given how thin he was, it must have been as much as his own weight; he'd stumble forward a few steps, slip, and fall full-length in the mud, sinking into it completely under the weight of the load. By the time I'd laughingly helped him to his feet, he was black from head to toe. Even Sophie was loaded down like a mule, and as she walked beside me she also slipped, and remained lying in the mud, waiting for God knew what. Her air of confusion made me laugh, and I just continued along my way; if she hoped for a gallant gesture, she'd just have to go on hoping, because I had better things to do.

The horses made the unloading a lot easier. Except for the motor. That fucker weighed more than four hundred pounds, and we had to drag it through the mud in a wooden handbarrow. It took us more than an hour to go the eight hundred yards, and I could imagine what the climbing would be like. Nizaro wasn't there, but all his enormous daughters were – somehow looking even fatter than before.

'Isn't there anybody up there to do the cooking?'

'No. Papa didn't want us to go up right away. He said to wait until the horses are rested. He's supposed to come back for us tomorrow.'

I had to admit that it would have been difficult for those two big cows to make the climb on foot. I didn't say anything, but it occurred to me that I had done well to hire Marcella.

All our stuff was stored in a shack alongside the house. I could see that very little had been brought up.

I yelled for Nizaro's wife. 'Señora, what does this mean? Haven't they brought anything?'

'Only a little – practically nothing.'

'But didn't Jimmy tell them to?'

'I have the feeling he couldn't get them to obey his orders and that they just laughed at him.'

Shit! What was the fucking idiot doing? I liked him well enough, but he'd ruin everything. I was in a hurry to get back up. After eating, we settled down for the night in the building used as a school. All evening Chita played the clown and hopped around like a devil, even making a pass at one of those enormous broads – who hauled off and clouted him. He brought me one cup of coffee after another and told some tall tales that made everyone laugh. The bastard was loony, but he had a lot of juice. He didn't go to bed until there was nobody awake to listen to him, and I could hear him still kidding around in the dark.

At three in the morning everyone turned out on the double. I'd requisitioned Nizaro's two horses, and Chita loaded them down heavily despite the complaints of Nizaro's wife, who wanted him to go easy. He paid no attention.

'I've got only two legs and I carry a hundred pounds. Since they've got four legs, they can easily carry three hundred pounds. Allez-oop! Let's go!'

Chita left with a large sack on his back, pushing the horses ahead of him.

'Señora, I'm going to send some men to get our goods, and it'll take several days. Feed them and keep track of the expenses – I'll pay you later.'

Each of us carried something. Miguel, an open-faced Indian of sixteen, was a real force of nature who effortlessly picked up a hundred-pound sack of rice and put it on his back. I loaded the others down until they said stop, then added a few pounds just in case they were trying to skive off. Miguel was different: he'd taken on a sack of rice, a twenty-pound miner's bar, and twenty pounds of sugar slung across one shoulder before I called a halt.

'Are you OK?'

'I'm fine.'

And he started off on a three-hour climb in the mud and the rain. Nicolas carried Marcella's little girl on his shoulders.

Just as we were leaving, Barbas the Bumblebee and the singer came from the opposite direction. They were glad to see me.

'You're just in time,' Barbas told me. 'I came to see if we could buy anything to eat here. There isn't much up there, we haven't had a hot meal, and the house isn't ready. Nobody knows what to do, and things are in a mess.'

He was ready to quit right then and there.

'You want to go?'

'No, now that you're here, I'll stay on.'

The two days of delay had been almost enough to ruin everything.

'Good. I'll straighten everything out. Load up. We're going back.'

Since they were there, I saw no point in their having come for nothing.

The mountain road had become a quagmire even more horrendous than the last time.

'It's been raining steadily for a month,' moaned Barbas, 'and all of it's like this.'

On the way we met Nizaro coming down.

'What the hell's going on? Why isn't the house ready?'

'We had some trouble with Barbaroja, and some of the men quit because they were afraid. The bastard doesn't want us to build here, and he didn't lose any time before showing up.'

'Where is everybody?'

'Jimmy settled the men in an abandoned ranch about twenty minutes from Barbaroja's place. They're waiting for you there.'

I could imagine the fucking confusion. Jimmy was a nice guy and he tried to be useful, but he didn't have the stuff of a leader in him. He might at least have made the men bring the goods up instead of letting them loaf around up there.

'Did you hire a new cook?' Nizaro asked anxiously.

'Yes.'

'What about my daughters?'

'Your daughters should have been there a long time ago. If we had to count on them, we wouldn't be eating much. Never mind – bring them with you when you come back up. They'll come in handy.'

We left Nizaro and went on to the camp.

When we got there, nothing was ready, nobody was working, and the men were scattered about everywhere. Jimmy smiled with relief when he saw me. I couldn't be angry with the poor guy; he'd been a lackey all his life and didn't know how to make decisions. When I put him in charge for a few days, he must have thought he could do it.

'I'm sorry, Juan Carlos. I've had some problems.'

I gave him a friendly tap on the shoulder.

'Don't worry, I understand. Take it easy now. First, let's see to the food.'

I looked around for the cook, but she was already in the house and busy making rice with the help of Chita, who was splitting wood.

The long-abandoned house was filthy, and a few of the men were napping on the ground. I fired a round into the air to wake them up and get everybody moving.

'OK, on your feet. You're in a house, and I expect you to behave that way.'

They were glad to see me, and soon everyone had gathered round. I began by passing some joints and opening a bottle of guaro; ten minutes later the atmosphere had relaxed, and they were kidding around with one another. I grabbed Sophie by the arm.

'Everybody stay here – I want to wash.'

They didn't seem to understand, so I spelled it out. 'I'm going to give this lady a good bang, and the first one of you who shows himself will get a bullet in his gut.'

We headed for the forest amid a burst of laughter. Sophie, who didn't know Spanish very well, hadn't understood a thing and trotted at my side. A little water, a little soap, a quick fuck, and I felt better. When I went back, they were all leaning over the railing – twenty-five men watching me with big smiles on their faces.

The arrival of food finished putting everyone in good humour. I'd had the cassette-player brought up, and I turned it on full force – fifty watts of punk music exploding in the jungle. Even the monkeys quietened down: it must have been the first time they'd ever listened to music – and what a selection! All night long Nina Hagen, the Sex Pistols, The Clash and the Rolling Stones screamed in the forest and could probably have been heard for miles around. The men were high on grass and pretty drunk; the place was like a nightclub, with people joking around and kicking up their heels. Chita played the clown, and while he was doing a trapeze act on the window-sill I put out my foot and threw him off balance. He went crashing six feet down, and everybody laughed. A few seconds later, covered with mud, he came back through the door and began fooling around again. After long days of tension, the men appreciated the celebration and let off steam like a bunch of kids.

Little by little, stupefied by dope and booze, they collapsed, some of them falling asleep on the table, surrounded by bottles. It was just as well, because the next day was going to be a rough one.

*   *   *

No sooner had I stretched out on my blanket than I felt insects running along my body. I lit a candle and saw a nightmare vision: the house was crawling with cockroaches, millions and millions of them coming out of every hole, out of every space between the floorboards. Once the sun had set, legions of them had attacked everything edible, and the walls were literally covered with a heaving black tide of voracious flying cockroaches that attacked everything and bit you in your sleep. Initially frightened by the light, they soon regained their courage and besieged the candles, gnawing away at their bases; when the candles fell, they were covered by a forest of cockroaches that devoured them in a few minutes, leaving only the wicks. Things were even worse in the kitchen, where the sacks of rice and sugar were seething with masses of cockroaches trying to penetrate them – a veritable moving carpet that I crushed under my heels. As for the plates and pots, they'd been completely cleaned by the hundreds of insects come to feast. To complete the picture, there were long processions of them promenading along the bodies of the sleepers. I couldn't understand how they could go on sleeping: Chita's chest was a constellation of bites.

It had been dumb of Jimmy to move in and, knowing what he did, he should never have allowed us to store the food there. I didn't want to sleep in that filth, but outside were the mud and the rain, and no place to take refuge. I spent the night talking to Nicolas. Sophie, who was terrified of bugs, began to see the kind of vacation she was in for.

At four in the morning I gently woke everybody up by firing off a few rounds; by the time they'd dressed, coffee and plates of rice were ready. I'd given orders not to spare the food.

'There should always be leftovers – nobody's to be hungry when he leaves the table.'

While they ate, I organized the day.

'Jimmy, go down to Guerra with ten men and bring up more equipment and supplies. You're in charge of this team, and I don't want to see anyone come back with less than fifty pounds on his back. If there are any problems, if anybody refuses to obey, let me know and I'll take care of it personally. Take Miguel, Wilson, Eduardo, Barbas, Chiche and Jeremiah, and don't waste any time. Begin by bringing up the picks and shovels, the rest of the food, my personal stuff, mattresses, sheets, pillows, some batteries for the cassette-player, and all the kitchen equipment. Eat at Nizaro's and start back immediately! Everybody finished his coffee? OK – hop to it and get going!'

It was still dark and it was still raining. Only half-awake and trying to protect themselves under plastic sacks, they were getting ready to leave when I called them back, a bottle of guaro in my hand.

174

'I can see you're going to need a little Dutch courage. Find something to drink out of.'

They rushed off to look for clean glasses and lined up in front of me in single file. I poured each of them a stiff shot, and they went off into the forest singing.

I turned to the others.

'White and Garret, go help Marcella. We have to move everything out of the house and get the cockroaches out. Do it carefully, item by item. We're going to transport everything to the camp, but I don't want to take along even one of these filthy bastards. Once you finish the clean-up, take the horses and begin moving the stuff. The rest of you go to the ranch, and I'll join you there later. I want to be sure everything's done carefully, because if we overlook even a few cockroaches it'll all have to be done over again.'

'Juan Carlos, what should I do with the men's clothes?' Marcella asked me. 'There may be cockroach eggs in them.'

'Roll everything up in a blanket and toss it into the water. Leave it there all day – that ought to kill them.'

She laughed, but I knew she'd do it.

When I got to the ranch, I could see how inefficient Nizaro had been. The frame of the house was ready, but that was all. The planks for the walls had been cut and were piled to one side; the framework of the roof was up, but nothing had been laid down for the foliage that was supposed to cover it – the long leaves called suitas, which are twisted in a certain way on battens attached to the framework, guaranteeing that the roof will be completely waterproof. We'd need a lot of them: the house was thirty feet by thirty feet, and the roof was constructed of four adjoining beams, which meant that a large surface had to be covered. A few bundles of leaves had already been cut and were waiting to be used.

'Omar, Daniel and Max – begin working on the roof! The others – look for more leaves. Chita, see to it that nobody takes more than an hour to gather a bundle, and make sure that each bundle is a decent size. Keep an eye out for snakes and, if you find any real pretty ones, bring back the skins.'

I hefted each bundle: if it was too light, or if the guy had spent too much time on it, he got a tongue-lashing and went back on the double. They had to go farther and farther away for the leaves, and they came back with bigger and bigger bundles; eventually they were dragging their arses, exhausted by the weight and the distance.

The roof made slow progress. I had them begin in the corner I'd chosen for my bedroom because I wanted to spend a comfortable night – it isn't often that you've got a piece of blonde tail available in the jungle.

I went into a rage if I saw one of the men not working.

'Carlos, what the fuck are you doing, taking a sunbath?'

'I don't have any more leaves.'

'There's plenty else that you can do. Help the carpenter. What's the idiot doing?'

I'd seen the carpenter standing in a corner, playing around with two boards.

'What are you doing?'

'I'm making a bed.'

'For whom?'

'For me.'

'Are you crazy? Where do you think you are? I suppose next you'll start knitting a blanket while you're at it?'

I smacked him on the back of the head and sent him flying towards the corner of my future bedroom.

'Didn't you see I've got a lady with me? Where's your brain, you selfish bastard? Nail up four walls here, then make me a bed – a big double bed – and a stool. After that, get busy on a fireplace for the kitchen and some shelves for the food-supplies. When that's done, finish the table and chairs. Move it – it's later than you think. You can get help if you need it, but it's got to be finished by this evening.'

I turned to Carlos. 'Stop farting around and lend a hand.'

Carlos was a former salsa musician whose voice had been ruined by alcohol and tobacco, but he could still manage a song and would bawl one at the drop of a hat. He was a goldbrick, however, and he and the lazy carpenter made a pair I had to keep my eyes on. . . . They picked up a few planks and walked off.

'Stay here – I may be able to give you some advice.'

'But it's better here!' replied Carlos.

'It's even better over here. I like you, and I want to be able to see you.'

Everyone had understood their manoeuvre, and the others all hooted. Someone called out: 'Cut off his tail so he can't fly away!'

The rain kept falling, and the whole interior of the ranch house, ploughed up by the constant coming and going, was nothing but a vast quagmire. Little Sophie, who didn't really understand anything that had happened after Guerra, kept getting in my way; I didn't like to see her without something to do.

'Don't just sit there – it's demoralizing for the others. Make yourself useful.'

I tossed her a bolt of cloth so she could make some mosquito-nets. She bitched but, if she didn't like it, fuck her! Which I did fairly often, because I thought she looked pretty cute in her mud-covered white jeans and with her blonde hair plastered down on her face by the rain. From time to time I'd interrupt her work and take her by the arm. 'Come along, kid, I want to show you the birds and the bees.'

The men caught on to my trick and profited from my absences to slow down. Every time I'd return with my little Swedish bundle looking muddier than before, I'd start to bawl them out and they'd begin scurrying. I wanted that bedroom finished in a hurry! The knees of my trousers were beginning to get dirty.

When White and Garret had finished their comings and goings between the house of cockroaches and the ranch, I immediately put them to work constructing a temporary roof to protect part of the kitchen. Everyone pitched in.

At three o'clock the team bringing up equipment and supplies arrived. Jimmy had really loaded them down, and all of them were exhausted and covered with mud from head to toe. A few of them wanted to change clothes, but couldn't when they saw the state of their things: my disinfection method didn't meet with everyone's approval.

'In any case, why change when the day's not over? Do you want to sleep indoors tonight?' I asked.

'Sure.'

'Then, everybody get busy on the roof.'

There were soon twenty-five of them swaying in the wind, hanging on to the beams. It was picturesque, like a sort of Christmas-tree.

Half an hour later there was a cry – Garret was bounching from beam to beam and hitting the ground some twenty feet below. Luckily he was built like a brick shithouse. Silence, then everyone burst out laughing. He wasn't hurt too badly, but his face was split from chin to forehead – and I didn't have a first-aid kit, not so much as a plaster.

'You want me to sew you up? I've got needles.'

'No, no,' he answered, terrified.

'Anybody got any ideas?'

'I know a cure,' said Chita. 'You have to mix up a plaster using ashes, oil and lemons.'

I'd have been surprised if that one didn't have some dumb idea, but – who knew? – maybe it would work. While Chita was applying his medicine, Garret was howling because the lemon stung. I felt sorry for him.

177

'Here, have a glass of guaro – it's a disinfectant. Feel better now?'

'Yes, yes,' he answered, eager to escape our attentions.

'So much the better. Get back up there and watch where you put your feet – you might have hurt yourself.'

My bedroom was now roofed over, and I next had them cover a strip about three feet wide in another corner so they'd have a little dry spot. Night was falling, and we'd soon have to stop work, damn it! Another guy, Omar, also took a tumble, but luckily it wasn't serious.

'OK, that's it for today. Everybody down. Bring the table under the covered part and we'll eat.'

I lit some candles, took out a few joints and a little alcohol, and things were soon more cheerful. Garret, whose head had swollen to double its size, was the chief target of the jibes, with the guys suggesting more and more weird cures – everything from a chickenshit dressing to cauterization with a red-hot iron. The cassette-player was going full blast, and the men forgot their exhaustion as they kidded around. But I was thinking of the next day and soon sent them off to bed – in a manner of speaking, because in fact the 'bed' each man arranged for himself was made up of plastic sacks, bits of board, and some leaves that offered a little protection from the mud and rain. They were jumbled together – actually piled up – under the narrow ledge of roof and on or under the table and benches.

In my bedroom a different sight greeted my eyes. A few planks on the ground isolated the mud; in the middle of the room, like a throne, was my bed, covered with mosquito-netting and white sheets. On each side, two candles set on miner's bars stuck in the ground gave the place a romantic glow. And the warrior's reward, wearing only a pair of white panties, was seated on the bed. This vision, after the sight of the men floundering in the mud, increased my desire tenfold. I turned up the music to cover the grunts and groans, and all night long the Rolling Stones provided the background for my wild galloping. The coke and the excitement had left me unable to sleep – and naturally Sophie didn't get any sleep, either. When I got her out of bed at four in the morning, together with the others, she didn't look too sprightly.

Nor was she the only one. The men who stumbled out looked strange; their hair was plastered against their faces by the mud, they were soaked to the skin, and they were barely awake. The night had done nothing to improve Garret's wound, and his face looked like a carnival mask. Frozen stiff, the men gathered silently around the table. I asked them: 'Didn't you sleep well?'

178

'It was freezing.'

'I was fine because I have my own heating system,' said Barbas, letting out a thunderous fart.

'Quit it, or I'll shove a cork up your arse. All right, I know it's hard, but we've got to keep at it. If we want a minimum of comfort, we have to work twice as hard, and in two days you'll be sleeping in dry quarters. Here, this should warm you up.'

I sent around the canteen of guaro. Comforted by the heat burning their guts, the men began to thaw out.

'OK, today – with the exception of Omar, Daniel and Garret – we're going to have a change of pace. Who wants to go down to Guerra for more stuff?'

Everybody volunteered. Once they got down there, they'd probably try to rest up, taking advantage of the fact that I wasn't around to get on their backs.

'All those who were on the roof yesterday will be part of that team, but today there'll have to be two round trips. If you leave now, you can be back before noon and make a second trip before night. Don't waste time, because you're going to make two trips no matter how late it is. Jimmy, the pipes for bringing water into the kitchen get first priority.'

'How are we going to get them here? There are a hell of a lot of them!'

'Take the horses, but don't load them too heavily. Attach the pipes to their rear ends. Bring up the canoa and everything else we need for work at the river. You can grab something to eat down there, then get on the road again.'

They downed their coffee and vanished into the darkness.

'Carpenter, I want more work out of you today than I got yesterday – I don't want to see you skiving off. You've got five single beds and sixteen bunk beds to make. Finish all the partitions, and I'll give you the plans for the doors. And see to it that you finish up the kitchen, too.'

Half an hour later everybody was busy and I felt better. Someone, however, hadn't shown up for duty – my little blonde slut. I found her sleeping in the bed she'd returned to right after breakfast, and I shook her feet violently.

'What are you doing here?'

'I'm resting. I'm bushed.'

'The hell you say! Nobody sleeps during working hours. Get a move on!'

'But it's four o'clock in the morning! At home I'm always asleep at this hour.'

179

'But you're not at home any more; you're with me, and this is the way things are. If you don't like it, take your stuff and clear out. You've chewed my ears off often enough with your talk about equality between the sexes, and now you're going to live up to it. Do you know how to weave?'

'Yes, a little.'

'Then, go up on the roof with the others and weave some leaves.'

Little by little the house was talking shape. Marcella had already pretty well arranged the kitchen, even though she was still paddling around in almost six inches of mud and there was still neither roof nor wall. Helped by her daughter, she hammered nails into the planks as soon as the carpenter put them up, and hung her pots and pans.

'Marcella, the men around here have been badly brought up, so keep an eye on your daughter if you don't want any problems.'

'Don't worry, Don Juan Carlos, these pigs don't frighten me. I always keep something to defend myself with close at hand,' she said with a big smile as she showed me a kitchen knife planted in the wall.

'I see – but it won't help me if you cut the balls off all these idiots! Just keep your daughter near you; she's your responsibility. Anyhow, I'm going to make the kitchen off-limits to everyone.'

One of my workers, Innocente, was a peninsula man who'd come with his son, Manolito, a boy of ten who was a wild uncivilized savage. I appointed Manolito to follow me around carrying the canteen of alcohol, and I tied a cup around his neck. He got a kick out of knowing that everyone looked forward to his arrival. Because he liked to hear me bawl the men out, he'd even point out the ones he felt weren't working hard enough.

By the time the equipment crew came from Guerra, the roof was pretty well along and the walls were slowly going up. A quick meal and a shot of rotten booze, and they left again for Guerra.

'But, Juan Carlos, we'll never make it before night,' Jimmy said.

'That's not my problem. I warned you not to linger on the way.'

'But the horses go so slowly!'

'Then, carry them.'

The afternoon passed at the same pace. I went from one to the other without saying a word, since I no longer had to bawl them out: all I had to do was look at a guy, and he speeded up. From time to time I'd send Manolito to give someone a well-earned shot.

Alone in her corner, Sophie was making slow and silent progress. As a matter of fact, she was actually doing pretty well. The sight of her frail body clinging to the roof beams made me feel a little guilty, and I decided to pay her some attention.

180

'Hey, kid, come down and rest a minute.'

She quickly came down from the roof, and I gently pushed her towards the bedroom. Three minutes later she was back on the roof. Work came first.

Night had fallen, but the men were still mechanically going on with their work. I would have let them continue, but some of them took advantage of the fact that I couldn't keep an eye on them in the dark to catch a little shuteye.

We skipped the celebration that evening. It didn't matter much because everybody was too tired. They ate quickly and silently, and even Barbas' trumpet solos had lost their oomph. The men set up the seven beds that had been built during the day.

'Off you go. Take advantage of those beds before the others get here and make things crowded.'

Thanks to the coke, I still wasn't sleepy, and I stayed up talking to Nicolas.

At about nine o'clock, the fire brigade arrived, dragging hundreds of yards of pipes and hose behind them. They were so tired they could hardly stand up; even the horses had had it, and one of them collapsed on the spot as soon as the unloading was finished. The men were mute, a band of phantoms who weren't even hungry. All they could think about was sleep. Some of them were even too tired to pull off their boots, and just collapsed in their damp and muddy clothes. After a short argument over the beds, silence reigned.

It was time for me to return to my Dulcinea, who'd taken advantage of my absence to nod off. I woke her up with a few rough caresses. Since I didn't want her moans to awaken the men and give them ideas – they were tired enough as it was – I again put on the cassette-player, which was a lot more cheerful than her groaning. The festivities kept her awake and active until four, when it was time to begin another work-day. Because dawn began at four o'clock and night fell at six in the evening, there was no chance to sleep late. Everybody was exhausted; even the alcohol couldn't shake off their numbness.

'Gentlemen, tonight we celebrate. As soon as the roof is finished, we'll take a break. The Guerra crew had better get moving. There'll only be one trip today, but the sooner you come back, the sooner you can help the others finish the roof. After that – fiesta!'

That's a magic word for Latins. The idea alone excited them, and when they started for Guerra they were almost running.

Sophie hadn't shown up for breakfast, and I was wondering if I ought to rejoin her. But I suddenly remembered my mother saying; 'If you want to go far, take good care of your horse.' I decided to let her sleep a little longer.

181

At about ten o'clock Raphael, one of Barbaroja's men, came to see me. I'd completely forgotten the old man, though his house was only fifty yards away.

'What do you want?'

'I was wondering if there might be any work for me.'

'Aren't you working for Barbaroja?'

'For the time being, I'm only looking after his house while he's away.'

'Do you know where he's gone?'

'He didn't tell me, but I think he went to get the cops. He was very angry.'

'Fuck him. As for you, you're welcome.'

'If you don't have enough planks, he's got a whole supply of them. You can take them if you give me a little something.'

I hesitated but, after all, it had been that son of a bitch Barbaroja who'd begun the cheating.

I called over the carpenter. 'Go along with Raphael and bring some wood from Barbaroja's place. Take only what you need, and let me know exactly how much you've taken.'

If Barbaroja decided to behave himself again, I could always pay him. Well, sure – *if* he decided to behave himself.

Following my directions, Chita and Cunado had put in running water by forming a dam way up on the quebrada with the aid of a half-barrel that served as a reservoir; from holes in the bottom, some 1500 feet of tubing ran down to the house, and this allowed me to install a shower near the kitchen.

When the Guerra crew returned at about two in the afternoon, the roof lacked only a few square yards. It could wait, especially as the rain had stopped for the first time in four days and a timid sun was trying to pierce the clouds.

'Fine, let's stop. That's enough for today. Clean up and let your clothes dry while there's still some sun.'

They hadn't washed or taken off their clothes in three days, and they were beginning to smell a little.

Encouraged by a few kicks in the arse, the carpenter and his helper had got a lot done. All the partitions were up, and except for the muddy floor the house finally looked like something. It was divided into three sections, ten by thirty feet each: in the centre, open on both sides, was the big main room that served as a dining-room and a common room; to the right was the kitchen and the men's dormitory; and to the left were the cook's bedroom, a bedroom for Jimmy and Nizaro, and my own bedroom.

When they all sat down at the table they were scrubbed and rosy, dressed in clothes that hadn't had a chance to get dirty yet. I'd sent Gabino, a brat whose family lived some two hours from the camp, back home to buy some pork, and the pig was already roasting.

'Men, you've done a good job. You've just about finished the house in three days, and tonight each of you will have a bed. Just remember that this is my place and that you'll have to respect my rules. I don't want to see any junk lying around this common room. Keep the dormitory clean, and don't turn it into a pig-sty. Nobody goes into the kitchen except the señora and Chita – the first guy I catch in there will remember it for a long time. You're also not to go into the left wing of the house, and my bedroom is strictly off-limits to everyone but Marcella and Sophie. If I ever catch anyone there, he won't remember it long, because he won't live long. I'm not going to repeat this, so remember – you've been warned. And now – eat up!'

When Marcella brought the plates of grilled meat, there were about sixty pounds of barbecue spread out on the table. Surprised by the abundance, the men hesitated a moment, then rushed over. I'd put out a ten-litre jug of guaro, and the glasses were soon full. The booze and the large joints going around quickly made them rowdy, and what had started as a family dinner soon became a free-for-all with everybody trying to out-yell and out-party his neighbour. I'd distributed cards, but the men were too drunk to play and soon began tossing them at one another. Some of them began to dance together or, rather, to stumble around clinging to each other. Eduardo was snoring on the floor, being trampled by the dancers.

'We need some women,' yelled Cunado.

'Go get the horses,' answered Barbas.

A few moments later, Chita, dressed in Marcella's apron, jumped up on the table and began a belly-dance while the others whistled and applauded. He still had his boots on, and he'd rolled his trousers up his fat hairy legs. Then he started to do a striptease, and Gabino, a rough mountain man, was sufficiently carried away by the illusion to put a hand on his arse. Chita immediately whirled around and gave him an enormous kick in the face that knocked him out and sent him to join Eduardo in the mud.

Marcella was really high and jumped up to join Chita on the table, which began to buckle under their weight. The men got excited; yelling their heads off, they tried to sing along with the music, which was Nina Hagen's 'Africa'. Though they didn't understand a word of German, they kept bawling 'Africa' as loud as they could.

When Marcella collapsed in a drunken heap, they rushed her. I'd

183

been laughing so hard that before I could stop them her tits were in the air and two of the guys were tearing at her underwear.

A few smacks on the head with a shovel cooled off the ones with the hottest nuts, and with Jimmy's help I carried Marcella out and threw her on her bed; we were laughing so hard that on the way we dropped her a few times. A little later the party wound up; exhaustion, booze and pot got the better of the guys one after another; and, though most of them managed to make it to their beds, a few just lay where they'd dropped.

'Chita, White, get these dumb bastards out of here!'

They unceremoniously dragged the men outside into the mud.

I went back to my room and my sweet nympho, who announced hesitantly as she was pulling off my boots: 'Juan Carlos, I'd like to leave tomorrow.'

Love of my life, why do you want to leave me when our romance is still going strong?

'Don't you like it here? Aren't you enjoying your vacation?'

'It's all right, but I'm worn out.'

The poor kid, I knew what she meant. She was the only one who worked day *and* night.

'OK. Tomorrow I'll have someone take you back to Guerra.'

I'd almost got used to the cosy little animal. Never mind – at least I'd sleep better. But I decided that I might as well profit from this last night before they took my little toy away: from then until dawn I played 'Heads or Tails' with her.

In the morning I was in a bad mood because Sophie had become little more than a lifeless puppet in my hands. Marcella was busy getting breakfast ready. When I entered the men's dorm I was disgusted – guys were stretched out in every direction, some of them even sleeping with their heads in their vomit. The ones assigned to the top bunks hadn't been able to make it into their beds and had collapsed anywhere and everywhere. I went for the kitchen hose to begin the clean-up. Under the stream of icy water, the men quickly came to.

'On your feet, you bunch of pigs. You have ten minutes to dress and have breakfast.'

They stumbled out, still drunk from the night before, and when they had all downed their coffee I took the floor.

'Today we start working down at the river. If anybody wants to leave, it's now or never. Afterwards it will be too late – I won't pay anyone off until December.'

To my pleased surprise, only three men spoke up: the singer, the carpenter – and Garret, who needed to to the hospital. (His wound

184

still hadn't healed, and it was beginning to turn green. The colour didn't show much against his black skin, but the odour of the infection was unpleasant; it was just as well that he wanted to leave because he was beginning to stink.) The other two were still trying to fuck off, and I was glad to see them go.

But the carpenter should have kept his mouth shut.

'After all, Juan Carlos, we're not animals. There are unions in this country, and rules about working hours.'

'You don't say! How interesting. Tell me more.'

Encouraged, he came within range. 'Here in Costa Rica, the laws say . . .,' he began.

I cut him short with a fist in the face.

'You're not in Costa Rica any more, you're in Quebrada del Frances, and the only laws are mine! If I say so, you'll work twenty hours a day. But, on the other hand, I guarantee you good eats, a place to sleep and a lot of laughs. Those who are willing to go along with that can stay – the rest, clear out. What'll it be?'

None of the others made a move; in fact, they looked at the three quitters with contempt. They were beginning to develop team spirit and were proud of what they'd accomplished in three days.

'Chiche, you're going to escort the señorita back. Take two horses, and when you return bring some stuff with you.'

I paid the three others.

'Follow Chiche to Guerra. Make arrangements with the pulpero for getting to Sierpe. And now beat it!'

Sophie, riding for the first time in her life, perched cautiously on the horse. The way she winced as she settled carefully into the saddle made me smile. Had I played 'tails' too often last night?

I was relieved to see her go. The unexpected little luxury had been great, but at the moment I needed all my energy for the job ahead. Now more than ever.

I turned to the men. 'We're going to settle down to some serious work. Daniel, you and your two sons, Max and Omar, will keep working on the roof.'

They were natives of the peninsula, and real pros at construction.

'Gabino and Miguel. I want you to take machetes and clear away the approaches to the house. Chita, dig us a latrine and make it a deep one. Jimmy, divide all the miner's bars, shovels and machetes among the other men.'

I decided to work Frenchman's River, my own river, and headed for it followed by all the men shouldering their tools and walking behind me in Indian file, happy at the prospect of getting close to the gold.

Manolito walked beside me, the Catiadora on his head. When we reached the river, I told all of them to take it easy: I had to do a little thinking and plan just where to begin, so I decided they might as well take advantage of such an unusual pause to rest up. . . . After studying the river and its banks I went upstream, accompanied by Manolito, to make a few tests. Oreros had obviously done some work there, and the underlying rock showed through in a few places.

I soon made up my mind. Where the valley grew wider the river flowed to the right, but the configuration of the terrain indicated that a few thousand years earlier it had flowed to the left. I decided to make it return to its earlier bed so I could work it.

When I returned to where I'd left the men, they were all down on their hands and knees busily examining the gravel and the rocks. Gold fever is more than a legend, as I'd noticed on many occasions. Some of them came running excitedly towards me, their pockets full of yellow stone; they didn't have the faintest idea of how to go about prospecting, and I must have been the only one who'd ever seen any gold-mining.

The first thing we needed was a dam. We had to pile up tons of rocks, mixed with leaves and branches, to a height of several yards. The barrier was not watertight, but it cut down the flow of the river considerably, so a pocket of water was soon created. Little by little, the water rose to the level of the old river-bed, and the first trickle flowed into its new route to the sound of a great hurrah. Then we cleared the terrain to facilitate the flow of the river along the cliff.

I counted on this water to erode down to the level of the auriferous gravel. My men, spread out along four hundred yards, hammered and broke the soil with mighty blows, lifting out the stones, one by one, so the current could swiftly carry off the soil and dig its new bed. I showed each of them how to go about it.

'Don't use shovels, just the miner's bars. Try to arrange the stones you take out to make a compact wall. The better it's made, the less risk there is of its tumbling down on you.'

The rapid action of the current and of the miner's bars worked fine. The men were quickly frozen stiff by the glacial water that came up to their knees, and by the incessant rain. So much the better: the only way they could warm up was to work twice as hard. They even had contests to see who could carry the largest stone while everybody shouted and yelled.

The racket of the work site was like music to my ears. Manolito, standing alongside me with a canteen of alcohol in his hand, distributed according to my direction small shots of guaro to warm up and encourage the men; but I was irritated because my little crew was scattered along the river, and it was impossible to keep an eye on all of them at once. The jungle, all that useless green, blocked my view.

I turned to two of the men.

'Chiche, Cunado, take an axe and a machete and clear this crap away for four hundred yards around.'

That's one nice thing about the Ticos. Tell any other worker who's got all his marbles to cut away hundreds of yards of trees with an axe and he'll laugh in your face. Here it was different; they had confidence in me, hopped to it, and asked no questions. One by one the trees went down, and the landscape began to change.

Manolito fingered the skivers and the gossips for me. I didn't mind them resting for a minute, but two minutes was too much. If it went on, a swift kick in the arse, a well-aimed stone, or a shot fired in the air brought them back to order. I was everywhere, and they became used to my omnipresence.

White, a loafer by nature, kept trying to keep out of my sight by going behind a tree or around a bend in the river – but the poor bastard was now the only black and, though I didn't know all the men, his absence was quickly apparent. Several times I found him asleep leaning on a miner's bar; a smack behind the ears invariably sent him flying into the water. I surprised Eduardo squatting in a corner and hand-picking some gravel, and I aimed a shot that grazed his ears; panicked, he rushed back to his place.

When I stopped work at the end of the day, the channel was about three feet deep, and the level of the pocket was still going down; the water would go on working during the night. On the way back, the men were less cheerful than they'd been in the morning: gold-prospecting had turned out to be more aquatic than they'd imagined.

At dinner I realized that someone was missing. 'Where's Chita?'

'He's still digging,' said Marcella with a laugh.

I went to see. The idiot had made a latrine more than ten feet deep – big enough for an army.

'Where are you going?' I asked as I motioned him to get out. 'Trying to get to China?'

'Don't worry. Nizaro's two daughters alone can fill it with shit in a week.'

The same work went on for the next two days, and we built a veritable Great Wall of China with the stones taken from the river. The jungle had been cleared away; I could see the heads sticking up over the channel, like in a carnival shooting gallery, and it was easy to keep track of everyone: I'd count and, if a head was missing, God help the man when I found him.

At the end of the third day, the channel was about eight feet deep and three feet wide, and the water had definitely chosen the new path.

The men were exhausted the stiff with cold, the ends of their fingers bloody from the effort of moving the stones. While everyone went back to the house, I did a little panning at the bottom of the channel, and a few grains of gold showed up. The time had come for some serious work.

After dinner that evening I gave a short speech.

'Tomorrow we're going to start taking gold out. From now on, nobody goes down to the river outside working hours, no matter what the excuse. If I catch anybody, I'll shoot him in the balls and leave him to die. I'm not kidding. If you want to wash, go to the other river – it's only ten minutes away. If you see gold in the canoa or alongside it, don't touch it – call me. The gold is mine and nobody else's. Got it?'

'Got it.'

'*In gold we trust, but nobody can touch,*' said White sententiously in his Caribbean English.

To break the silence brought on by my announcement, I sent around several joints and a canteen of guaro.

The men were living better; they were beginning to get used to the working conditions, and the house was pleasant. The dormitory was clean and well kept; everyone had his own bed and his own clearly defined territory, which was a luxury in the mountains, where several oreros often shared the same bed. The mud was beginning to dry, and I'd forbidden anyone to wear boots in the house.

It was the big day. I was setting up a ten-foot canoa in the river. Eduardo, the only one who knew how to use a saw or hammer in a nail without killing himself, had been promoted to carpenter. The canoa was V-shaped. The wider end, about four or five feet across at the opening, was made of aluminium. The narrow end, the 'head', was made of wood and rested in the aluminium part. A synthetic carpeting helped trap the gold particles.

Up front a dozen men armed with shovels and picks were assigned to load the canoa. At its head, where the nuggets remained, I put those people I trusted completely: Daniel had his two sons, Omar and Max. I'd known Omar and Max at Drake, and when they'd heard I was on the peninsula they'd come looking for work, bringing their father with them. He was a funny sort of guy who seldom spoke – probably because he had nothing to say. A native of Panama, he'd never in his life worn shoes or taken a shower: his feet were as large as flippers, and he smelt like a goat. The men he shared the room with had once dragged him under the kitchen hose.

To them I added Manolito's father, whose name, Innocente, fitted him like a glove: he wouldn't have harmed a fly. I told them exactly what to do and what motions to make to help pass the gravel through.

'Take out the large stones and the pebbles one by one after you've had a look at them. Don't ever throw out a handful without examining it carefully.'

I knew the area had many nuggets, and since the idiots couldn't tell what they were by touch they might easily toss them away, so I spent a long time explaining this: it was hard for them to take in new information. The important thing was for them to understand the movements, even if they didn't understand the reason for them.

After a while, three others took over the same job, just as a simple security measure. Behind them, two guys with shovels cleared away the rejected pebbles so they wouldn't impede the flow of the current. Barbas and Jimmy kept an eye on everyone who worked the canoa, while I settled myself in a rocking chair – from which, with a cup of Java in my hand and a joint in my mouth, I minded the store; I could see everything from where I sat.

The work went on like that all day. In the water the men with the miner's bars kept hacking away at the ground; downstream the others kept shovelling stuff into the head of the canoa, where Daniel, Max, Omar and Innocente seemed to have got the idea of what had to be done. They all talked and fooled around as they worked – except for Innocente, who was too busy following my instructions to allow himself a moment of distraction. When the rhythm slowed down, I'd get off a couple of rounds a few inches over their heads; they'd jump, then laughingly speed up again.

About noon that day, as we were getting ready to leave for lunch, Nizaro and his two fat daughters appeared. He was amazed at the quantity and quality of the work that had been done since he'd left, but didn't seem to understand my methods. He started playing the know-it-all grandfather.

'Why did you go to this side? You should have started on the right.'

'Why?'

'Because that's the way it's always done.'

'Well, my intuition tells me that the gold is here; if there's any down below, there must be some here as well.'

'Well, what's done is done. I wasn't here, and you couldn't know.'

Keep talking that way, you old wreck, I thought, and I'll have you picking up gold with your teeth. But, rather than take a poke at a senior citizen, I preferred to end the discussion.

'We'll see in a couple of days.'

189

Barbaroja showed up in the afternoon, claiming he'd been to see his sister in Puerto Cortés about some property deeds. He was impressed by the size of the house and the extent of our work, but he didn't say anything. Which was just as well.

At five o'clock I sent away everyone but Jimmy and Nizaro and lifted out the canoa. The old man did some quick panning and showed me the result, his eyes gleaming with irony: a few grains, two or three grams at most. I wasn't disappointed since I felt we hadn't yet reached the level I was interested in, and I hoped soon to show the old man that I was right – and that I was the better man – without having to beat his brains out.

The next day, to save time, everyone ate down at the river. The meal was brought by Nizaro's two fat girls, who complained because walking a few hundred yards with a pot in each hand was more work than they were used to.

At the end of the day the hole was larger but the results were pretty much the same as they'd been the day before. The old man looked even more ironic. Barbaroja, who'd come to see what was up, must have been convinced that he'd soon be able to return to his solitary life, but I was feeling more and more sure of myself.

Two days later, at about eleven o'clock, Jimmy's brother Wilson, who was working the canoa, suddenly shouted and, with an expression of absolute joy, held up a nugget – the first one. It weighed seventeen grams, and I knew there were more where it came from.

When I lifted out the canoa that evening, a galaxy of bright spots appeared on the carpeting: there were more than a hundred grams in grains and in ten-to-twelve-gram nuggets. It was a triumph, though I'd never for a minute doubted that my reasoning had been correct.

The following days confirmed the success: 100 grams, 120 grams, 80 grams. . . . I was euphoric, and my joy spread to the men, who all felt very involved.

They worked just as hard – if not harder – but the atmosphere relaxed; and I have to say that if, as I'd promised, I made them break their backs working I also kept my other promises.

The food was plentiful: in the morning, at 4.30 a hearty breakfast: at ten, coffee and enormous stomach-filling tacos; at 12.30 lunch at the quebrada, served by the two fatties; at 3.30, more coffee and a snack; and finally, at seven, dinner.

The camp continued to improve. The jungle had been forced back, the approaches to the house cleared, and the danger from snakes considerably diminished: in a week only twelve 'deadlies' had been killed, one of them right under Nicolas' bed. Eduardo had made

190

ventilation openings, which had completely dried the mud. He'd also added a little overhang to protect the horses' saddles and begun work on a tool shed.

Since the work-day ended at about 4.30 – though this varied – the men had plenty of time to wash their clothes or improve the menu, often returning from the jungle with stalks of bananas, cassava roots and hearts of palm.

They were even beginning to like the punk music that endlessly pounded their ears. At the beginning, nobody cared for it, and they kept asking me for their everlasting salsa, which of course I refused. But after hearing my music in the house and down at the river they had got to know the words even if they didn't understand them.

Only the working conditions remained the same. Their clothes were always soaked through; the rain began every morning at about ten, sometimes earlier, and went on until late at night; the hole became larger and deeper, and they had to stand in icy water up to their chests for twelve hours on end, warmed from time to time only by a shot of guaro. I wondered how they managed to end each day with a little party.

After dinner, I passed the joints around and they played cards, losing and winning their salaries over and over. They could stay up as late as they wanted, so long as they were in the hole by 4.30, and I'd hang around and kid with them.

The water in the hole was really very cold. I'd tried to wash in it, but I have to admit that I couldn't take it. As for the men, they didn't complain too much since they had no choice. I had to select those men who worked in the hole carefully because it had become so deep that the smaller ones got a mouthful with every shovelful.

One day a snake fell off the cliff and right into the hole. I drew my gun and fired, while everybody hot-footed it out of the water. Later they told me they'd been more afraid of my richocheting bullets than of the snake. They must have wondered just how crazy I was, because from then on they scattered on the double as soon as I got the gun out. . . .

Only one problem bothered me as much as it bothered them, because it cut down on production: since they were always in their wet rubber boots, their feet began to rot with a kind of infection that covered them with scabs oozing a greenish liquid. Nothing seemed to help, and some of the men began working barefoot because they couldn't get their boots on. The only way to disinfect everything was to boil it, and nobody was willing to try that.

*   *   *

191

Things had been going well for ten days, and Nizaro had finally shut up. Better yet, he told everybody who'd listen that he had suspected that the gold was there, and that it was because of him that I'd discovered Frenchman's River. The old liar.

Barbaroja was amazed: he had never seen so much gold. According to his own words, I was a magician. He felt raw about having lived so long right on top of all that wealth, but what he wouldn't admit was that, even if he'd known about it, he'd never have been able to undertake a project of such magnitude. Every night he'd come to the ranch to eat with us and join in our daily celebrations. He loved alcohol, and I occasionally gave him a litre of guaro, which he'd polish off before dawn. The former local terror no longer terrorized anybody; he'd stagger home, and his morning hangover had become routine. Though his life had improved and – thanks to us – he now had running water, what really mattered to him was my supply of booze.

Miguel's father supplied me with bootleg guaro, and he also sold me two horses at a good price because I had to return Nizaro's nags to him. None too soon, either! They were in pretty bad shape by now. Someone went to Guerra every day to bring back supplies and equipment; and, though the men took turns, the horses were always the same: their backs were bloody and they looked worn out.

After we reached bedrock, work began at 5.30; I wanted to be alone during the first hour. The irregular form of the rock and the opacity of the muddy water prevented the men from raking the bottom carefully, and some of auriferous gravel escaped their shovels. In addition, as the miner's bars broke up the soil, some of the gold would mix with the smaller particles and settle even more deeply, and as a result it couldn't be taken out with tools.

Every morning, before the others were up, I went to the quebrada on my own. Marcella, already up and around, was supposed to make sure that nobody followed me – an easy assignment because the men were too exhausted to sacrifice a minute of precious sleep.

Once there, I smeared my body with grease as a protection against the freezing water, put on diver's goggles, hid my revolver nearby under some leaves, and went fishing for nuggets. The water was clear, because the mud stirred up the previous day had settled. Once under water, I swept gently, to avoid stirring up the soil again, and bared the rock uncovered the day before; an unbelievable harvest of nuggets would be waiting for me in the cracks or right on the surface of the rock. Those were moments of intense excitement, not just because of the gold but because of its quantity; every morning I collected about

192

twice as much as had been taken out the day before: if there had been eighty grams, I collected 150 grams or more.

I don't ordinarily get carried away, but this was fabulous! Back in my room, which the others were forbidden to enter, I studied the nuggets, the largest of which was 260 grams. I was very familiar with gold and had already seen rich sites, but never a lode like that one.

I knew that large companies worked on the basis of a return of one gram per cubic metre. It's not the density that counts but the amount of gravel worked.

Here the mine was extraordinarily rich, maybe too rich for one man. It was an immense potential fortune, an inexhaustible treasure; I was sitting on top of hundreds of millions of dollars. At the beginning I'd thought it was simply one rich pocket, but the daily production remained more or less constant; some days were lower than others, but that was to be expected when you worked on the upper layers, which weren't as rich in precious metal.

I'd been lucky enough to have money very young – large sums obtained in lucrative affairs; but, whatever the amount, it could be calculated in advance and never came as a surprise. But this was completely different, and the results surpassed all my expectations.

Until then, no sum had been so large that I couldn't see myself rapidly spending it – or, rather, wasting it – on pleasures. For the first time, I could plan ahead: this mine could bring in enough to allow me to realize my dreams – without having to scrimp and save, something strictly against my principles. That was what had kept me going, what had excited me every morning: the possibility of preparing for the future without having to give up the present. That and only that had given me the tenacity to stay in such a Godforsaken spot no matter what.

You can't live an adventurous life without making enormous demands on your body, and mine had taken a lot of punishment. You can't go beyond your limits without having to pay for it later, and I knew that, when it came, the bill might be high – so I had to keep pushing ahead as long as I was in full possession of my strength, and my last adventure had to be grander, more insane than all the others. Maybe Frenchman's River was it.

I wasn't home safe yet. You don't get 50 per cent of a fabulous fortune without arousing envy, and I knew from experience that when a deal reaches astronomic proportions neither word of honour, nor written contracts, nor promises mean anything for very long. And, having come to that conclusion, I stopped brooding; it was 5.30, time to wake the others.

193

Every morning I went through the same routine: on entering the men's dormitory, I fired off a single round from my .357 Magnum and everybody jumped out of bed. If it's true that stressful awakenings are bad for the heart, my workers would never see their old age. I always aimed at the same plank, which became a sort of calendar.

For obvious security reasons, the gold and I were never apart. I carried it around in a padlocked iron box bought in San José. My bedroom was off-limits to everyone, but I knew the powerful attraction of gold – and that the best way to prevent a theft was to eliminate temptation. Nobody knew about my morning harvests, and the regular weighings took place without witnesses. The only access to my room was through the one shared by Jimmy and Nizaro, which was also off-limits to the men; thus isolated, I was protected from unwelcome visits.

Though nobody knew the real grade of the ore, all the men were aware of its abundance. Their first contact with gold hadn't been disappointing but, once the initial excitement of knowing that at any moment they might come upon a nugget had passed, their enthusiasm was moderated – or, rather, the focus of their interest changed. What concerned them most was the sum total of the day's production, which they saw as a personal challenge, a daily record that had to be beaten. They knew that the site was the richest on the peninsula and our production higher than that of the other sites, so every evening the announcement of how much had been taken out was received with shouts of approval: they got the glory, I got the profit.

Only White, the cleverest of the lot, kept a clear head. One day as he was examining his shovel-callused hands I said to him: 'Come on, don't complain. Think of all the memories you're storing up. You'll be able to tell your kids that you worked one of the richest gold mines ever found.'

'And suppose they ask me where the gold is? Who'll look like an arsehole then?'

In any case, not me.

I wasn't fooled by the notion that my men were disinterested. Even if they were enthusiastic and kept that way by my constant attentions, I knew that the first time a nugget came into their hands without any witnesses nearby it would find its way right to the bottom of their pockets. A hundred-gram nugget represented ten months' wages, and it would be a great temptation.

That was only human, but I didn't want anybody helping them-

194

selves at my expense; and those who might try knew that, if they failed, the punishment would be extreme – as I made clear. 'I know you're tempted, but remember that, if I catch you at it, there'll be no second chance.'

It was up to me to see to it that they didn't have the opportunity. I was there all the time – the first to arrive and the last to leave. I set my rocking chair on the banks so I could overlook them all; as soon as a man raised his head, his eyes met mine. That omnipresence was more helpful than any threat, and like a good overseer watching his slaves I beat out the cadence.

One day they learned about dynamite. An enormous immovable boulder was interfering with work, so Miguel took charge of matters. Straddling it with a pike and a five-pound hammer in hand, he bored a hole and pounded away at it as regularly as a metronome, not stopping once that whole day. By the end of the afternoon, the hole was large enough to get some dynamite into it, so I put in some sticks and a detonator and attached a two-minute fuse. The men were nervous and, though they went on working, they kept an eye on me. They knew nothing about dynamite, but they thought of it as having some terrible power. I was amused by their fear, and masked by Jimmy I lit the fuse.

'Señores, you have one minute and fifty seconds to find shelter. Take your tools with you.'

A wise recommendation, because they went mad, jumping out of the hole and racing off in all directions. Nicolas and I lit cigarettes from the smoking fuse and calmly went to stand behind a tree. After a violent explosion that shot a geyser of water fifty feet into the air, the boulder was pulverized and the whole gorge filled with smoke. Having got over their terror, the men applauded, shouted their approval, and – stimulated by the noise and the smoke – joked about their earlier panic. However, they never got used to the explosions and were always scared shitless by them; like children, they were excited and frightened by power and noise, and between the fanfare wake-ups and the dynamite they got plenty of both.

The team worked well together; everybody knew his job and everybody earned his salary – except the two Nizaro girls. The irritating sight of those two big cows turned my stomach; they didn't do a fucking thing all day long and, just as Chita had predicted, they spent their time stuffing themselves and shitting. Though they were afraid of me and would pretend to be busy when I was around, I knew damn well that once I turned my back they never moved again.

195

I'd warned them against exciting the men by wearing skin-tight pants, because I didn't want any relationships to develop. The idea of one of my employees fucking those mounds of repugnant flesh actually disgusted me. They knew this and hated me for it – as well as for having often discussed them, in extremely unflattering terms. Luckily, Marcella could do all that needed doing in the kitchen. I'd told her to supervise the food at all times so the two sacks of shit, as I publicly called them, wouldn't be able to poison us.

The strongbox got heavier and heavier; it became impractical to carry it with me all the time, and in any case I didn't want to keep all that gold with me. The best thing would be to put it in some secure place in San José; and, besides, I wanted to show my partners just how rich the mine was, so they'd speed up the administrative process.

I decided to send Jimmy to telephone Herman and at the same time reinforce my position with the cops. Barbaroja worried me; I wasn't taken in by his apparently submissive attitude, and I suspected he was preparing a mess of trouble. He'd already intimated that because the site was so rich he should get more than the 35,000 colones we'd agreed on, but I pretended not to understand. I would stick to our agreement, but I had no confidence in the word of a Tico.

'Jimmy, here's a hundred and fifty grams of gold. First, go to Palmar and phone Herman. Tell him the operation is profitable and I'd like him to come talk it over – and, while he's at it, he might as well bring along the boat. Be sure to tell him there are no more snakes or other nasty things around, so he needn't be afraid. Next, go to Jiménez, sell this gold at the bank, and bring back a receipt. Finally, here are three envelopes: one is for the man in charge of the police in Jiménez, the other is for the chief in Golfito, and the last is for the big shot in Palmar. Make sure they understand that it comes from me.'

I'd slipped ten thousand colones – my monthly contribution to the cops' charities – into each envelope and written my name on the back in capital letters. Just in case Barbaroja started anything, I wanted the cops to remember me.

I also told Jimmy to bring back a sack of cement. At that point, the dynamite was stored in my room, under my bed, where a spark might set it off at any moment. Those two hundred sticks could easily have turned the camp into a fireworks show – and us into living torches – so I had decided to build a small padlocked and watertight bunker.

Jimmy was also supposed to bring back about a hundred lightbulbs, because the time had come to install electricity. The reason for this was simple – I had too many workers. Even discounting those whose foot infections had made them useless, I couldn't use more than ten

196

in the hole and four on the canoa – but I didn't want to fire anybody. In addition, the thought of that big hole naked in the dark made me sad, and I'd decided to set up two teams, one of which would work at night. It seemed to me that fifty lamps and reflectors ought to light up the area sufficiently, but to do this the generator would have to be set up – and that would be no picnic.

At first glance it seemed impossible, but you had to have faith. I'd have to handle it myself; knowing my men, I was sure they'd never manage it on their own, and discouragement would make them desert – literally, because they'd abandon the motor in the mountains and never dare show their faces again. I decided to wait until Jimmy got back before beginning.

After dinner the night before, just as everyone was getting ready for bed, a man came out of the rainy darkness. It was Demesio, who lived about two miles away and who sold me meat wholesale. I wasn't particularly fond of him: he was a small-time local crook, degenerate, thief and liar.

'Don Juan Carlos,' he said, coming up to me, 'is it true you need horses?'

'True. Do you have any to sell?'

'I've brought you two handsome animals, and I'll sell them for sixteen thousand colones.'

'Why should I pay that much when I just bought two for nine thousand colones?'

'Because mine are different. They're bigger, and they can carry over six hundred pounds apiece.'

'Six hundred? You're sure? Don't forget that we're neighbours and, if you cheat me, I'll know where to find you.'

'I swear in front of everybody that I'll take them back if you don't like them,' he said, turning to my men. 'I give you my word.'

'All right, but at that price I also want two leather saddles and two wooden pack-saddles.'

After a little dithering, I gave him seventeen thousand colones for the horses and their equipment. Before leaving, he renewed his promise and I repeated my warning.

The next morning I got a good look at them in daylight. One of them really was a very handsome animal, considerably larger and more solid than what's usually available on Osa, but the other was an old nag that could hardly stand on its feet and was ready for the glue factory. The son of a bitch! If he thought he was going to get away with it, he had another think coming. For the moment I had more important things to attend to, but he'd get his.

But first, the electricity. After dinner I announced my intentions.

197

'Gentlemen, tomorrow we're going to bring up the generator.'

There was a heavy silence as each man considered the effort that would be required.

I assigned seven of the more sturdy men whose feet were in good shape. 'Miguel, Chita, Chiche, White, Gobino, Omar, and Barbas – you'll go down tomorrow. Get to bed early, because we leave at three in the morning. It's not going to be easy, but it has to be done.'

That sentence had become a leitmotiv; whenever they heard it they knew they were going to sweat bullets. But the fact that I was going to be with them reassured them.

I went down on horseback, my men walking ahead of me. I left Jimmy in charge back at the camp. Nobody was supposed to work at the quebrada; everybody was to be kept busy on construction. Early the previous morning I had cleaned off the rock, and during the day we'd only worked the unproductive top layer – from which, barring an unusual stroke of luck, it was practically impossible to get any gold out. Even so, I'd instructed Jimmy to keep the men away from the river. Jimmy had become more and more efficient, and his initial failure was only a bad memory. I'd helped him gain self-confidence, and he'd established himself with the men, who respected him; his good nature made up for his lack of forcefulness.

When I got to Guerra, I examined the generator and we experimented with a few ways of transporting it. It was too heavy for one man to carry and, given the state of the route, it was impossible for several men to carry it. I tried different things, including a little cart borrowed from Mario, but it quickly got stuck in the mud. There was only one solution – a litter. I had the men cut two stout long poles and placed the generator between them. Four men up front and four in the rear carried the poles on their shoulders. My horse followed us, and to set an example I took my turn with the others. It was six o'clock when we began; five hours later we'd covered two and a half miles – and that was on flat ground. It was awful. Crushed by the weight of the generator, we sank deep into the mud that grabbed at our boots: tear your foot loose, take a step forward, tear the other foot loose, take another step forward. Every few feet someone lost a boot and crumpled into the mud, which meant that the others had to balance the generator until he got up, then start moving again until the next fall. Every hundred yards, our legs trembling with exhaustion, we had to stop and put the generator down. Omar, who because of his size did more carrying than the others, collapsed in exhaustion, and despite our efforts he remained sprawled in the mud, barely conscious, his arms outflung. I loaded the ends of the two poles on both my shoulders and we continued; it took two hours for him to catch up with us, stumbling. Finally we got to the bottom of the hill and, though we were at last out of the mire, I knew we could never crawl up the mountain.

'Chita, take my horse and ride up to the camp. Tell Jimmy to come here with all the men as fast as possible.'

'All?'

'Every one of them. Tell them to take flashlights and bring lots of coffee and tacos. Hurry!'

After an hour's rest I stood up.

'Gentlemen, it's not going to be easy . . .'

'. . . but it has to be done,' they chorused.

'One final effort. Let's start up the hill before the relief gets here.'

By the time Jimmy arrived with the rest of the men, nobody could stand up straight; we'd done a quarter of the climb more or less on all fours, with plenty of slides and falls. Dog-tired, we ate and had some coffee while the others replaced us. Everyone took a turn. Manolito went back and forth to the foot of the mountain and brought us canteens of water from a river down there.

We did the last stretch by flashlight, some of the men doing the carrying while others lit the ground beneath their feet; those in front warned those behind them of holes and roots. At a particularly steep slope, one of the carriers stumbled and fell, another followed suit, and with the balance gone all the others collapsed like dominoes and let the generator drop. Chita, courageous but not very smart, tried to keep it from falling and was crushed beneath its weight; he lay there with bulging eyes, gasping for breath.

We quickly got him out from under. By a great stroke of luck, he'd fallen into a deep rut, the edges of which had caught and held the generator so that he wasn't completely crushed; he escaped with just a cracked ribcage. He'd been badly scared, and he recovered slowly. We left him propped up against a tree and continued on our way. It was 10.30 before we got to the camp; it had taken sixteen and a half hours to bring up that fucking generator. Nobody had escaped without injury. Even I had a crushed fingernail – but we'd achieved the impossible, and I was convinced that from here on my men would think they could do just about anything. We downed our dinner quickly, and everyone turned in without saying a word.

As a special treat, I let them sleep an hour longer the next day; they'd earned it.

I formed two teams. One worked at the quebrada as usual, while the other got busy installing the electricity. I'd put Barbas in charge and made Eduardo, the ultimate handyman, responsible for the technical details. They were told to build a shed for the generator halfway between the house and the river.

Fifteen men were assigned to the installation. During the day they laid electric cable from the generator to the house, then to the quebrada, where fifty bulbs in four reflecting panels were waiting for the electric current. I stopped the crew on the canoa at five o'clock and everyone gathered round the generator, looking at it as if it was some invention of the devil: they had no confidence in the strange gadget that made electricity, and were reluctant to touch the wires and the bulbs – especially the people from Osa, who even hung back a bit.

Omar, a professional boatman, was the only one who had any sort of familiarity with that kind of thing.

'OK, start it up,' I told him.

In complete silence and with a very professional air, he grabbed the crank and turned with all his strength. One turn, then two, and it kicked back, hitting him right in the face. He fell, blood flowing from a split eyebrow. He didn't look too pretty.

I calmed the general hilarity with two words: 'Next man!'

The men were on the defensive, and rightly so; one by one they tried to start it up, but timidly because the fear of getting their heads split open had sapped their strength.

'OK,' I said after several useless attempts, 'we'll try it another way. Who's left-handed?'

Because of the direction in which the crank rotated, there should have been less risk. Nobody answered, but Eduardo, with a big smile, said: 'White! He's left-handed, but he doesn't want to admit it.'

It was true. White, usually right up front, was trying to hide behind the others; he was ashen with fear.

'Is that true, White?'.

'I guess so.'

'Well, then, show us what you can do.'

He turned the crank timidly, without conviction, several times.

'A double ration of grass for you if you start this fucker up.'

It was the only thing that could get him moving, and this time he put his heart and soul into it. Thirty seconds later the sound of the first generator ever installed on Osa was heard in the mountains, and the entire camp lit up: it was a bright beginning. Joy reigned triumphant, the men singing and yelling hurrahs. In town, electricity is something ordinary, something you don't pay much attention to; in the jungle, it's an unheard-of luxury, and we'd all sweated blood to make it happen.

There were several lamps in every room in the house, and the unusual brightness gave the place a new look, festive and comfortable. Barbaroja looked in amazement at the bulb we'd strung in his shack, then we all went down to the quebrada, where the spectacle was greeted with loud shouts; the muddy hole, lit to daylight brightness by four floodlights, made a fantastic sight – the only thing lacking to make it look like a Hollywood production was a half-nude starlet prancing around in the water.

'It's beautiful!' Chita said emotionally.

'It's going to be even more beautiful when fifteen men are working in that hole. OK, night crew, in you go!'

Instead of a starlet, my bearded crew was going to take the plunge. They seemed surprised by my order: carried away by the pleasure of installing electricity in the jungle, they had almost forgotten we were there on business.

After some hesitation, the night crew climbed into the icy water. But, excited by the new set-up, the daytime squad jumped in with them, and for an hour both groups worked together.

From now on there were always two teams, and the hours changed: the daytime crew worked from 6.30 to noon and from 1.30 to 4.30, when the night crew took over until dinner at six and then went back from seven to midnight. Every man had his time preference, and there was no trouble in setting up the two crews. The weather had improved; there was sunshine between showers – and fewer showers, at least at night – and the water wasn't quite as cold.

Everything was fine – but something bothered me. I didn't like seeing all those people doing nothing during the day. I was down at the quebrada for both shifts, and I learned that during my absence all hell broke loose up at the house. All that physical labour and good food had turned my men into athletes; the skinny little guys of the early days had disappeared, and they were now bursting with vitality. That overflow of energy had to be used, if only because boredom and inactivity are the worst vices – they leave too much time to think.

So, little by little, I began assigning the night-shift men to duties around the ranch. At the beginning, they only lent a hand, but after a week they were doing more – and soon they were working both day and night. Except for some cynical comments – expressed in a joking manner – they quickly accepted the situation, knowing that the more they worked the more I liked them and that the more I liked them the more presents I gave them. For example, I had previously deducted their cigarettes from their wages, but now I distributed them at no cost.

To prevent jealousy, the day team was given the same treatment: they worked around the camp from six o'clock to midnight.

201

Acting through the pulpero Mario, I bought twenty-four sacks of cement in Palmar and had them brought to Guerra. Every day, two sacks were brought up and put to immediate use: I'd decided to pave the floor of the house. Since the house was on ground with a slight slope, we first had to use some gravel from the quebrada as fill, and that's the task I set for the crew not working in the hole; day and night the men went back and forth with enormous sacks on their backs.

Not wanting to leave the river, I couldn't supervise the work at the camp, but I could judge each man's efficiency by how often he came and went. Except for a few who fell asleep at the dinner-table, the men tolerated this new schedule pretty well. As for myself, I never slept at night. I'd occasionally snooze off in my rocking chair, but I was often awakened by the feeling that the rhythm of the work had slowed down – in which case I'd fire off a round almost as a reflex. My target was an enormous tree-trunk balanced on the cliff, and every shot sent a shower of splinters down on the men; more than one of them jumped under the impression that he'd been hit.

The gold kept rolling in, morale was good, and the two teams were even competing. I'd become a little less rigid about work time: at every coffee- or meal-break, I stopped the canoa and inspected the results; if a big nugget showed up, I stopped work for the day.

There was gold everywhere. While cleaning up a small slide from the cliff in a spot we hadn't even worked, Jimmy found a 62-gram nugget, which convinced me more than ever that it was important to keep everyone away from the quebrada when I wasn't there. My dawn dives were still fruitful, and one morning was exceptional: I found a 420-gram nugget around which, wide and flat like a saucer, were a multitude of shiny points – 200 grams in nuggets of from five to ten grams each.

As a souvenir of those expeditions, I attached five nuggets to a chain that I wore around my left wrist; and around my neck I wore a beautiful fifty-gram nugget shaped like South America.

I felt great. I hadn't had any worries about the richness of the strike for a long time, and Barbaroja, who showed up regularly when the canoa was taken out, couldn't get over it; he and Nizaro kept talking about Beta Madre, the legendary lode of gold. Nizaro himself, though, was becoming a pain in the arse, nagging me about how he'd been the first to know about the spot, about how I was only there thanks to him, and so on. One evening I heard him complaining to Jimmy: 'I sowed the gold, Don Juan Carlos is harvesting it.'

That was too much! The next day he was in the hole with a pan in his hand, and from then on he spent his time doing catiadoras where the shovel hadn't been able to clean up. Since he got about ten grams a day – about six times his salary – he stopped complaining, but he was a thief, and I was on my guard: Nicolas, sitting on the boulder about a yard away, never took his eyes off him. The constant surveillance and the new work assignment finally made him realize that he was no longer in my good graces; he regularly complained to me, and I just as regularly sent him back to work. At first I'd intended to assign him to an easy job, but his daily boasting – to say nothing of his inefficiency – had changed my mind. He was useless; I'd thought that his thirty-five years of experience in the mountains would come in handy, but I now realized I knew more than he did, and at that point, as far as I was concerned, he could drop dead.

Barbaroja invited me to eat some chicken at his place, and I knew exactly what he wanted to talk to me about. The sight of so much gold had convinced him that he should have made a better deal with me, and he was undoubtedly working up his courage to make new demands. I could have given him a little more, but then there'd have been no reason for him not to keep on asking for still more – and, besides, what I paid him every month was already a lot by local standards, and he ate and drank free of charge every day. I would have been ready to help him set up a pulperia, but I wasn't prepared to give him a colon more than what we'd initially agreed on. I had to make him understand this – gently.

As I'd expected, after five minutes of chitchat he began to unload all his complaints and demands. Christ, what an arsehole! Well, too bad for him: I had a log in my hand, and I gave him a big whack on the back of the neck, making him fall to his knees. The second blow KO'd him; the impact made a funny noise, and he stopped moving. Shit, suppose he's croaked, I thought. I didn't want to touch him, so the only thing I could do to bring him around was piss on him – but he still didn't move. So I grabbed the pot in which the chicken soup was simmering and tossed it at his head. The boiling water did the trick, and his scalded cries reassured me. Taking his carbine, I splintered the butt against the central pillar, then picked up a mallet, smashed the mechanism, and broke the trigger and the hammer. When I left the house he was wiggling around on the ground; I felt sorry that I had wasted the soup – it smelt good.

Back in the house, I took my usual seat in front of the men, who were eating together.

'Chita, you get along well with Barbaroja, so I want you to go to his shack. Tell the son of a bitch that I never want to see him again either here or at the quebrada. On second thoughts, better tell him I never want to see him again, period. While you're there bring back his light and the electric wire.'

Then I turned to the others.

'From now on, Barbaroja is no longer our friend. He's not to come here, and nobody's to go over there. Is that clear? If you see his pigs near the house, chase them off – they make the place filthy.'

In the morning, while everyone was having breakfast, I noticed that Barbaroja's horse wasn't there and decided that he must have gone for the cops. I was wondering just how to punish him when one of his pigs stuck its head through the kitchen door. To everyone's surprise. I jumped up and shot a bullet into its groin. Marcella burst out laughing, but the two big fatties were horrified because on Osa animals are allowed to roam free and everybody respects his neighbour's property.

'Clean it,' I told them. 'It's a present from Barbaroja.'

'But we don't know what to do!'

'Then, this is a good time to learn. White, Chiche, Cunado – get the rest of the planks at Barbaroja's. They're ours now.'

The pig was nice and fat, so we had a feast that evening. There was plenty of meat, and the men liked my way of shopping for it. They were also happy because the next day and the day after – Saturday and Sunday – I was going to give them their first weekend off: I had a little fever and I could feel an attack of malaria coming on.

We were in the middle of dinner when Tonio, one of Nizaro's sons, appeared and immediately came over to me.

'Good evening, Don Juan Carlos.'

'Hi, Tonio. What's up?'

'Some people have come to Guerra by boat – Herman Weinberg, Orlando Caracas and Pablo Garcia. They want you to send some men with horses this evening so that they can come up tomorrow morning. They also want a few men to load the equipment and supplies. And they want everything now.'

'Hold it. What do they think they're doing? You can go back if you want, but you go alone. Tell those idiots I'll send everything down tomorrow, but right now we're resting. You might also tell them that we have work to do up here!'

The next day I didn't feel too well; every muscle hurt. I sent five men on ahead with two horses, and Nicolas and I left on the other two a few hours later. We met the men, and our visitors, about halfway along the trail. With all the stuff they brought, they looked as if they were going on a suburban picnic: Omar was even balancing a television on his head. Herman and Orlando were on horseback, and

Orlando had a case of dynamite on his saddle. The third man, a chubby type they introduced as the accountant, was slogging painfully through the mud and kept mopping his brow with a big handkerchief.

The sight of those three city slickers, red and sweating, contrasted sharply with that of my men, who were striding along effortlessly. Dead tired before beginning the climb, our visitors stopped at the river.

All three of them wore denim shorts and boots, and Herman — who'd stuck a revolver in his belt — was even sporting a pair of dark glasses. The accountant, Pablo Garcia, stopped every ten yards and quickly fell behind; Orlando Caracas soon joined him, because he rode very badly and during a difficult stretch slipped slowly from his horse, clinging to the case of dynamite. Struggling to get upright, he called for help; but, knowing what was in the case, instead of coming to his aid the others dropped everything and scattered to take cover behind a tree. There was no danger, because that's not the way dynamite goes off, but they weren't taking any chances. Orlando looked surprised, then collapsed into the mud with a noisy splat. He was offended; he, the nephew of the president, had never before been treated this way, and he raged against the workers, who just kept laughing. Vexed, he attached the case to his horse and, leading it by the reins, continued on foot.

I left a man behind to show them the way, and we went on. Herman asked me a whole bunch of questions to which I scarcely replied because I wasn't in the mood to talk. A better horseman than the others, he managed to keep up with us; but the terrain was treacherous, and while he was proudly prancing along the horse stumbled and dragged him down as it fell. He tumbled some thirty feet as we watched indifferently, and when he picked himself up his dark glasses were gone and he was covered with mud. Smiling grimly, he got back on his horse as the men looked on with amusement. After a few tumbles, he lost his smug manner and proceeded cautiously.

I took advantage of that to speed up and escape his questions. Nicolas, who was riding alongside me, was having a great time, and we were joking as we rode into camp long before the others.

Out of habit, I went to see what was going on at the quebrada. When I got back to the house, everyone had arrived, and they were all making a lot of noise. Orlando was using my chair, and I asked him to get up so I could sit there. He didn't much like that, but there was little he could do about it.

Herman, all smiles, launched a popularity campaign. He plugged in the television and began fiddling with it, making a lot of fuss and noise but getting nowhere. The men looked on with great interest since many had never seen a television and the novelty excited them, but at the end of an hour Herman was still getting nothing but splutters and the men began scowling, obviously annoyed that their hopes had been raised for nothing. I could sense they were ready to smash the thing over his head. Eventually, they lost interest and began asking for music.

'It needs an antenna,' said Herman. 'You and you,' he said, pointing, 'attach this to the roof.'

Nobody budged, and the men looked amused by the chubby little guy shouting orders. He began to get angry, and I came to his assistance.

'Chiche, Cunado, put this thing up for the gentleman.'

Herman came to sit next to me.

'This is unbelievable,' he said. 'They know I'm your partner, and they ought to obey me. I wonder how you manage with them.'

'Look, you're in the mountains here, not in your office. These men don't work for wages but because they like the atmosphere. Respect and authority can't be taken for granted – they have to be earned. If you go on talking to them like that, watch it. You could be in for some nasty surprises.'

He backed off and changed the subject.

'What about the gold? Is there a lot?'

'An enormous amount.'

'Are you going to show me?'

'In a while. There's no hurry. How long are you staying?'

'Two days.'

'More than enough time.'

'Tell me when you begin working so we can be on hand to watch.'

'Nobody's working today. I promised them two days off. Maybe we'll do an hour or two tomorrow just to show you.'

Disappointed, he insisted: 'One day off ought to be enough. I have a feeling you spoil them: meat at every meal, a bed and a mattress for each man. . . . You know, they're only animals; they're not used to so much comfort.'

The oncoming attack of malaria was tiring me, and I didn't feel like discussing or explaining my behaviour. But the men had overheard his comments and had begun to look at the newcomers with hostility. They didn't really fit into the décor; my boys worked hard, but they were used to a certain family atmosphere, to kidding around together like buddies, and they were irritated by the snooty way the city people spoke to them. Even physically they were an eyesore: three chubby guys in shorts that exposed unhealthy white skin were

206

revolting to look at. Except for Nizaro, who kept bowing and scraping, the men began to ignore them.

'What a pity we have to put up with these slugs,' I said to Nicolas. 'To think that people like this run the country!'

'I certainly thought the president's nephew would have a little more style! Did you notice how the men disliked them from the very beginning?'

'What do you expect? They show up here like they've conquered the place, but, as far as the men are concerned, Weinberg and Caracas are less than nothing. All they see are two ridiculous city men they'd love to boot in the arse just for the fun of it.'

Just then Herman brought over the third jerk, to whom I'd not yet said a word.

'Juan Carlos, I've brought Pablo Garcia along to take care of the accounting.'

'What accounting? What are you talking about?'

'The papers for Malessa and also those for the men. We're going to do a count. Tell them to line up with their identity papers.'

'You're making a big mistake. Nobody's going to do that. Half my men have records and are running away from something – alimony or the cops. Nobody's really clean, and they won't want their names on legal documents.'

'But we have to do this according to regulations. Suppose one of them has an accident.'

'I think they'd rather run that risk than the risk of prison. Anyway, we'll look into it tomorrow. Right now it's time to eat.'

'Are you going to set up a separate table?'

'Hell, no! This is one big family, and we don't believe in segregation.'

When dinner was over, Herman broke out two bottles of whisky. 'This is to celebrate the mine. I brought it along for us.'

'Great idea. Hey, boys – bring your glasses. Herman's brought us a present.'

While they pressed around me, delighted with the windfall, I could see from Herman's face that it really hurt him to share good whisky with the workers.

Looking unhappy, Chiche came over to talk to me. 'Herman says we're going to work tomorrow. Is that true?'

'Absolutely not. I promised you two days off, and you'll get them. We'll just do a one-hour run-through to show them.'

The evening went on, and the men, looking forward to another day of rest, were relaxed and unruly. The two bottles were quickly emptied, and I got out the bootleg guaro, filling all the glasses to the brim as Herman watched in fascination and sniffed his glass.

'To the mine! Health!'

I emptied my glass with a gulp and all my men imitated me: their throats had already been scorched by the 90 per cent alcohol, so they could take it. Orlando, a heavy drinker, was nevertheless surprised; turning turkey-red, he almost suffocated as the men looked on and smirked. Herman prudently took only a small swallow.

I refilled the glasses, and we went through the same routine again. After half an hour Orlando, done in by fatigue and alcohol, was completely out of it; he sank under the bench as the men hooted, and losing all sense of dignity he broke into maudlin drunken sobs and incoherent babbling. He was laughable.

Jimmy and Herman dragged him off to bed. Nizaro and Jimmy had given their beds to Herman and Orlando, and Pablo didn't know what to do: two of the men reluctantly teamed up so he could have a bed.

Before turning in, Chita came to see me.

'Juan Carlos, I'm going to leave.'

'Why?'

'I can't stand those two big shots. They just talk nonsense, and they treat me like dirt.'

'You're not going to let these jerks get the better of you, are you? We'll talk about it tomorrow.'

My malaria was still acting up and, though it wasn't a very bad attack, every bone hurt. Marcella came to give me a massage. She had arms like a wrestler and, though I'm pretty solid, her delicate treatment really knocked me out.

The house was quiet, and I was just about to drop off when I heard the sound of some heavy snoring. Without moving from where I was, I shouted: 'Who the fuck's making that racket?'

'It's Pablo,' Chiche replied.

'Wake him up and make him stop it.'

Ten minutes later the snoring began again, even louder.

'Chiche, put a gag on that arsehole or there's going to be trouble.'

I could hear the sound of a sharp slap followed by an exclamation from Pablo and bursts of laughter. Ten minutes later it began again. This time I'd had it.

'Chiche, White, Cunado, Miguel, Raphael, and everybody else who's not asleep – grab that bastard and throw him outside.'

There was a lot of scurrying and cursing, and I had the feeling they must have pushed him out of an upper bunk: he was screaming bloody murder as they roughed him up.

'Keep it down, dammit, or go play somewhere else!'

The noise – a symphony of screams and laughter – continued

208

outside, and I looked out the window. Leaning on the sill, I watched a spectacle of rare beauty: they'd all piled out and were giving the unfortunate accountant a lesson he'd never forget. Four of them had him by the arms and the hair, while the others worked over his face. At first, in their hurry to get the job done, they were doing it helter-skelter, but they soon organized themselves and went at him methodically, lining up in a single file, politely waiting their turn, punching him a couple of times in the head, then going back to the end of the line. Pablo's eyes closed, his nose split, and I could see the men were going at it hot and heavy; Pablo soon stopped screaming. I guess they really didn't like his attitude and were happy to show him as much!

Meanwhile Herman had come out and was trying to stop them by screaming at them, but he was afraid to get too close, and when he saw me at the window he called: 'Juan Carlos, do something or they'll kill him!'

'I warned you they could be rough. They don't get much sleep, and Pablo was disturbing them. There isn't much I can do about it.'

But I was beginning to think they might really finish him off, so I intervened.

'OK, boys, that's enough. Toss him into Barbaroja's place and go back to bed.'

Taking him by the legs and arms, they rushed off to Barbaroja's, barely took time to open the door, and with one heave threw him unceremoniously inside. The show was over, and I could go back to bed.

It was a little rough, but he had no right to snore that loud. Pablo didn't show up at breakfast, and Marcella came to tell me that he'd locked himself in Barbaroja's shack and refused to come out.

'His head's all blue and he's lost two teeth,' she told me with a laugh.

Still, I hadn't forgotten why my associates had come, and that morning I took everyone down to the quebrada.

As I left the house, I found a pile of shit a few yards from the door. What disgusting slob had come to shit there? It couldn't have been one of the workers, because they'd been taught to respect their environment. Orlando had been too loaded and had crapped in his pants, and it seemed unlikely that it had been Pablo; I decided that that pig Herman had been afraid of snakes and had lacked the courage to go as far as the latrines. . . .

At the quebrada the men quickly took up their positions, I sat in the rocking chair, and the two big shots settled on a tree-trunk. At the end of three hours I stopped work; I'd promised the men two days of rest and I intended to keep my word. And, besides, I couldn't bear the sight of those two loafers sitting there and doing nothing. Though my men were kept hopping, they all had their personal dignity; the fact that I was sitting there overseeing them was something natural and normal, but those two pigs had done nothing to earn that right, and it was humiliating to have my men working as they watched.

I sent the men back to the house and took out the canoa. The demonstration was positive: there were about ten grams on the carpeting, and Herman and Orlando couldn't believe their eyes; it was the first time they'd ever seen raw gold, and in a state of intense excitement they examined the nuggets and exchanged knowing looks.

I explained the richness of the site and its possibilities. It was hard for them to realize that they were standing on a gigantic lode and that there were millions of tons of gold-bearing material that would have to be processed, but little by little they became aware of what I had done for them and went mad with joy, their eyes burning with gold fever.

When they got back to the ranch they'd regained much of their lost assurance.

'I've heard you've had problems with Barbaroja,' Herman said. 'If you like, we can get rid of him for you. All we have to do is bring false charges against him. I can take care of that, and he'll get twenty to thirty years in the slammer – nothing could be easier.'

Or sleazier.

'No, I hate those cowardly methods. I fight honestly, and I won't use that kind of treachery. I prefer to settle my own scores.'

He sensed my contempt and tried to retrieve the situation by changing the topic.

'Look,' he said as he dug through his stuff, 'I've prepared some papers that can help you. The best thing would be for us to collaborate closely. A mine like this has to be administered in an organized manner, and for that I can be a lot of use to you.'

He gave me a wad of documents printed on Malessa-letterhead stationery: schedules, work rules, and a lot of other crap bearing his signature. Where did this idiot think he was? This wasn't his office in San José, he couldn't really think I was going to post such nonsense on the wall? And just what did he think the signature 'Herman Weinberg' meant here? I tossed the stack on the table.

'Gentlemen, Herman's brought us some toilet paper with fancy designs on it.'

I motioned him to follow me and we went to my room.

'Just take a look at what I've done in my own unorganized way and without the benefit of your help.'

I emptied the strongbox on the bed.

Dumbfounded by what he saw, he kept picking up the nuggets one by one, saying: 'It can't be true, it can't be true.'

Then, shaking off the stupor into which he'd been plunged for several marvellous minutes, he asked me excitedly: 'How much is there?'

'About seven thousand grams, my fat friend. One month's work.'

He clammed up and kept looking at the wealth spread out on the bed. I didn't think he had any more doubts about my efficiency.

'Well, I've fulfilled my part of the contract. I've found the gold and got it out of the ground. Now it's your turn. Where are the papers and the concession?'

'Don't worry about that. We're working on it, but it takes time.'

'Stop fucking around! Spend whatever you have to, but make sure this doesn't slip through our fingers. Who's in charge of granting concessions? There's enough here to buy him. Toss him ten or twenty thousand bucks if necessary, but don't waste time. And, by the way, where's my residence permit? Have you taken care of that passport business for me?'

'We're working on it. There are some legal channels that just can't be avoided. To smooth the way, we're going to make you president of a banana company we own in Panama.'

'And my gun permit?'

'We're looking into it, but —'

'In other words, you haven't done a fucking thing!'

'Look, Juan Carlos, don't take it that way! In any country in the world, even here, it's hard to legalize a weapon with a filed-off number. After all, there are rules and regulations!'

He was getting on my nerves, but I had no choice but to go along with him for now.

'OK. I'm counting on you for the machines. Working this by hand will soon be impossible – the rock is farther and farther down, and we'd lose too much time clearing away the soil. In addition, I can't keep my men going at this rate for more than three months – they'd crack on me. I need the work permit and the machines as fast as possible.'

'I've already thought of that and I'm preparing a surprise for you. My best mechanic is putting together a machine that combines suction and hydraulics. It's a secret prototype that we're going to try here and commercialize later.'

I wasn't all that hot for that kind of thing. There were already

211

excellent suction pumps on the market, and I didn't see why I should play the guinea-pig. But, still, he seemed so sure of his mechanic – the best in Costa Rica, he said – so I was willing to try it.

We agreed that he'd send me a caterpillar tractor with a front shovel capable of clearing away the non-auriferous dirt and gravel.

We weighed the gold. There were 7853 grams in nuggets. I turned it over to him, keeping only a little gold dust for mining expenses.

'Put it somewhere safe, and we'll share it out after we've deducted expenses when I get back in December.'

As I handed him the gold, I noticed a worried expression on his face, the expression of someone asking himself some questions. I was sure the son of a bitch was wondering if I hadn't held out on him, and that really got my goat.

'Now, listen carefully. You haven't done much to earn this manna from heaven, but I've given you everything without a receipt. I'm warning you right now, don't try to cheat me.'

'You needn't worry,' he said with a big smile. 'We need you too much. Only you could have got such results. You've really done a fantastic job.'

And he was off on a string of arse-kissing compliments. They're somehow always pleasant to hear, but coming from a hypocrite like him they sounded hollow to my ears.

They left the next morning. Pablo reappeared and went off on foot. Herman, to whom I'd lent my horse, put on a Lone Ranger show, standing in the stirrups and making sweeping gestures of farewell. I'd given him another warning before he left and, though I was glad to see the back of him, something made me uneasy.

Herman had seemed surprisingly well informed about life at the camp – about the Barbaroja episode, the Sierpe brawl, and a lot of other things that were none of his business. It wasn't all that important, but still it bothered me.

I called Jimmy.

'Did Herman ask you a lot of questions?'

'No, he hardly said a word to me.'

I told him what was eating me.

'I swear I never said a word about any of that. I know when to keep my mouth shut, and I don't sell out my friends.'

I believed him. I decided someone else in the crew must be running off at the mouth. . . .

I had to get my men cracking again. Those two days of semi-vacation and the presence of those idiots had played hell with production.

When the day shift was ready to leave, Chita came to see me.

'Don Juan Carlos, I've made up my mind. I'm leaving.'

'You're sure?'

'Yes. I can't stand Nizaro's daughters, and I don't feel appreciated around here.'

I tried to talk him round, because until then I'd found him satisfactory and I liked him well enough, but nobody is indispensable. Because he'd behaved so well, I paid him off despite my previous warning to the contrary.

'Where are you going?'

'To work with Barbaroja. I know gold better now, and I've decided to throw in with him because he's had experience.'

'Remember, if you join up with him, the same bans apply to you from now on: you're never again to set foot either here or at the quebrada. Understand?'

'I understand.'

And he left.

Two days went by, and I forgot about him. It was the evening rest hour and, having sent the men off to eat, I was down at the quebrada taking out the canoa. Only Jimmy, White, Chiche and Nizaro were with me. I was overseeing the operation when I saw Chita coming towards us. He was carrying a machete, and as usual he was naked to the waist.

'I want to talk to you, Don Juan Carlos.'

'You've got no business here, you son of a bitch! Beat it!'

'As the guardian of Barbaroja's house, I've the right —'

'You've the right to beat it before it's too late!'

'You can't frighten me,' he said, raising his machete.

That was going too far. Unholstering my gun as I jumped the low wall, I aimed at his leg and fired. The ball ripped his trousers at the knee, and his face showed first amazement and then fear when he realized I'd fired at him. Panic-stricken, he dropped everything and ran, stumbling, falling, then scrambling to his feet in sheer terror. Expecting a second bullet to cut him down, he flew across the four hundred yards separating him from the forest, and by the time his wild race was over and he disappeared behind the trees he must have broken a few speed records.

For the next five minutes nobody said a word, and the work went on in silence. Then the others relaxed and began to crack jokes. An hour later, when we got back to the house, we were greeted with smiles. The men had seen Chita proudly enter the forest despite Marcella's warnings, and then they'd heard the shot and seen him come racing out of

213

the forest like a madman. They almost died laughing just describing it. He was evidently covered with blood caused by the numerous spills he'd taken during his hasty retreat.

After we'd eaten, I noticed that the men were a bit tense, and little by little I got the explanation. Chita had been threatening to poison the water and set fire to the ranch; and the men, who'd seen him prepare a torch, were frightened because the house was built of wood and leaves and it would go up in a minute. They also knew that there was a case of dynamite under my bed, and some of them refused to go to sleep. As I saw it, those were only the threats and boasts of a guy who didn't want to lose face but, though I doubted he would do anything about them, I had to calm the men down.

As I walked towards Barbaroja's shack, a box of bullets in my hand, they stood in the doorway and watched me. I took one shot at the roof, then invited Chita outside for a talk. Since there was no answer, I warned him to give up his ideas of revenge. To add more weight to my words, I settled down directly opposite the doorway and riddled the house with bullets. I began with the door, which disintegrated under the impact, and went on with the walls in a thunder of explosions. Each bullet from my Magnum tore away a piece of plank. When I stopped, the box of fifty cartridges was empty and the front of the house sagged sadly. I hoped poor Chita had had a chance to take cover. When silence returned, I told the men they could go to bed.

The next day, Chita had disappeared. He couldn't be found, and I decided panic had made him run. When Manolito came running to warn me that Barbaroja had shown up with a cop, I decided it was showdown time. A few minutes later, there they were. Seated in my rocking chair, I watched them approach. Barbaroja looked sure of himself, and with a sweep of his arm he showed the cop the quebrada. I didn't know the guy, but he was a young fellow of about twenty-five who was hiding behind the prestige of his uniform.

'Julio Cortés, of the Sierpe division,' he said, giving me a military salute. 'Are you Don Juan Carlos?'

'What the fuck are you doing here? Didn't they tell you this is private property?'

My response threw him off balance. Clearing his throat, he tried to regain the upper hand.

'I've come on a complaint from Señor Gerardo. There are some illegal things going on here. I've seen the condition of his house. Until the courts can decide, I'm going to have to stop work here.'

I got up and went over to him. I was a head taller than he was.

'You're going to do what, cocksucker?'

214

The men had stopped working and they surrounded him, laughing. Suddenly he looked a little lonely. He was learning that enforcing the law in the jungle is somewhat different from doing the same thing in the city: in the jungle the uniform isn't enough to ensure authority.

He began to stammer. 'Well, I was just saying that . . . that maybe we can reconsider the question and talk it over quietly.'

He shot an angry glance at Barbaroja, the one who had led him into this hornets' nest.

'Maybe we'd better, because if you keep running off at the mouth I'm going to put you in the water.'

Delighted with the way things were going, the men began to chant 'In the water, in the water'.

The poor cop realized that he'd completely lost control of the situation and tried to save his skin.

'My apologies. I didn't know. I was only doing what I was told to do. Maybe I was given the wrong information. He's the one who brought me here.'

He pointed to Barbaroja, who had seen how things were going and was discreetly trying to sneak away.

'Catch him and bring him to me,' I said to the men.

Before he could make a move, ten pairs of arms had grabbed him and dragged him trembling before me. I made him turn round and gave him a mighty kick in the arse; then, carried away by my example, the men did the same, booting him to their hearts' content. He struggled, left the torn remnants of his shirt in their hands, and escaped. The men turned towards the cop, who was beginning to feel he was in for trouble.

'You were right,' he said. 'He deserved a good beating. He's a liar, and I'll say as much in my report. Well, I think I'd better be getting on. I've a long way to go.'

'Not at all, you've got plenty of time. Stay with us a while. Relax,' I said, grabbing his shoulder and forcing him to sit down.

The guys began to act up, and his cap went flying into the water. They were almost all two-time losers, and they hated uniforms. And because Costa Rican cops get no training and are constantly changing around – one day they're cops, and a few months later they're masons or something else – he had no experience in how to handle such a situation. A few friendly whacks on the back of his head had made him completely lose his composure.

'Don Juan Carlos,' Cunado, the horniest one of the gang, said to me, 'White and me think he's got a pretty face and we'd like to slip it to him a little. All right?'

It was an amusing idea. The cop turned green as Cunado ran a hand through his hair. I hesitated a little before replying, to leave him in doubt for a few moments.

'No, that wouldn't be right – we shouldn't get too intimate with the law. Let him go. He's got a long trip ahead of him.'

The joke had gone on long enough, and I didn't want things to go too far – the cop might have remembered he was armed.

He shook my hand, apologized, thanked me, and after another handshake quickly walked away, his sweat-soaked hat on his head, happy to get off so easily.

When we returned at noon, the men wanted to celebrate.

'A pig, a pig,' they demanded.

They ran after Barbaroja's herd and brought back two by dragging them along on a rope tied to their feet. Acceding to the general demand, I shot one – then, after a second's reflection, the other. After all, it was Barbaroja's treat.

In the evening we had a ball. The two pigs, cut into chunks were spread out all over the table. Thanks, Barbaroja.

And then Nizaro cracked up. For several days he'd been panning without interruption under Nicolas' inquisitorial eye. The day before, he'd found an 82-gram nugget – which had scarcely appeared in the catiadora before Nicolas grabbed it and brought it to me, showing a lack of trust that must have hurt Nizaro. The following morning, when everyone was getting ready to leave, he hesitated a while, then asked to speak to me in private.

Once we were alone he burst into tears.

'You've no confidence in me, Don Juan Carlos, I feel it in my bones. Why? There's nothing I wouldn't do for you.'

The old man crying unrestrainedly on my shoulder irritated rather than touched me. I found his tears revolting.

'Don't worry, it's not you. I don't have confidence in anyone, and no less in you than in anyone else. Get back to work – we've lost enough time.'

Ten minutes later he was at the catiadora, his back obviously bothering him, and I decided he'd soon leave on his own. The poor bastard – on top of everything else, he was probably worried about the health of his daughters. . . .

I have to admit that the Nizaro family no longer had a place in my heart: they'd too often mistaken generosity for weakness. In their trips to and from Guerra, the men would stop to eat with Nizaro's wife, and the fat lady's total bill was a little excessive. Thanks to me the Nizaros were in the process of building a new house, but instead of being grateful they kept getting on my nerves.

216

I could no longer stand the two daughters, who'd become so fat that they'd gone from being indecent to being obscene. Their obesity bothered me – it was like a disease – so with the help of White and by means of a purgative Jimmy had brought back from Palmar I decided to administer treatment. The stuff was meant for animals, and the doses I gave them for several days running would have been enough for an elephant. The first few times White mixed it with their food the results caused an upheaval – it looked as though Chita's predictions about the latrine were going to come true. In a few days the girls turned green.

Worried by their unhealthy looks, every morning I made them a medicinal tea – the composition of which you can imagine – and quietly kept mixing the purgative with their food. They spent their day in the latrines; every ten minutes one or both of them, propelled by a torrent of shit that wanted out, ran towards the crappers. They were running only in a manner of speaking, because with those big arses of theirs all they could do was comically waddle, buttocks clenched, as quickly as possible. As time went by, they became thinner and ran faster. The men complained that the crappers were always occupied by the two shitbags dumping their loads; they commented laughingly on the cows' sudden departures for the latrines and on the little symphony of noises they emitted. The sight of one of those fatties lurching to her goal became a permanent part of the landscape.

Their cheeks hollow, their complexions waxy, they moved in a constant odour of shit, a perfume that seemed to suit their physiques. Marcella, who shared the same room, justifiably complained, and to tell the truth it was pretty disgusting. Just as I was about to accede to everyone's entreaties and send them away, they announced their departure – as soon as they could get up the courage to leave the crappers. And after a last bowl of my brew they did leave, buttocks tight, under a hail of laughter. Max unhappily accompanied them, returning late because they'd been obliged to stop so often on the way. But the trail down was now permanently marked out, he explained: all you had to do was follow the stink.

The unappetizing episode of the Nizaro girls, plus my prohibition against having anything to do with women within the confines of the camp, drove up the popularity of La Puta; little by little I learned about the camp's only love-story.

Our four horses were called Pingón ('Big Cock'), Huevon ('Big Ball'), Cabrón ('Dirty Bastard') and La Puta ('Whore'). The last, the only mare of the group, was the nag Demesio had sold me. She had a long mane, big black eyes, and really looked like an old whore. Barbas, who was responsible for taking care of the animals, was a former Guana-

217

caste cop who was wanted for the sexual abuse of minors; in addition to being an incessant farter, he was a sex maniac. Though I'd noticed that the others kidded him by calling La Puta his fiancée, I'd never really paid much attention.

Marcella let the cat out of the bag. Ever since La Puta had come to camp, Barbas had been fucking her regularly. I'd been right to turn the horses over to him – he really did love them.

Cunado, who'd originally emptied slops in a brothel, soon joined the list of lovers – probably to the great joy of La Puta, because he'd been endowed by nature with an impressive tool: as a matter of fact, the others nicknamed him Three Legs.

Eventually, about ten of the men were disputing the favours of the mare, who seemed to take it all in her stride; given her age, it was an unhoped-for opportunity. The men had even organized things and built a special stool so they could be at the right height; White, a former pimp, tried to set up a partnership with Barbas so those moments of relaxation would be paid for, but he gave up the notion when the men threatened to substitute him for the mare.

The idea of those little Ticos standing on a stool and jiggling away amused me, so I made no effort to interfere. The risks of lovers' quarrels were minimal, and as long as they kept their hands off my horse it was OK with me.

Anyhow, La Puta didn't seem to mind. As I saw it, she purposely turned them on. In the evening I could see the men openly head for the meadow, a big smile on their lips, the stool in one hand and a lasso in the other. They spoke about it openly; and, if Barbas was proud of having had her first, Cunado could boast that he was the only one who made her whinny.

I continued my early-morning collections, and the mine kept making me presents: on the forty-second day I found a 3500-gram nugget, a chunk of gold as big as my hand. I had no idea how far those surprises might go, but I was sure I had the richest mine in Costa Rica.

The biggest nugget every found in Osa weighed five thousand grams, so I still hadn't beaten the record; but I knew that somewhere, hidden under my feet, there were even bigger ones and that it was only a matter of time before I found them.

Driven not only by desire to improve productivity but also by a desire to know the potential of the mine and the size the nuggets might reach, I was impatiently awaiting the machines.

Jimmy and four men had gone to Palmar to get the skidder – a sort of caterpillar tractor with a front-mounted shovel – that had been delivered on a truck by the mechanic. From Palmar they were supposed to take the new government route through the forest from Piedras Blancas to Rincón. At that time it was only a twenty-mile stretch of mud somewhat wider than the others; with its caterpillar treads, the tractor – originally built to transport wood in the forest – should be able to make it. Afterwards, from Rincón to Vanegas, the road was easy because it was flat and clear. The real difficulties would begin when they got to the stretch between Vanegas and Rancho Quemado, where the road was little more than a path snaking between the crests, and no motorized vehicles had ever passed that way. The tractor would have to make its own road. The men had gone off with shovels and miner's bars, and the mechanic was supposed to bring some chainsaws.

It was night when Jimmy arrived, drawn and mud-splattered.

'Well, Jimmy, where's the tractor?'

'It got stuck crossing the river in front of Demesio's, about three miles away. We've been trying since morning to get it out, but it's sunk up to the motor and can't go either backwards or forwards.'

'OK, get some rest and we'll all see to it tomorrow. Did you leave anyone to keep an eye on things?'

'Yes, all the others are there, but they'd like to be relieved. We didn't get much sleep the last few nights.'

'Right. Eduardo, Raphael and Ramon – take your blankets and go sleep on the tractor. Send the others back to me. Take this along to help you stand the cold,' I said, handing them a bottle of guaro.

While they were on their way, Jimmy told me about the trip.

'It was easy at first, and we took only a day to get as far as Vanegas. But after that it was rough going. It took three days to get from Vanegas to here, without eating and hardly sleeping. Between the trees that had to be cut down and cleared away and the ditches that had to be filled in, it was insane. To say nothing of the fact that the skidder isn't powerful enough to go up some hills, so we sometimes had to detour! Still, we managed – then this happened, and we really got stuck.'

The next morning all the men were assembled and I distributed the tools.

'Jimmy, saddle three horses and attach La Puta behind yours. You can change her at Demesio's on the way.'

I'd already sent Demesio word to remind him that he was obliged to give us a new horse, but he'd turned a deaf ear. When the men heard what I said, they gathered together, and then Barbas, Cunado and Max came to speak to me.

'Don Juan Carlos, are you really set on exchanging La Puta?'

'Yes. She's too old to carry anything.'

'But we like her and, if you'll keep her, we promise to carry more stuff ourselves when we come from Guerra.'

Ah, the power of love!

'OK,' I said with a laugh, 'we'll ask Demesio to give us an additional horse, or to exchange this one for another mare.'

My romantic nature made me loath to interfere with such a love-story.

An hour later we got to the skidder, which made for an impressive spectacle. They'd chosen the worst possible place to cross, and the tractor had almost completely disappeared in the mud. It was an imposing Russian-made monster, meant to transport wood in the snow. I wondered how it had ended up here. It looked like an assault-tank without a turret: two enormous treads on which were set a platform and a winch; at one end a cabin; and at the front a large shovel to open the route. The platform was loaded with merchandise – sacks of cement to finish the house, two drums of gasoline, and a lot of other things; in the middle was a strange collection of iron, pistons, belts, and soldered pipes – all of it painted yellow. Was Herman sending us a work of modern sculpture to decorate the ranch?

'What the hell is this gadget?' I couldn't help asking the mechanic.

'It's the machine,' he replied, swelling with pride.

I took a look from closer up: except for the two wheels on each side, nothing was familiar. It looked like a cross between a combine harvester and the latest-style can-opener.

'And this *works*?'

The mechanic was offended by my scepticism.

'I'm the one who invented and constructed it.'

So this was the famous mechanic, the best in all Costa Rica! I could only hope he was a better inventor than driver. . . . For the moment, however, the problem was to set the tractor free. Some of the men unloaded the platform, while others cut branches and tree-trunks to place behind the treads; then they planted some piles deep in the ground and attached chains to them.

When everything was ready, the mechanic got on and started it up. With the help of the chains and the branches, after several tries the skidder moved a yard; then we had to stop and change the position of the chains, reposition the tree-trunks, and begin all over again. The contraption was ten times too heavy: the trunks disintegrated into splinters under the treads.

Five hours later the tractor had been worked free. I sent some men to the ranch for coffee, and we were having a break when I noticed that a son of Demesio, our dishonest horse-trader, had come to watch the operation.

I called him over.

'Tell your father to come see me. We've got some problems to settle.'

'He's not there,' said the boy, grinning. 'He left two days ago to go to Jiménez, and he won't be back for a week.'

'That's not true,' said Cunado. 'I saw him this morning while I was bringing the coffee. He hid behind his house and watched us go by.'

'All right, since he refuses to co-operate, we'll help ourselves.' I called Jimmy. 'You want to have some fun? Take White and Chiche with you and ride to Demesio's place. Pick out his best mount and bring it back here – it's time to settle accounts. Do what I said, but no rough stuff. You're in charge.'

Delighted with this unexpected treat, the three of them galloped off. I had the men place dozens of tree-trunks downstream, where the mud wasn't as deep, and this time the skidder made it across the river without any trouble. We were ready to leave when our horsemen reappeared – each of them with a horse attached to his saddle.

'Everything go all right?'

'We began by sneaking up so we could spot the horses from a distance, but we couldn't see a thing, so we lost patience and galloped into the courtyard. There were three horses, and since we didn't know which one to choose we took all three. The only one we left behind was an old nag – probably La Puta's mother.'

'Good! Any reactions?'

'When we got to the courtyard, we only found his sons and a neighbour busy trying to hide the horses. When we took them, Demesio came out of the house with a pistol in his belt, yelling that nobody would ever steal them and threatening to shoot – but nothing happened. But he said that he forbids you to come to his place and that if you do there will be trouble.'

'OK, we'll make a courtesy call,' I said to the men who'd been listening to the story. 'We'll even make the road pass his way, since that's the shortest route to the Quebrada del Frances. Let's go!'

The skidder moved off. Everyone hopped on except Innocente and Daniel, who'd never seen a contraption like it and were scared shitless. On level terrain it worked wonders, clearing everything – even trunks and mounds of earth – in its path, and we quickly came within sight of Demesio's place. The first fence flew apart, and the skidder stopped in the courtyard. We made an impressive sight: I was sitting on the cabin; some twenty laughing men were crowding behind on

221

the platform; and an escort of six horsemen was galloping alongside us.

Ready to react if Demesio tried anything, I bawled: 'Demesio, come out so I can talk to you!'

No answer. I figured he must be hiding somewhere.

'OK, let's get going,' I told the mechanic.

'Which way?'

'Straight ahead. Lay out a new road.'

A granary and a chicken-coop disappeared under the treads in a symphony of splintering wood, after which we disposed of a variety of useless and unaesthetic sheds.

The house was temping, but the faces of the two terrified kids peering out of the window saved it.

When I turned around after the pulverization of the second fence, I noted with satisfaction that, thanks to me, civilization had changed the face of the country: progress had finally come to Demesio's.

In a mood of civilizing euphoria, after having flattened everything in our way, we reached the camp and I noticed Barbaroja's chicken-coop. What good was a chicken-coop without chickens? A few minutes later it had ceased to spoil the landscape.

'The house! The house!' yelled my excited lads.

I hesitated for only a moment. Ever since Chiche, very pleased with his joke, had gone to shit in Barbaroja's boots and piss on his bed, I'd been using his house as a personal crapper, and it was beginning to be unhealthy. But this tank assault was becoming monotonous and called for a change. With the help of Chiche, I attached a dozen sticks to the main pillar with a seven-minute fuse. All the men took shelter in the ranch and watched through the windows. In an explosion that seemed to announce the end of the world, Barbaroja's house flew apart: the roof sailed off and the walls squirted in every direction as the hut opened like a flower in the morning. When the smoke cleared there was nothing more than a little pile of straw and planks; one well-placed match, and fire rid us for ever of reminders of Barbaroja.

Finally, you could see around you, and I felt more comfortable; I've never liked the excessive closeness of suburban houses. All I spared was his shed – because it had been used to store planks that now belonged to me. I made sure that the mop-up was complete, and I almost regretted the absence of the two fatties. Though I was sorely tempted by the shed, I knew that if we stopped to remove the planks the spontaneity of the celebration would be ruined. Too bad, but I'd find other amusements.

*　　*　　*

We tried the skidder in the afternoon, and the power of my new toy amused me. It displaced several tons of rocks in ten minutes; but then, during the eleventh minute, it came off one of its tread.

The mechanic was dumbfounded. 'That's something that never happens,' he said in embarrassment. 'Logically, it can't happen.'

'Well, my friend, even logic is different here. This isn't any ordinary work-site – it's Osa.'

It took an hour to fix it – and five minutes later the other tread showed the same independence. Later a shovel piston snapped, and that threw the mechanic completely. I didn't know where they'd dug up such an antique, but you obviously couldn't count on those jerks for anything.

While I was wondering if I ought to dynamite it, throw it into the ravine, or make the mechanic eat it piece by piece, some guy who said he came from Vanegas handed me a letter. It was from Herman Weinberg, who was in Vanegas with Ureba. They'd followed the track of the skidder up to that point in a land-rover, but they were afraid to go on because they'd already spent one night stuck in the mud; they politely asked if I could send some horses.

I would just as soon have left them there to take root, but the work-day was all fucked up anyhow, so I decided I might as well fetch them. That way Herman could see for himself just how useful his equipment was.

'Jimmy, saddle four horses – we're going to pick up Herman and Ureba in Vanegas. Miguel, take something for the rain. You're coming with us.'

I left Chiche to watch over the camp, and fifteen minutes later we were on our way to Vanegas. Thanks to the earlier passage of the skidder, we could make the whole trip on horseback. Though we did it at a gallop, it was pitch-black when we got to the Vanegas pulperia, where the two lard-arses were sitting around with beers in their hands.

Herman still had his revolver on his hip. Ureba, looking fierce, had a knife stuck in his belt, but it was masked by his prominent belly.

'Glad to see you,' said Herman. 'I've got blankets in the car, and we can bed down here without any problem.'

'Who said anything about bedding down? I brought horses for everybody. Get into the saddle. Miguel will follow on foot.'

Ureba stared at me in terror.

'But that's insane! You can't see a thing. It's dangerous, there are snakes, we could get lost and. . . .'

'Listen, chubby, I don't intend to leave the mine without anybody to watch it! If you want to come along, this is the time. If not, you can wait here till Herman gets back.'

'No, no, I'll come. But how will I manage? I've never ridden horseback!'

'Don't worry. Just sit tight and the horse will do the rest – or would you rather be tied on?'

After a few beers we started back. The horses, tired from their day's galloping, moved slowly; and Ureba, who was too heavy for his horse, was soon left behind – despite his protests. I could hear him shouting: 'Hold it! Wait for me! Be nice! You're going to lose me! Wait up, will you!'

His complaints sounded funny in the night. Little by little, the distance between us grew longer, and eventually we stopped to wait for him. By the time he reached us he was pale with fear, his teeth were chattering, and he was no longer talking.

The next day we had breakfast together at about nine o'clock. Herman and Ureba, exhausted by their previous night's efforts, asked to sleep later, and because I didn't want my men working while other people loafed I took advantage of the wait to dress and cook personally two of Barbaroja's white rabbits, slaughtered that very morning.

We were ready to leave for the quebrada when a troop of about twenty men appeared on the road and headed for us.

'I see somebody with dark glasses,' Jimmy said to me. 'It's Barbaroja.'

'OK, get the weapons out of their hiding-place and distribute them to their owners – but tell them they're not to do anything without orders from me.'

Most of my men had brought arms, but as a security measure I'd forbidden weapons in the camp, and they'd been hidden away in the forest. After the cops' first visit, I'd also contrived a special watertight and unfindable stash – only three of us knew where it was – for the grass and coke.

The newcomers had stopped some way off and seemed to be consulting. When they started moving again, I noticed two uniforms; the others were in civilian clothes. Nobody said a word when they reached us. At the head, I recognized Villanueva – the lieutenant in charge of the Jiménez post, whom I'd been paying off regularly since Nogales had introduced me to him – followed by his assistant, who'd been present when I was arrested in Cerro de Oro. Alongside Barbaroja was a well-dressed city slicker and behind them were some fifteen men – peninsula types who looked like candidates for the hangman. Gobino pointed out four who were from the Vargas family I'd heard about: brothers, buddies of Barbaroja and cut from the same cloth – a quartet well able to use strong-arm methods to settle their problems. I baptized them the Dalton Brothers. All of them were armed, looked menacing and were ready for trouble.

Pretending not to know me, Villanueva came up and presented himself military fashion.

'Good morning, gentlemen. My name is Lieutenant Villanueva and I'm responsible for seeing that the law is obeyed here on the peninsula. Which one of you is Don Juan Carlos?'

I played along with him.

'I am.'

'Well, I'm here at the request of Señor Gerardo. May I speak to you in private?'

While the men dismounted, I took Villanueva to the kitchen. As soon as he couldn't be seen, he dropped his formal manner and again became friendly and deferential. He explained what was going on.

'I'm sorry, but Barbaroja has lodged about a dozen formal complaints, and I must say you go about things with a heavy hand. I came along personally so I could control the situation and help you out. Barbaroja is terrified and doesn't want to live here any more. He's hired a lawyer – that young fellow who's with him – and they've come to make a deal. They've asked their friends along to protect them. I'm supposed to defend this bastard Barbaroja and see to it that there's no trouble. Watch out for the henchmen, but don't worry – we'll take care of everything.'

He was obviously fond of that monthly envelope.

When we rejoined the others, the atmosphere was tense. The newcomers had gathered before the entrance to the compound and were being watched by my men, who never took their eyes off them. I briefly explained the situation to Herman, then invited Barbaroja and his lawyer to come to my room so we could talk.

As we were about to go in, there was a little comic interlude. Herman asked me not to leave him alone with Barbaroja, who in turn said he wouldn't go with me unless the lieutenant came along. Not a pair of balls between them! The violence of my first reactions had terrified Barbaroja, and he watched the discussion in silence.

Barbaroja's counsellor was confident at first. He came from San José and had some property on Osa; a freshly turned-out university arsehole, he still believed in the law and was probably the only honest man in the country – at least, for the time being.

He began in a firm tone. 'What you've done is indefensible. You're in a democratic country, and the fact that you're a foreigner doesn't mean you don't have to obey the law.' Resolutely xenophobic, he went on with a strong indictment of gringos and the violence they perpetuated, then spoke of the disastrous influence of Europeans on Costa Rica.

225

The sight of what remained of Barbaroja's house and the state of his domestic animals – now down to a cow and a very suspicious hen – flabbergasted and enraged him.

'What gave you the right to burn this house?'

'It bothered me and, since I anticipated that Señor Barbaroja was going to sell it, as the only possible buyer I considered myself the future owner of the plot and I cleared it.'

'What about my client's personal belongings and his furnishings?'

'I assure you that nobody touched them. Everything is where he left it,' I replied, pointing to the pile of ashes that indicated where Barbaroja's house had been.

My irony both disconcerted and infuriated him, though he didn't quite dare lose his temper.

Villanueva diplomatically intervened.

'You'll have to excuse Don Juan Carlos. He's not from here and doesn't know all the laws of our country. Keep in mind that he comes from another continent, where customs are different.'

Eventually the lawyer got the idea that all he could do was arrange things as well as possible and save what could still be saved.

He asked 2 million colones for Barbaroja's land. Herman, happy to see that the discussion had taken a less dangerous turn, was almost ready to accept, but I offered 200,000 colones and remained inflexible. The mine legally belonged to me and couldn't be involved in any transaction.

'If I've understood correctly,' said the lawyer, 'this land is very rich, so the price asked doesn't seem unreasonable.'

'Oh, but that's where you're mistaken! Nobody's said anything about buying a mine – a mine I happen to be the sole owner of! Barbaroja never exploited the resources under the soil, and there was no mine here previously. This transaction has nothing to do with the mine. What we're dealing with here is simply the purchase of the land on which I've built my house. This land had been rented from Barbaroja by mutual agreement – if he wants to sell it now, I'm offering two hundred thousand colones and not a penny more. That's ten times what it's really worth!'

The discussion continued, but I refused to budge. From time to time I glanced at Barbaroja, who immediately lowered his head, obviously wishing he was somewhere else.

When I stood up to stretch my legs, he jumped, and I suddenly realized just how frightened he was. He didn't look well and was a lot thinner than when I'd last seen him; trouble didn't seem to agree with him.

In the next room the atmosphere was very tense, the two groups

226

silently watching each other as they awaited the results of our palaver. Ureba, sitting on a bed, bit his fingernails until they bled, and asked himself in anguish how he'd got mixed up in all this and how it would end. Every time I put in an appearance, he showered me with questions and irritated me with terrified advice; those were probably some of the hardest moments he'd ever lived through – he'd even forgotten to eat.

I thought the time had come for a little refreshment, so I had the two rabbits brought into the bedroom where the discussion was going on, and I invited Ureba to come and join us.

'I'm too nervous to be hungry,' he said.

'Get a grip on yourself. Everything will be all right.'

'I've got a feeling that everybody's going to start shooting in a minute, and it makes me lose my appetite.'

'That's too bad, because you're going to miss the best rabbits that have ever been cooked on Osa.'

'You mean you're going to serve Barbaroja his own rabbits?'

'Sure I am! He was very fond of them, so he might as well take advantage of this last possibility of contact.'

Meanwhile, in the large room the two groups were seated at the table face to face, everybody swallowing rapidly, keeping an eye on his opposition, then quickly going back to his place.

At about eleven in the evening we reached an agreement – in other words, the lawyer finally gave up, and we bought the land for 200,000 colones, payable in several monthly instalments.

As the company was still not a legal entity, the land was bought in the name of Herman Weinberg. I didn't care for that, but there was no other solution.

Barbaroja was pleased and relieved; this had been his last attempt and, having cheated and lost, he hadn't expected to get off so easily.

Since it was dark by then, I suggested to the lawyer, who'd given up his high and mighty manners and was behaving decently, that he sleep at the ranch. At first he said he couldn't because he had too much work, but eventually he told me the real reason for his refusal.

'You can understand that, given your reputation, I took some precautions. I warned my family and my friends that if I didn't return this evening they were to alert the police and come looking for me. My apologies. Don't take offence. There was no way I could know, and Barbaroja seemed so terrified. . . . Everyone's afraid to come near the Quebrada del Frances.'

To the great disappointment of the men, who were looking forward to a brawl, he left in the company of his escort and of Barbaroja's friends. As for Barbaroja himself, he went off to sleep in his shed, his only remaining shelter. The two cops were about to follow him, when I invited them to sleep at the ranch.

'Thank you, Don Juan Carlos, but we have to go with Señor Gerardo,' said Villanueva.

He walked a few yards, then turned back and confessed.

'It's not that I wouldn't prefer your hospitality, but we have to protect Barbaroja. He's paid us for that.'

No doubt about it: Villanueva fed at every trough.

In the morning Barbaroja tried to gather together his last possessions. There wasn't much left: his pigs – seventeen in all – had been slaughtered, his rabbits and practically all his hens were gone. The ones that had escaped, warned by a sixth sense, had returned to the wild, to live among the banana-trees. The only thing that remained was his cow, which he attached to his horse before leaving to look for survivors. The two cops were waiting alongside his stuff, so I went over to speak to them. As we talked, I looked at the cow. She had a nice friendly face, and I kept thinking about all the trouble waiting for her during that long exhausting descent to Vanegas – so, feeling sorry for her, without warning I put a bullet in her head. She jumped, and collapsed. The two cops were dumbfounded, then began to laugh.

I signalled my men. 'Carve that up for me, and hurry.'

Five merry men came running up with machetes and skinned it in a matter of minutes – and just then Barbaroja emerged from the patch of banana-trees carrying a rooster. The spectacle sent him into shock. There was nothing attached to the piece of rope dangling from his horse, and five men were chopping away at his cow, his beautiful cow, with mighty blows of their machetes. Bloodied to their elbows, one pulled at a leg and another at the tail, shouting with joy. That was hard to take – the cow that had given him his milk every morning for years being hacked to pieces right in front of his eyes by those bloody madmen.

Turning to the cops, who'd wiped the smiles off their faces, he asked for help. Villanueva went over to him, and I could see he was struggling not to laugh. Placing a hand on Barbaroja's shoulder, he began in a solemn voice: 'Don Gerardo. . . .'

Then, unable to restrain himself any longer, he cracked up. Shaking with laughter, he tried in vain to mumble vague excuses. The laughter grew, as Chiche stepped up and politely attached the animal's head behind Barbaroja's horse. As for Barbaroja himself, he was completely demoralized; clutching his last fowl in his arms, he mounted his horse and rode off without responding to my invitation to stay for lunch. Still laughing, the two cops followed him, and as I watched

228

him disappear I decided he wasn't leaving a moment too soon: by dinner-time I would have been ready to serve up his horse.

The next day we all went down to the quebrada to try Herman's wonder machine. I was curious to see how that contraption would work. Though I was still sceptical, I'd nevertheless marvelled at its capacities as described by the mechanic, and since I don't like manual labour I prefer to believe in technicians. . . . If it worked, I could put on three shifts a day.

When we got to the quebrada, Herman launched into a speech.

'My friends, from today manual labour is over. I've brought you progress. Thanks to this unique machine developed by José, your job will be simplified and considerably easier.'

He was all worked up, and as he told me about his great expectations for the commercialization of the invention the enthusiastic workers, laughing and shouting, brought the machine to the pit – not an easy thing to do, because it wasn't adapted to broken terrain.

When José started it up, everybody watched with enormous interest. On one side a big tube was supposed to suck in water and gravel and discharge the latter into the canoa; on the other, two horses ended in nozzles from which pressurized water was supposed to spurt, attacking the earth and facilitating the work with the miner's bars. At first sight, it seemed clever but after two hours of effort the machine had almost emptied the hole of water and tossed only three bits of gravel into the canoa; as for the two rickety jets that came from the hoses, I could see no use for them – except maybe for washing your ears.

Herman and José had to put up with the catcalls of the disillusioned men. There was no denying that the gadget was unique. What a bunch of jerks my partners were!

Herman tried to save face.

'It works,' he said with an uncomfortable smile, shouting over the noise of the motor. 'Do you think you can use it?'

'Of course we can. Marcella's going to be delighted to have a pressure jet for her dishwashing.'

Suddenly, no doubt aware of its uselessness, the pump stopped on its own with a loud groan of tortured metal. Pandemonium broke loose, with the men hooting Herman openly and suggesting he take a turn in the hole before trying to play engineer.

I quietened them down. 'Gentlemen, you've been privileged to witness one of the marvels of civilization. Now clear this shit away.'

'Do you know what you're going to do with it?' Herman asked me.

'I sure do! Boys, throw this crap into some ravine. It's a blot on the landscape.'

229

Pulled, rolled and carried, the machine quickly got to the old river-bed below, into which it smashed after an unsuccessful attempt to fly.

Two minutes later, the men were in the hole and working hard to make up for lost time. Eduardo handed a shovel to Herman, who ignored it, and the mechanic wept over his disappointed dreams as he stood in water up to his waist and plied a miner's bar under the supervision of White, who instructed him on the use of machines that worked on elbow grease.

At noon Herman, to whom I'd shown the state of the skidder, was depressed and spoke of going back to San José that very day. I returned to serious business.

'OK – now, where are the papers?'

'We're making progress. If you want, I can bring them in a week or two and you can sign them.'

'No, no, in a few weeks it'll be Christmas, and I'm going to go to San José. I'll take care of it there. I'd rather you didn't come back here – it plays hell with my schedule, and we lose time and money. By the way, how much did those two scrapheaps cost?'

'Fifteen thousand dollars for the skidder, ten thousand for the pump.'

'I don't believe it! That makes twenty-five thousand bucks you've wasted. Stop all this bullshit! I'm breaking my balls to get this dough out, and just because the mine's rich that's no reason to waste everything by piling up mistakes. Keep out of the operations side from now on – you've already made enough of a mess. Luckily, the mine is still productive. Here.'

I handed him the 3500-gram nugget. He took it, looked at it for a moment without realizing what it was, then started turning it around in his hands. When he finally understood, he let out a shout of joy and danced around the room, kissing the nugget and clutching it to his chest. I wondered if the shock had been too much for him.

'Are you giving me this one, too?' he asked when he came to a stop.

'There isn't much I can do with it here. Put it somewhere safe in San José.'

He went back to his dancing, and wriggled all around the room; I was just about to slap him to bring him back to earth when he calmed down.

After weighing everything, he took out two big account-books and said cheerfully: 'You know, this is a really big find, maybe too big. We'll have to be careful not to arouse envy. Our request for the concession has already attracted attention, and I'm leery of the other branches of the Caracas family, who are also very influential. I suggest we set up two different accounting systems: the one for the two of us will have the real figures and remain secret; in the other we'll exaggerate our expenses and report lower production. That one will be for those who come poking around – remember, there are spies everywhere. What do you think?'

'Whatever you want – you're the one who knows these people. That family must be something – after having seen the sons, I can imagine what the father is like. Do what you think is best. But get this straight: I'll sign your account-pages in advance, but I want you to keep the fuck out of here. Take care of all this paperwork and don't come around playing cowboy.'

He was irritated when he left; he hadn't cared for the way his mechanic, his machines and he himself had been treated. It was hard for the confidential agent of the powerful Caracas family to get used to the contempt we had shown him. Ureba, much relieved, went along with him; the snakes, the jungle, and the tension of the previous day had been too much for him, and he even seemed to have lost weight.

Christmas was near, and everything had gone well. There had been many changes in both the men and the site in three months.

The camp was very clean; the house, completely paved and ventilated, was well run. The men had made it their home, and many of them had never lived in anything so luxurious; some of them had never even had a roof over their heads. Compared to other buildings on Osa, the place was a palace. The men voluntarily took their shoes off when they went inside, and the dormitory was always impeccable – washed and waxed. It was their room, and I only entered upon invitation. When they weren't too tired, they organized little celebrations. They gambled away their salaries, and some of them had already lost three-quarters of their wages in the all-night poker games I started. Alcohol was permitted, but everyone knew that a hangover was no excuse for doing less work.

The men showed personal initiative when it came to maintenance: the insects were slowly eliminated and, if a colony of termites attacked a wall, there was no need for me to give any orders – they destroyed the vermin on their own. All the approaches had been cleared, the jungle pushed back, and the danger of snakes considerably reduced; in fact, the walls were decorated with the dried skins of 122 such beasts, hanging alongside other animals that had been killed. The collection went from monkeys to boas, and the common room began to look like a hunting-lodge.

The work was more relaxed, even though the men were putting in

231

as many hours as ever under conditions that remained difficult. Each man had developed his own rhythm, and I no longer had to intervene; if they stopped for two minutes to catch their breath or take a leak, they caught up on their own. They had come to take pride in their work.

The dry season had begun; it was warm, so working in the hole was no longer disagreeable. Also, they knew that conditions were supposed to improve after Christmas and that those who had hung in during those three crazy months and who came back after the holiday would have privileged positions. Out of habit, I still kept firing over their heads, but I no longer met with the sneaky attitude that suggested a guy was trying to rob me. They worked without thinking of the gold – in other words, mechanically, without coveting it.

I could even leave them on their own for a few minutes, and on one of those occasions I heard happy cries coming from the quebrada. When I returned, they were all grinning broadly, watching me out of the corners of their eyes as they worked.

'Where's the gold?' I said, suspecting the reason for their joy.

'Here,' they replied, pointing towards the cliff.

A little landslide had detached a few stones from the face and exposed the end of an enormous nugget. Everyone had seen it, but nobody had touched it; they'd waited for me to return and dig it out myself.

I profited from some of those respites to tour my domain on horseback, because among my projects were plans for a landing-field.

A forest inspector came to see me. On his first visit, he pointed out that I didn't have the right to cut down a tree or clear land without written permission but that he was ready to close his eyes to what had already been done. The second time he came, the jungle had retreated another fifty yards, and he was upset by the size of the ecological damage. (I should mention that I had two men doing nothing but supplying wood for the camp.) He seemed on the verge of a heart attack, so I promised I'd stop. The third time he came, he preferred to talk about other things and pretended not to see the hundreds of planks we had prepared. When an enormous tree that was probably over a century old came crashing down, he looked elsewhere and we went on talking about ecology. I hadn't converted him to my way of thinking, but the ranch was the only place for miles around where he could sleep, and those small concessions made it possible for him to avoid a night in the jungle.

I've always liked to change things around me, and those weeks I had spent directing the men from my rocking chair had resulted in a clear improvement of the landscape. Everything in that green valley grew in anarchic confusion, but my strong desire for order had transformed it into a desert of precisely arranged stones and mud; it was neater that way and looked like a lunar landscape. Nevertheless, I gave some thought to planting a lawn.

My men didn't complain because the camp gave them a feeling of total impunity. They'd previously ignored the law but never so openly. Here they could smoke and carry on without any problem. The conquest of the jungle, our troubles with the neighbours, and the constant pressure had all forged a fine team spirit.

They were sturdy now – men who without a second thought carried stones they would only recently have considered immovable. They were habituated to gunshot, rain, mud, ceaseless work – everything except dynamite. Every time I lit a fuse there was a wild scramble.

One day Chiche made me a phoney stick of dynamite, a length of wood covered in brown paper and equipped with a real fuse. Without warning, I lit the fuse and tossed the stick into the dorm the morning after a celebration when they were having trouble waking up. The room emptied in a matter of seconds, some men going through the windows, some climbing the bunk beds and going over the walls; only a few had thought of the door.

We were lucky enough not to have had anyone seriously hurt. The generator had claimed three pairs of eyebrows and a row of teeth, but nothing more – which was just as well since we had no first-aid kit. Miguel, who'd driven a miner's bar through his foot, dosed himself with bootleg booze; attacks of malaria, initially frequent, were treated with aspirin and eventually disappeared.

Only Barbas' brother, Ramon, came in for a little attention. As he was hammering in a nail, the wall shook so badly that an enormous loudspeaker fell right on his head. His scalp split, he dropped like a stone, then got up looking dazed and collapsed into a coma. I had him carried to his bed. He seemed certain to die of a cerebral haemorrhage – and we had nothing to treat him with but aspirin. Initially compassionate, the commentary from the others soon became ribald. As Ramon grew paler and paler, each man pronounced himself the victim's best friend and therefore entitled to his salary; Barbas shouted the loudest and, as a brother, won his case. The others immediately began to place bets, first on Ramon's chances for survival and then on the hour of his death.

It was a long night of watching. Never had Ramon been the centre of such interest: every other minute, someone went to check on his

233

condition. A few claimed that he was dead, and his feeble life-signs had to be checked. As the hours dragged on, those who had lost their bets began to curse him. I watched to make sure that nobody cheated. By the time he awoke at noon the next day, he'd made many enemies. He got an afternoon off to rest up.

When Ronald Reagan came to Costa Rica, we had the pleasure of a visit from an anti-terrorist squad. As we went down to the quebrada, some twenty cops in combat uniforms came out of nowhere and encircled the ranch. History was repeating itself, but I could see that I'd made progress since Cerro de Oro: the previous time there'd been twice as many of them.

The tension quickly subsided when they saw they were only dealing with an inoffensive camp of gold prospectors. The chief explained why he'd come: the use of dynamite, plus the exaggerations spread by the people of Osa, had given rise to the story that we were a camp of guerrillas armed with heavy weapons, and the news had reached the ears of the Minister of Security, who'd been rendered somewhat paranoid by Reagan's visit.

The officer informed me there were helicopters filled with troops ready to take off should the first assault-wave be wiped out.

Ureba later told me that the radio had announced an important operation aimed at mopping up a terrorist camp; they'd actually mobilized half the armed forces in the area. However, given the weary state in which they arrived – exhausted by the weight of their combat equipment – they wouldn't have stood up to real guerrillas very long.

I also learned that an incredible number of complaints had been lodged against us.

'I imagine there's been a great deal of exaggeration,' the officer told me, 'but there are charges of theft, violence, attempted murder, and rape.'

'Rape? Except for La Puta, I don't see who could have been fucked in this camp!'

'La Puta?'

'Yes, our mare. But I doubt that she lodged a complaint, and anyway she's of age.'

A little investigation showed that the guy who had accused us of having raped his wife wasn't even married. . . . The officer became aware of the falseness of the accusations and decided we were a peaceful group. I invited the cops to dinner and got them drunk on bootleg guaro. At night Chiche suggested they settle into Barbaroja's old woodshed. Since it had been invaded by thousands of fleas after it had been abandoned, in the morning, to the great pleasure of my men, the twenty cops, their bodies covered with red welts, were busy washing their clothes in the river. They left as suddenly as they'd appeared, without even searching the ranch.

The last day of work before the Christmas break had finally arrived. The hardest part had been done, and I was really pleased with the results obtained in three months: an excellent work-crew, a comfortable camp, and above all a very promising mine. I'd taken out seventeen thousand grams of ore with only shovels and miner's bars, and we'd washed some forty square yards of auriferous soil – more than I had hoped for in my wildest dreams.

I was a budding billionaire, because when we began to use machines I expected enormous increases in production. Nevetheless, I knew that nothing was certain. My partners might easily cheat me, yet I unfortunately needed them; all I could do was hope they wouldn't be dumb enough to kill the goose that laid the golden eggs. Later, when things had been carefully organized, I'd have to watch my step.

I was sorry to have to call a halt, but in this country nobody works during the Christmas season because it's when the men get paid off. Most of them knew that their wages would be cut in half by debts to the company, gambling debts, and purchases Jimmy had made for them on his trips from camp, but to their great surprise I gave each of them their whole pay, plus a bonus; it was only fair. They'd held up under tough conditions, and I had grown fond of them. In three months they'd been metamorphosed in one way or another: White, a former pimp, loafer and thief, had worked for the first time in his life; Eduardo, a professional gaolbird, had never spent so much time out of the slammer; Chiche, a pickpocket, no longer even looked at the gold; Ramón, the rustic playboy, had lost all his front teeth and most of his side-hair; Jimmy, a one-time lackey, had won the men's respect. . . . Even Barbas the Bumblebee, Three-Legs Cunado, and Miguel the Indian all announced their decision to return after Christmas – though three months ago nobody would have predicted as much – and put their personal belongings into a box that they each had set up in the dormitory.

My advice to them was to spend the Christmas holidays in the south: their new life-style oughtn't to make them forget that most of them were wanted by the police. I stayed on a few days to wait for the two cops Lieutenant Villanueva had promised to send to guard the mine during my absence. It wasn't that I was afraid of anyone working my mine, because I'd taken care to discourage amateurs by

235

collapsing a portion of the cliff over the hole; but I was concerned that my friends and neighbours might take advantage of the opportunity to pillage and destroy the camp.

The lieutenant sent us his own son and one other cop. After having completed the inventory and explained everything, I went down to Guerra with Jimmy and Marcella. Nicolas left for San José and telephoned René with instructions to prepare a super-celebration – well earned after those three months in the jungle! I had six thousand grams of gold, and I fully intended to spend most of it.

When I got to Palmar, René was waiting for me in a friend's house. He had brought everything I'd asked for. Five members of a mariachi band had come by truck to begin the celebration; he himself had come by plane with three of Mamma's protégées, as well as some coke, some grub and a case of French champagne – exactly what I needed. In town I'd run into several of my men high on rotten booze and clinging to the arms of local whores, but I wanted more stylish pleasures: one of Omar's cousins had left me his house, and I intended to lock myself in for two days and enjoy the sweets I'd been deprived of.

I took over the largest room with three of my former girlfriends, who seemed as pleased to see me as I was to see them. They'd dressed in their best undress and smelt of French perfume, something very rare in this country.

The five musicians were in a curtained-off room next door, and they had instructions to go on playing as long as the celebration lasted. I'd seen to it that they had coke, food, booze and even a local prostitute to help them stand the pressure. My three fresh little things still bore no stigmata of sin and were having a lot of innocent fun – the luxury dazzled them, and they liked the idea of the musicians. René, who'd orchestrated the celebration, had left nothing to chance, even providing a big bathtub filled with warm water. . . .

At first it seemed I'd be able to enjoy those pleasures for a long time, but the repertory of the musicians wasn't very extensive – and, besides, there are limits to human endurance. When for the hundredth time they began a husky rendition of 'La cucaracha ya no puede caminar', the rhythm of the maracas – and my own rhythm – had both, alas, slowed down.

While René settled accounts and took care of the damage, my three nymphettes and I got into a taxi and headed for San José. The ride seemed shorter than usual.

Upon my arrival I immediately went to see Herman so I could get that out of the way. The sight of his foul face after two days in which my eyes had been filled with beauty wasn't particularly pleasant, and I was in a black mood as I entered his office. As usual, he was all smiles and politeness and, all things considered, I preferred seeing him there, wearing a shirt and tie; his physique went better with these surroundings.

'Juan Carlos, welcome back to civilization! Did everything go all right?'

'Yes, of course.'

I told him what had happened during the past few weeks and about the arrival of the cops.

'I heard the announcement on the radio, but it was too late to do anything. We'd wanted to stay out of the limelight and we did, but it will be hard to keep the secret now.'

'In any case, don't you think it's time to drop the anonymity and make the company known?'

'Yes. And, by the way, we have to settle accounts. I hear you paid the men more than what had been agreed, and that's contrary to all the rules of economy.'

'Economy, my arse! You're a fine one to talk after all the dumb things you bought! You're making enough to give a present to the men, who didn't "economize" in their work. If necessary, I'll pay it out of my part of the gold.'

'Speaking of gold, was production good?'

'Yes, as usual.'

'Great! How much were you able to take out?'

'About six thousand grams.'

'That's really fantastic. Were there any nuggets?'

He was circling around the question without having quite enough courage to plunge in. Since I didn't help him, he eventually had to come out with it.

'Well, where is it?'

'I've got it.'

'Aren't you going to give it to me?'

'No, it's my share and I'm keeping it.'

'But, Juan Carlos, that isn't the way things are done. In a company each man can't decide for himself. Everything has to go through the accounting department, the board of directors, and all the rest. . . .'

'Oh, come off it! What are you trying to feed me? Why are you talking about the company? I made you a present, and you've had more than your share. I've taken six thousand grams, and that's less than my share. There are still four thousand grams in the till for future expenses, so stop all this crap about accounting. I've had

237

dozens of companies and I know how they work. By the way, what's happened to those papers since the last time we spoke?'

'Things are moving along. It's only a matter of days.'

'What the fuck are you trying to pull? It's been three months now, and you haven't kept your promises. I get out the gold, and you live on it without giving anything in exchange. That's a hell of a partnership; I might as well have joined up with any garbage-collector – he'd have done as well! You've spent the dough on one dumb thing after another and haven't done anything I asked you to. You talk of protection – what a phoney you are!'

I'd had enough, and I got up before I gave way to the itch to rough him up a little. As I was going through the shop, he came running after me.

'Come on, don't take it like that. We're going to get results. Your papers are almost ready. Don't get angry – our job isn't always easy.'

'And I suppose mine is?'

'Listen, there's no point in losing your temper,' he said with a big smile. 'Forget all this and relax. Let me invite you to my house on the twenty-fifth for Christmas dinner. My wife wants to meet you – I've been talking about you for so long. . . .'

The whole idea turned my stomach, but he was so insistent that I eventually accepted out of politeness. A guy can live in the jungle and still know how to behave.

After leaving his office, I wondered where to go. The pleasures of the city had lost their interest; the casino bored me, and I knew all the whores. After thinking about it for a while, I decided to treat myself to something out of the ordinary, and I went off to settle in at René's.

I won't go into details about the delights of those few days, which – despite the amused Mamma's generous home cooking – wore me out physically as well as financially: a king's pleasures have to be paid for royally. But I felt comfortable in that family atmosphere, and I had the time to get to know the rest of Mamma's protégées. I stayed there for ten days without budging, leaving only to go to Herman's dinner.

He introduced me to his wife, a famished thirty-five-year-old vagina who kept staring at my nuts all evening long. Stimulated by the aphrodisiac virtues of coke, she began to play footsies under the table, but I was revolted by her obvious intentions and quickly left to return to the purity of my whores. I didn't blame the poor thing; her husband looked as if he couldn't get it up, so she probably didn't get a workout too often.

After those few days of daydreaming, I decided to get down to business again. I hadn't lost sight of the mine and my impending return to

Osa. In a little while, I thought, I'd get the permit for the machines, then work could begin in earnest: with a good mechanical excavator and a giant canoa I'd be able to wash several tons a day. But I decided to discontinue my twenty-four-hour work-day; the hardest part was over, and I planned to exploit the site at a more relaxed pace – though one that would be every bit as productive. For that I needed more people I could depend on, people who could supervise the different shifts. I thought of Lars, the old Dane I'd met in Punta Burica, and decided to go look for him.

Leaving the gold in a San José bank safe-deposit box, I went down to Golfito, where I hired a Tico to take me to Penas Blancas by boat on New Year's Day 1983.

Lars spotted the boat coming in and was glad to see me again. He'd built a new house on the hill that overlooked the beach and invited me to have some coffee while we talked. I began explaining my plans for the mine, and he immediately became enthusiastic, admitting that his hermit's life was beginning to bore him and he was tired of scraping along without any money. He told me that what he really wanted was to leave this continent and go to Australia – he wanted his son to have a better education than he could get in Costa Rica – but he needed money for that.

We agreed that Lars would meet me in San José a few days later. I spent the night at his place, then took the boat to Puerto Jiménez because I was concerned about the mine and wanted to check on it.

When I reached Jiménez I hired the village's only taxi. It was the dry season, and I thought that a land-rover could take me a good bit of the way before bogging down – it would just have to follow the skidder tracks.

The taxi-driver wasn't eager to make the trip, but he finally accepted, quoting me a hefty price. I agreed to it, but I already knew he was in for trouble: his tyres were smooth, and his battery wasn't worth a damn. Just what you need in the jungle! And, of course, three miles past Vanegas, following in the wake of the tractor and crossing a muddy strip too slowly, the land-rover sank up to the doors. It was stuck, and stuck fast. Despite my advice, he kept gunning the motor until he was blue in the face, but he only sank deeper. I climbed out and watched him struggle. When the overheated motor conked out there was about half a foot of muddy water in the car.

Night was rapidly falling as I started into the forest on foot. The driver quickly caught up with me.

'Hey, you're not going to leave me here, are you?'

'Sure, why not?'

239

'But I'm afraid to spend the night alone in the jungle – there are tigers and snakes!'

'Then, come with me,' I said, walking off. 'It's only a four-hour hike.'

He threw a last look at his taxi and ran to join me.

Not at all equipped for such an expedition, he had on a pair of shorts and was wearing sandals that soon disappeared in the mud. Since I was used to the terrain I walked along at a rapid pace while he had to run alongside me, barefoot.

When we got to Demesio's there was still three miles to go and I was tired. I decided to rent a horse from him. After all, neighbours should help one another out. My shouting woke him up, and he was very surprised to see me. I knew he hated my guts, but I also knew human nature: the price I was offering for the hire of his horse would make him forget all desire for revenge.

He obviously wanted peace, and he took advantage of the occasion to smooth our difficulties.

'You understand,' he said in a honeyed voice, 'I'm not a rich man, and I told myself I wasn't doing you much harm by selling you that horse.'

'But I warned you.'

'Yes, but I don't think I deserved such a punishment – I think we're even now. You wrecked my farm and took my horses – maybe we can arrange things so you return one or two of them. These mountains are unfriendly, and it's not a good idea to be on bad terms with your neighbours. We have to help one another, and for my part I'm very fond of you.'

Hypocrite and double hypocrite! I assured him that all was forgotten and that we'd iron things out when I got back. He disgusted me, but for the time being I needed him. Later we'd see.

I took the taxi-driver up behind me, and we soon reached the camp and woke the guards. To my surprise, Lieutenant Villanueva himself had joined his son in protecting the mine. They weren't in uniform and, instead of their usual weapons, were armed only with carbines. After listening to a confused story about a theft and a brawl, I understood that he'd been dismissed from his police post for corruption. What injustice! He must have gone a little too far and another conniver had got his job – one of the most envied in the country.

Well, it didn't matter that much – all I'd have to do was change the name on the monthly envelope. The funny thing about it was that Villanueva kept assuring me of his good faith and honesty.

Even though it was dark, a rapid tour of the quebrada assured me that everything was in order. My worries had been unfounded, but I still felt better for having checked.

I left the driver in the camp, suggested that he hire Demesio's sons to pull the taxi out of the mud, paid for the trip, and added a generous bonus for his trouble. Taking my own horse, Pingón, I started for Vanegas, dropped the rented mount off with Demesio, and reached town by dawn. Maybe it was exhaustion due to those round trips or maybe the weather was acting up, but I'd been terribly cold and had spent the night clinging to my horse's neck and withers to take advantage of his warmth. I turned him over to the owner of the Vanegas pulperia, who drove me to Jiménez in a car. After a boat to Golfito and then a plane, I arrived in San José on 3 January, 1983.

I went directly to Malessa because I'd decided to settle all the problems involved in the next trip to the peninsula as soon as possible; I wanted to be ready to leave in a few days, about 10 January.

Herman was waiting for me with Jimmy. He explained his new scheme.

'Juan Carlos, you told me you'd noticed some pre-Columbian cemeteries on the concession?'

'That's right.'

'Then, it seems to me that we've got a double opportunity. Jimmy's father – you've met him – is very good at robbing tombs. I think we can ask him to work with us, don't you?'

'It might be a good idea.'

'But there's a problem. The old man's half-crazy and he does pretty much as he wants. It would be a good idea if you went to Limon with Jimmy to see if you can convince him. He likes you, and you're the only one who can talk him round.'

I had two free days ahead of me, and the Atlantic coast near Limón is pretty; besides, the old man really was a character. Jimmy and I left for his father's place the next morning.

After pretending to say no, so he could be begged a while, the old man finally agreed: he'd come join us on the mountain. The old guy was completely nutty, alternating between periods of lucidity and attacks of insanity during which he believed he was the reincarnation of an Indian chief in contact with the God of Gold who helped him find the figurines in the tombs. Although he was seventy years old, he was married to a fifteen-year-old Indian girl, his third wife. Foul-minded and nasty, he was also dangerous, because he would shoot at his neighbours; and he was a born troublemaker with a viper's tongue.

Those faults made me like him all the more. He was the kind of childlike, intolerable and capricious old man who'd decided to give everybody a hard time until his dying day, and who simply refused to

241

grow old. Most likely he'd be out of place in the camp. Jimmy, who was a little afraid of him, assured me that despite all his faults he was very good at pillaging cemeteries, and I could easily believe him, because the son in turn had an extraordinary feeling for gold and attracted it the way other people attract trouble. We spent the night at the farm listening as the old man, caught up in an esoteric delirium, told stories about divine protection.

Before we left, Jimmy asked me for some money so he could buy some dope.

'My father grows a lot of the best stuff, and Herman wanted me to bring him back a key.'

'It would be better to buy it in town so we don't have to carry it past the checkpoints.'

'We can easily hide it in the car, and Herman knows that it's a help to my father, who needs the dough.'

'OK. After all, it's your business.'

We reached San José in the afternoon and went directly to Malessa. Jimmy gave the grass to Herman, and we tried it. It was really good stuff, and all of us quickly felt its effects. The atmosphere was relaxed as we laughed and talked about the old man's nonsense. Herman was glad to know that Jimmy's father had agreed to come, and we got things ready for the return to Osa.

'I don't know what you've done to your men, but they keep phoning here to ask when they're supposed to leave. They all want to go back up and they're afraid of missing the departure date. I really don't know what to say to reassure them.'

'Tell them all to be here on January tenth.'

I was glad to hear that there had been no desertions. It wasn't just the pay that made them want to come back; in all modesty, it seemed to me that they'd never found a similar atmosphere on any other job and that they really liked me. (Nicolas, however, I didn't expect back. He had come to Osa on a lark, but he turned out to be too fragile to do any work at the mine. In fact after he left the camp for San José I never saw him again.)

While we talked, Herman handed the somewhat shrunken packet of grass back to Jimmy.

'Here, hold on to this for me. The safe is closed, and when I leave here I'm going directly to a reception at Juan Caracas' house. You can return it to me tomorrow.'

Just as we were about to leave, Pablo, the toothless accountant, took out some papers and said to me: 'Don Juan Carlos, since you're here, we have some accounting to go over together.'

242

'Not today. I don't like papers, and I need a shower and a change of clothes – I've got an appointment tonight.'

'If you're going to disappear with your women for another week, we won't be able to find you. Nobody knows where to reach you when you're in town, and I'd like to get this settled this week. What hotel are you at?'

'Tonight the Astoria – after that, I don't know.'

I could imagine what chubby here would do if he learned of the existence of Mamma's protégées, and I preferred to get in touch with my associates when and if it pleased me.

We went back to my room at the Astoria, where René was going to pick me up because I was turning over the car to Jimmy, who lived outside the city. Jimmy was just about to leave when there was a knock at the door. After slipping the package of dope under the pillow, I opened the door thinking it was René. A guy with a pistol in his hand immediately came in and went to the far side of the room while another armed man stood at the door.

'Narcotics!' he said.

After a quick search of the room, he came up with the package of grass, then rapidly slipped the cuffs on to us as the other guy relieved me of my gun. It all took only a few minutes. This wasn't the first time I had been caught *in flagrante delicto*, and I knew how to smooth things over with a little diplomacy and a lot of money – but it was impossible to get a conversation going, and we soon found ourselves at the Narcotics Bureau.

We were left in a big room in which all the agents, supposedly undercover men, were parading past us – the kind of stupidity typical of Costa Rica. I knew several of the men because I'd had coffee with them on occasion, and I tried to use the opportunity to familiarize myself with the faces of the others.

They played with my Magnum and made a lot of comments – they'd probably never seen such a beautiful piece. Then, after filling in a lot of forms, they took us to a room containing several beds and looking much too spacious to be a cell. Jimmy was beside himself, and I tried to build up his morale. I wasn't worried because I'd got out of this kind of situation before, but something about this one smelt fishy. I wasn't surprised that the police had come knocking, but why the Narcotics Squad – and especially at that time of day? In addition, I'd had the distinct impression that the cop had been looking for something specific, and both their speed and their refusal to discuss things surprised me. It wasn't like the local cops, who never let any opportunity slide to pick up a little something on the side. Could I have come across the country's only zealot in search of a promotion?

I discussed my suspicions with Jimmy.

'Jimmy, forget your feelings about Herman for a moment and tell me frankly if you think he could have set us up?'

'No, impossible. He'd never do anything like that. Why, we grew up together and were friends as kids. He and Tino Caracas were witnesses at my wedding, and I've been working for him these past ten years. No, forget it. I can assure you that's not Herman's style.'

'Maybe you're right. Then. . . .'

Then, what? An extraordinary coincidence? I'd known strange things to happen, and the most improbable, even mathematically 'impossible' coincidences have nevertheless occurred. Bad luck sometimes comes in strange ways.

And, besides, since they still needed me, I couldn't understand what Herman and his cronies had to gain by keeping me locked up. I thought about it all night, but in the morning I still hadn't come up with an answer.

When I got up, I saw that Jimmy hadn't slept either, and I was amazed by how he looked. He'd aged ten years in a night: his face was drawn, he had deep bags under his eyes, and he was obviously very worried.

'Don't look like that,' I told him. 'It's not so dangerous, and everything will work out.'

'It's not just this, Juan Carlos. You probably don't know about it, but some time before I met you I was tried for having torn off a man's finger in a brawl. They let me out on bail and gave me a three-year suspended sentence, but at the first sign of trouble, the first contact with the cops, I have to start serving my actual sentence immediately. I'm not afraid of gaol, but I've got a wife and two kids to take care of. What'll happen to them if I'm locked up?'

Poor Jimmy – now I knew why he was so upset. I liked the guy and was touched by his domestic worries. Also, he was dependable and deserved my help, so after thinking about it for a few minutes I said: 'Don't worry. I'll take all the blame; you'll be free in an hour.'

Of course I was completely innocent in the affair, and I wasn't the one to have made the original mistake, but I couldn't abandon Jimmy: given his record, he had no chance of getting off. It was up to me to do whatever had to be done, and it wasn't just a matter of stupid generosity leading me sheeplike to the slaughter, because I had confidence in my ability – I knew I could figure a way out. All I was up against was human brains, and I had outwitted more and bigger brains in my time. In addition, though Costa Rican law is very strict about dealing in dope, it's vague when it's only a question of possession.

Could they really believe that a mine-owner, the president of a company, would stoop to selling a few grams? I was neither a criminal nor a tourist – I had settled in the country and, if necessary, the names of my partners could serve as a guarantee.

During the interrogation, I followed my usual line of defence: yes, I smoked a lot, and this package was part of my personal supply; I'd been using grass ever since I was a child; I lived in the jungle and needed it to fall asleep and tranquillize my sick body. To support what I said I could cite hospital statements attesting that I used the drug to ease my discomfort. I denied the accusation of resale and, taking all responsibility on myself, declared that I'd bought the grass in Golfito.

The weapon with the filed-off numbers intrigued them.

'To whom does this belong?' asked my interrogator.

'It's mine. I've had it for years.'

'Why are the identification numbers filed off?'

'It's neater that way.'

Little by little the atmosphere lost its tension; the cops relaxed and began to make jokes. I asked for and was denied permission to make a phone call. The chief of the Narcotics Division, Colonel Altamira, came to talk to me. He was a well-known and much-feared son of a bitch. I knew he was connected with the Partido del Pueblo Unido, but he turned a deaf ear to all my allusions to my contacts.

When I saw Jimmy again after my questioning, he looked a little calmer. The cops had told him that I'd cleared him of any responsibility and that he was going to be freed.

'You can take it easy now. As soon as you're out, get in touch with Herman. If I haven't been turned loose by the end of the day, tell him to step in, but for the moment I prefer to handle it myself.'

We were kidding around when who should appear but Luis, the young inspector who'd interrogated me in Golfito and to whom I'd lent money for his fiancée's abortion. He was surprised to see me.

'Juan Carlos! What are you doing here?'

I explained the whole story.

'Look,' I said, 'I'd like you to do me a favour. I've got a feeling that this whole thing's a set-up. Can you check to see where the search warrant originated? They told me I was denounced by the hotel employees, who thought I looked suspicious. They're supposed to have talked about my 'shifty looks', but I don't believe a word of it. Will you see what you can find out?'

'Sure. I owe you at least that. Get in touch with me at the house as soon as you're out. How much grass did you have?'

'About five hundred grams, and I only accepted responsibility for possession.'

An hour later Jimmy was released, much relieved but very embarrassed.

'I don't know how to thank you, Juan Carlos. What you did is really decent.'

'It was nothing, buddy, and don't worry about me – we'll meet again soon.'

Then the cop who'd been in charge of my interrogation came to see me.

'We know you're not a dealer, but nevertheless we're going to bring you before the judge. Altamira said to eliminate the gun from the report, so you won't be charged with carrying an illegal weapon.'

I guess Altamira liked my Magnum and wanted to keep it for himself, which was why he left it out of the report. In any case, I never got it back.

The cuffs were put on again, and I was taken to the courthouse, where I waited several hours in the company of a uniformed cop who moved with me from place to place. Finally, I was brought before the judge – a sympathetic young woman whom I quickly won over.

'So far as I can see,' she said, 'the accusation of drug-trafficking doesn't stand up, and I'm going to ask that the charge be dismissed. Unfortunately, the final decision doesn't rest with me – only the tax inspector can set you free.'

'When can I see him?'

'He's not here today, but don't worry – I'm sure you'll be leaving us in a day or two.'

Shit! Things were becoming complicated.

I was taken to the central prison, where a clerk who looked more like a thief registered my things. I had my knapsack with me, and in it was everything I owned except for the gold left in the safe-deposit box. I had to hand over everything, including my jewels. (I had a small bag with a few emeralds bought as presents for my little mistresses.) I realized just in time that the cocksucking clerk had casually recorded them as merely 'green stones', while the nuggets I wore around my neck and wrists were described as 'yellow stones'. The son of a bitch must really have taken me for an idiot, but I had no intention of letting myself be robbed.

I got permission to telephone Jimmy, who came for my stuff. Both of us laughed about how I was dressed: I'd had to take off my own things and put on a pair of blue overalls that were too small for me, but I was allowed to keep my boots because they had no shoes my size, and my leather jacket because the gaol was none too warm.

* * *

When I arrived, it was too late to open a file on me, and I spent the night in a bare room with a cement floor: no cigarettes, nothing to eat, and no bed – I had to stretch out on the ground. Things were off to a bad start.

In the morning I had my first argument. The gaoler poured some slop they called coffee through the bars and spilled it over my sleeve with a purposely awkward gesture. I tried to grab him, but he retreated beyond my reach and all I could do was swear at him. Next we went on to the check-in formalities, and I was measured and photographed front and side with a big number across my chest. They even photographed my arm, to immortalize the Hong Kong tattoo on my wrist: a flower decorated with two marijuana leaves. It was my first police record, and I wasn't too happy about it. Sure, I'm an outlaw – since I tend to follow my own law, which I consider more just – but I'm certainly not a criminal.

As we were being transferred to a large room, I noticed that morning's gaoler watching us. I'd slept badly, I was irritated, and his superior air didn't sit right with me; I cursed him, he replied, and I grabbed him and started to choke him. Frightened, he called for help, and ten or more guards came running. I managed to calm down and diplomatically smooth things over in time, but the incident worried me: I always react violently to a lack of respect, and in prison there was always the risk that a guard would deliberately provoke me so he could have an excuse for shooting me down.

We finally got to a common room with about sixty beds, where the prisoners awaited their trial or the judge's decision.

On the third day I had a visit from Herman. When I got to the visiting-room he was seated behind the glass and for once he wasn't smiling. Irritated, I quickly got down to business, accused him of negligence, and demanded that he get me out of there immediately.

'It's all your fault and has nothing to do with me. You should never have had the grass bought in Limón, or given it to Jimmy, who was at the hotel. The only reason I'm here now is because I wanted to save Jimmy, who's serving a suspended sentence, but it was your grass! I've had to take all this shit in your place, so now get me out of here. You keep talking of protecting me, assuring my security, and here I am in the slammer! What he hell does it mean? Why haven't you got our people to intervene?'

'It's not that simple. Tino represents the puritan branch of the Caracas family and he's absolutely against any sort of drugs, so I can't speak to him unless we really have no other choice. The problem is

247

that the taxman has refused to let you go because he's convinced there's been dealing.'

'That's bullshit. You tell me you've got the best lawyers in the country – well, get them busy! There's absolutely no proof to support a charge of dealing, and it should be easy to get me out.'

'I'll do what I can, Juan Carlos.'

'You'd better, because there's something strange about all this. Now, listen, and listen hard. I have no intention of staying here any longer because of you. If I'm still here at the end of the week, I can promise you that *my* troubles will be nothing compared to yours. Just because I'm in here doesn't mean I don't have friends on the outside. You know me, and you know that I'm a man of my word.'

'But I assure you that it's a series of coincidences. I swear it.'

'That's not the problem. This is your fault – it's your grass and your stupidity, and that's enough for me. Get your arse in gear!'

Considering the interview closed, I got up and went back to the 'provisiona' detention room. I wasn't making idle threats: I could easily have got in touch with Wayne or René, who'd have been glad to help, and that's exactly what I intended to do if I wasn't out by the end of the week. Meanwhile, I got busy organizing myself. I still didn't know where the trouble was coming from, and I preferred to take my precautions, because for a few bucks it was very easy to have a prisoner put out of the way. I had won over a social worker named Maria, who helped me get some tranquillizers; that way, armed with a pair of scissors I stole from the infirmary, I could sleep a good part of the day and be awake at night, which was a good time for settling scores. I also convinced Maria that I couldn't keep prison food down, so she got me a special medical certificate that allowed me to have stuff sent in from outside.

The beds were only cement pallets fastened to the wall, but I'd managed to get a mattress and a blanket. I soon became popular because I had the guard buy ping-pong balls and rackets for the playroom, some soap and toothpaste for everybody, and some cleansing products for the toilets and the showers, which were really filthy. The guards knew me and let me move around freely, from the dorm to the recreation room – normally open only two hours a day – where we played ping-pong or watched television.

People were being held there on a variety of charges. I met an Osa gold prospector imprisoned for a ridiculous debt of 150 colones (about three dollars), so I gave him the money and he got out. Many of the men asked to work for me once they were free. I often strode around shouting 'Liberty for the Frenchman!' and after a while it became a sort of refrain. Sometimes one of the other prisoners would take it up, then everybody would chorus it.

By the end of a week I'd really had it. Herman had sent news that I'd be out on Thursday, but at seven that evening I was still cooling my heels. I seriously began to consider my theory of a trap. But, my God, how did they expect to profit from it? I was brooding over various schemes of vengeance when a guy dressed in civilian clothes asked to speak to me.

'Good evening, señor, I've come to tell you you're free.'

I was surprised and suspicious.

'On the level? Who are you?'

'Señor Garcia, from the Rosenberg office. Herman asked me to take care of your case and I got it thrown out. Get your things ready. You'll be free in an hour.'

I could have kissed him. I went back to the dorm yelling 'Liberty for the Frenchman' as loud as I could. Five minutes later, the whole room was roaring it, and it was to the tune of that music that the guard came to get me so I could complete the exit formalities. It was none too soon!

Herman was waiting for me at the gate, once again smiling.

'Look,' he said, leading me to his car, 'I've brought something to celebrate your liberation with.'

From the back seat, two women of easy virtue watched us and giggled.

'I've also got some coke,' he confided. 'The four of us are going to have a great time. I've reserved a suite at the Balmoral.'

The idea of celebrating with this big pig turned my stomach. In addition, I still had my suspicions about what had happened – so I accepted the coke but refused the celebration.

'You're making a mistake,' he said. 'The girls are great – they're lesbians and they put on a super show! I've had them both.'

All the more reason for saying no: I'd never take sloppy seconds after that pile of lard!

He was as friendly as could be, but I stayed cool and we mostly spoke of the mine. He gave me the latest news.

'Jimmy and the men left for Osa three days ago. They showed up on the tenth, completely broke. Lars, the Dane, came to see you, but I couldn't get him to wait. I told him you were in Nicaragua and having some trouble getting back in, some problem with a re-entry visa. He said he'd go up to the Quebrada del Frances about the nineteenth or the twentieth.'

*   *   *

249

Once I was alone, I tried to contact Luis, my buddy in the Narcotics Division. His wife answered the phone and said he'd been sent on a special mission to the Atlantic coast and that he'd left no message for me.

I picked up my stuff, went to celebrate my liberation at René's, and distributed my salvaged gifts to the little darlings.

René, to whom I told the story, warned me to be careful and made me promise to call on him for help in case other problems should spring up. I knew I could count on him.

I went back to Osa in a jeep driven by Fabio, a Malessa mechanic who was going to work at the mine. I'd brought along a new friend, King, a young Dobermann I intended to train in the mountains. He'd spent all his life cooped up, and was now a year old and as aggressive as you could want.

I went to Palmar to pick up a new employee, an accountant hired at Herman's request so he could look after my books: then, dropping Fabio, I left alone for Golfito to visit Wayne.

I'd withdrawn all my remaining gold – 3500 grams – from the bank because my celebrations had been expensive. I didn't want to keep it up on the mountain, but I did want it close at hand, and I had complete confidence in Wayne: he'd have been glad to take care of Herman if I'd asked him to. Since the police had kept my revolver, Herman had lent me an old .38 in such rotten condition that the chamber no longer turned automatically. Because I was used to the .357 Magnum, this felt like a toy to me, so Wayne sold me a second-hand .44 Magnum – a magnificent weapon, in perfect shape, that made even more noise and did more damage than the .357. Compared to it, the .38 seemed like a starting-gun.

I picked up the mechanic and the accountant in Palmar, and we went to Osa. Because it was the dry season, we had no problem following the road linking the Pan-American Highway to Puerto Jiménez. Our jeep was a Russian army model – big and solid but hard to manoeuvre because it was too heavy. With a heap like that a picnic becomes an adventure. Later Herman was supposed to send us something that would equip it to ride in the mud but, as it was, it was no more efficient than that taxi had been, and it only went a few hundred yards farther before grinding to a halt. For the second time, I had to do the stretch on foot, and my two new recruits were a little chilled.

When we got to Demesio's, I saw his horse. The owner himself wasn't there, but we'd presumably made peace, so I figured he'd have no objection to lending it to me and I finished the journey more comfortably.

* * *

The next morning I got up in a foul mood. There'd been time enough for me to see that camp discipline had broken down during the two weeks of vacation and that I'd better take my men in hand.

Such were my thoughts when I suddenly heard yelps of pain from King. Running out, I saw that he had a big gash on his nose.

'Barbaroja's cat scratched him,' Chiche told me, 'but the dog had it coming.'

The men were afraid of the dog and therefore all the more ready to take the side of the cat, which had gone feral after Barbaroja left. I could see it on the roof. I was itching to try my new revolver, and one shot flung the cat into the grass, where it limped away, wounded. Too bad, we'd never get to eat it. When Jimmy asked what he should do with Demesio's horse, I had it brought to me; a final pat on the head, and the thunder of the Magnum accompanied it to its last round-up. I'd made peace with Demesio, and as a good neighbour, he surely wouldn't want to see me go without meat.

The men were dumbfounded. They'd seen cows, pigs and chickens slaughtered, but never a horse. Horsemeat isn't generally eaten in Costa Rica, especially not in the country, where the animal is considered a work-tool, but I wanted to test the usefulness of Villanueva's son, Glandulon ('Fathead') – a former butcher – who'd decided to stay and work with us. He had the horse completely quartered and dressed in less than two hours. The table looked like a butcher's block, and the work was interesting to watch. I'd have liked to keep the hide, but that would have been pushing the joke too far. Demesio would probably guess who'd swiped his last horse, but it would never occur to him that it had been eaten. That's the way I am – I'm not spiteful, but I like to settle my accounts completely, and the thought of Demesio reduced to travelling on foot made me feel good.

Those two gunshots following one on the heels of another, gave the men a jolt and put them back in the mood. Once they'd got over their surprise, they joked about the trick played on Demesio and seemed pleased to have recovered their old team spirit so quickly. We went back to work that same day.

I'd promised the men that the operation would quickly be mechanized, but I no longer had any confidence in my partners and knew it might very well be months before we saw the first suction machine. Old Nizaro had told me he had one. Thanks to my money, he'd been able to build one of the handsomest houses in Guerra and no longer had to work, so I bought the machine from him.

It was a fairly old but serviceable model, and in exchange for it Fabio fixed up the motor of Herman's old prototype so that Nizaro could have electricity. The new machine made the work a lot easier; the ground still had to be broken with miner's bars, but the suction pump replaced the shovel. Because we were in the dry season, there was very little water in the quebrada, which made things difficult; and as I had a few doubts about the honesty of my partners I was reluctant to bust my balls working. All in all, getting the gold out by no matter what means was no longer the goal; the richness of the mine had been proved, and the time had come to exploit it industrially.

My most major and most immediate goal was to get ready for winter. I was tired of the mud and all the rest of it, and if I had to settle in for a year or two it would be in the greatest comfort ever known on Osa.

I therefore started building with a will. While Lars, who'd shown up with his son, supervised the reduced team at the quebrada, I had all the rest of the men busy clearing land and preparing the new installations; the camp became an enormous construction site. I called in all the Osa people who had chainsaws, and everyone cut down trees and prepared planks. I routinely signed on all the available help who showed up from the neighbouring villages, and I sometimes had as many as forty men running around every way from morning till night. The newcomers never stayed more than a day or two since they weren't used to the pace we worked at, and the old hands would palm off the hardest jobs on them. They'd been toughened by the ordeal of the first few months and felt vastly superior to the others, refusing to make things easier for anyone. When a newcomer complained, they proudly told him the story about how the generator was brought up, and other similar episodes. Faced with this tightly knit team, the others felt like intruders, so fewer and fewer people asked for work, and soon there was nobody but the old-timers.

In the mean time a number of buildings had sprung from the soil. The skidder had been repaired and came and went all the time, transporting material. Every day thousands of leaves were cut to make roofs, and as soon as the planks of a building had been put together the floor was immediately cemented: the city grew like a mushroom. The camp was completely surrounded by wooden and barbed-wire fences, and enormous red and white signs warned future passers-by: PRIVATE PROPERTY, NO ENTRANCE, BEWARE OF GUARD DOGS. Though I had only the one dog, he was fierce enough for two. In the middle of the jungle, the sight of those signs placed five yards apart was more than a little surprising.

There was only one entrance – a swinging gate with a guardhouse

252

alongside it. Octagonal-shaped and five yards in diameter, the attractive building was the only round house on Osa, and in it lived Mario, a new employee whom I'd appointed guard because he was an extraordinary shot: he could do marvels with a .22 and never missed, whatever the size of his target. His orders were to prevent anyone from entering the camp by using a very simple method – first, a warning shot over the head, then a bullet between the eyes.

Marcella hadn't come back, so he also took on the duties of cook, and since there was nobody to take care of my personal affairs I asked him to bring his wife. He was reluctant, since she would be the only woman, but a little speech to my men and my public authorization to Mario to shoot the first man who was disrespectful to his wife reassured him. Between the two of them they handled the duties of guard, messenger, gardener, valet, cook and household help. They were very well paid but, on the other hand, they promised to take no vacations for a year.

The men now had a separate dorm – a fifteen-by-thirty-foot house, in which each of them had his own bed, sheets and mattress. Jimmy, Lars and the accountant shared one wing of the first building, and I occupied the rest after having the interior partitions knocked down. My quarters were off-limits to everyone except Mario and his wife. An electrician had come to install a battery-operated internal phone system that linked the quebrada, the guard's house and my room. Its original function was to make it possible for Mario to warn me, wherever I might be, of the possible arrival of a visitor; in practice, it was mostly used in the other direction: I didn't fall asleep until late in the evening and, if in the middle of the night I felt like having a cup of coffee, all I had to do was crank the handle and a few minutes later Mario or his wife, their eyes heavy with sleep, would bring it to my bedside. Such small comforts eventually made the jungle quite inhabitable.

Among the other constructions were a shower-building, a kitchen, storage sheds, etc. I began work on a mess-hall, an enormous round building with a sloping roof of the kind never seen on Osa. Buildings were set down as the land was cleared, and there was one amusing result: the dynamite-shed had initially been off by itself, but as the other buildings went up it eventually ended right in the middle of the camp.

Despite all the construction, I had by no means called a halt to production. I made only one inspection tour a day down at the quebrada, but there was always one team working under the supervision of Jimmy or Lars, who proved a very efficient assistant.

Dumbfounded by the amount of work being done, he said that in his twenty-five years in Costa Rica he'd never seen Ticos sweat so hard and enjoy it so much.

I didn't push to raise the gold production because I was counting on the machines and didn't want my men to bust their balls. In addition, I had no intention of overwhelming Herman and company with gifts as long as I still had even the slightest suspicions. I did just enough work to cover the outlay for supplies and labour.

Every new hand who signed on with us for a while did a training stint in the hole. Fabio was surprised by that requirement: because of his status as a mechanic, he considered himself above it all, but he soon learned that at the Quebrada del Frances everything had to be earned. On his second day that little guy watched the others struggling in the mud.

'Why the hell are you standing around doing nothing?' I asked him.

'I was signed on as a mechanic. In Malessa I was told that I'd be chief engineer.'

'We're not in Malessa, so dive in and pray you get results if you ever want to get out of the water.'

The accountant also had to have his egalitarian bath. A pure-blooded Indian who'd had considerable schooling, he was very thin with arms like wires and a supple stride that soon won him the nickname Pink Panther. His fairly long hair was carefully combed, his features were regular, and he wore the large spectacles of an intellectual. A timid fellow, he said very little, and because he was well brought up he never uttered a vulgar word – in other words, a dreamer who'd somehow wandered into a world of brutes.

In the beginning, I had to protect him and give him his own room, because his feminine facial features had excited Barbas and Cunado. Though hired as an accountant, he did just about everything but accounting, which was the least of my worries. Since he was incapable of lifting a shovel, I put him on the canoa, gently explaining that he could do the accounting if he wanted to – but only after working hours. Initially reserved and calm, he soon changed and quickly became as vulgar and crude as the others. As his muscles developed, he asserted himself and proved to have a nasty vicious personality; it wasn't a good idea to turn your back on him if you'd been less than polite. At first, he kept up with his accounting, but after a few weeks an overindulgence in booze and grass turned his once impeccable account-books into a fucking mess, and he soon got rid of them.

He and Fabio were subjected to the usual tricks. As a professional mechanic, Fabio was invited to start up the generator while his friends and buddies looked on and then collapsed with laughter when the crank split his cheekbone. When Chiche suggested that he try his new muscles, the Pink Panther had no more success. To the great joy of White, who felt he'd discovered a blood brother, for a week the Pink Panther's lips looked like two purple-red sausages.

For Puntarenas, the training period had been different. A Drake fisherman who was always laughing and kidding around, he'd come with his chainsaw to turn out planks. When we'd built up an ample supply, he asked as a favour if he couldn't take a turn in the hole. I immediately agreed. Unfortunately, he was barely four feet four and kept losing his footing; despite his desire to do well, he was of no use because the water came up to his lips, and since he couldn't stop kidding around he often got a mouthful. I had to put him on the canoa before he drowned. His constant good humour won him everybody's affection, yet he also knew how to make himself respected.

Glandulon, the son of former Lieutenant Villanueva, was the fifth of our new recruits, as dumb as he was strong – and God knows he was sturdy! Because he was naïve and credulous, the others always took advantage of his simplicity, but they never went too far since he packed quite a punch. He was probably the only one of the crew to have an honest past, though his father more than made up for it. As a former butcher, he was an ideal recruit because, thanks to Mario's rifle, there was an abundance of game. He wolfed down everything in sight, and he was one of the few who voluntarily ate the horsemeat. To keep the latter from going to waste, I had had to have it dried and mixed with game, but nothing bothered Glandulon: his stomach could take everything – even Barbaroja's cat.

It had in fact shown up again while we were all eating; my bullet had taken off its two rear legs and it crawled around on stumps, miaowing wretchedly. On one side, the wound had healed over, exposing white dry bone; on the other, gangrene had set in, and the odour was unbearable. Cats are said to have extraordinary resistance and, having seen that one, I could believe it. It had been dragging around like that for a week, and I quickly gave it the relief it had come looking for. Only Glandulon was tempted to see what it tasted like; the others were nauseated. With Glandulon around, I felt that if one of my boys ever had a fatal accident I'd have to count his limbs before burying him.

Thanks to the skidder, which valiantly struggled to earn the price of the gasoline it used, I'd improved the road leading to the camp and was able to have the jeep brought in. It was soon equipped with tractor tyres, which made it look like an enormous insect, but it was the only automobile that could climb the mountain. Within my property I travelled only by car. White – whose diplomacy and efforts to obtain an easy job merited reward – piloted me around to the different work-sites. Every time we stopped, White, standing on his seat, would read a passage from the Bible to the men, then tear out the page and roll an enormous joint that I lit up and passed around. White always took several deep puffs, and by the end of the day, collapsed on his seat, he would have trouble spotting the trees.

We were no longer as isolated as we'd been, and while the dry season lasted it was easy to drive to Puerto Jiménez, about twenty-five miles away. A good driver could make the round trip in a day, and Jimmy, White, Barbas or Fabio would often go in the jeep to sell the gold at the bank or make some purchases. They always used the buddy system, and in case of an accident or a breakdown one would go for help while the other stood guard over the equipment. Jimmy was once again turning my envelope over to the new chief of police, from whom I also bought coke, which Jimmy brought back. That was what enabled me to put up with all the delays while I waited for Herman to get things moving.

From time to time, to keep the boys from growing soft and to swell the gold receipts, I'd decree an extended work-day. For a week I'd have everybody work at the quebrada in three eight-hour shifts. As for myself, stimulated by the coke, I got no more than an occasional hour's sleep here and there, which increased my bad humour. My constant outbursts frightened everyone: when I decided to slow down again, all the men were relieved – until the next time.

One evening I suddenly decided to change my appearance, and I shaved my head. In the morning everybody kept looking at me, uncertain as to whether or not they ought to laugh. At noon I picked up a pair of scissors and called to Puntarenas, the only one who'd made fun openly. A smile on his lips, he came over and sat opposite me. A few snips of the scissors, a touch-up with a razor – and Punt-arenas looked a lot different. Then it was Cunado's turn, and eventually they were all given the treatment. At first a few of them hung back, but soon they were horsing around and shoving to be next. In a little while, everyone looked like a billiard ball. They cut each other's hair, and the appearance of each shiny new head was greeted with shouts and cheers.

The new look suited some but not others. Though Miguel ended up with something that looked like a big pumpkin, Cunado's skull looked like a big cock with ears. The atmosphere became festive, and it was great. They felt each other's head or rubbed them against one another, enjoying the new sensation, pointing to one another, and bursting into laughter. Almost all of them had had long hair, pounds of which were now heaped up in the room. Puntarenas suggested weaving a blanket of it and hanging it on the wall with the other trophies; Barbas stuffed some into a T-shirt to make a comfortable pillow.

The spectacle of those twenty-five smooth round heads was amazing. White, the only exception, had an Iroquois cut, and it actually made him look more intelligent. Jimmy had used his elephant ears as an excuse for escaping the clippers – the only one to do so; I'd spared him because he so often had to go into town. Three guys who had come from Vanegas for a few days also got the treatment. Carried away by the general enthusiasm, they joyously joined in, and I later learned that when they returned home their wives had wept and the whole village had treated them as though they had the plague. The fashion caught on, and all those shaven heads added to the image of the group. Even more than a uniform, it became a distinguishing mark.

In the mean time camp life had become easier, and every Saturday we slaughtered one another in an organized fashion: I had a piece of land cleared and built two soccer goals. Jimmy brought a ball back from Golfito, and the men divided into two teams for some friendly matches – friendly only in a manner of speaking, because the games were often very violent. As good Latin Americans, they were all extremely enthusiastic, but with the exception of myself – whose career as a soccer-player had come to an abrupt end when I was unfortunately expelled from the league – nobody had ever touched a soccer ball. The games were something between Rugby and boxing matches, because the rules were very flexible. Taking advantage of their respect for me, I scored goal after goal, kicking everything that got in my way. God help the man who did the same to me – he risked being in the hole for a week.

Among themselves, the men went at it hot and heavy, and as often as not the matches ended in a free-for-all. Nobody dared serve as referee, because the decisions of the first of that breed had been contested rather roughly – and in any case my side always won, because I'd forbidden the other team to score too many points lest it be deprived of its weekly relaxation. I hated losing, and they knew it.

Originally reserved for Saturday relaxation, the matches were eventually played several times a week if I was bored and my men not too tired. It was during one of those matches, while King the guard dog was busy persuading Barbas not to score, that a small white piece of arse surmounted by a blonde head came into view walking along the road from Guerra. Sophie!

My favourite nympho in the flesh. She explained that she had a week's vacation and had come directly from Frankfurt to see me. More than six thousand miles, to say nothing of the walk through the jungle, just so she could be treated like an animal! It showed that she was either an adventuress born and bred – or a masochist.

Apparently, my feminist had come to be dominated and mistreated far from the eyes of others, I decided in amusement. I could see no other explanation. I don't want to boast, but I've been around enough to know how to make any woman worth the trouble get her jollies. Unfortunately, my egoism and my misogyny tend to make me most concerned with my own pleasure, and at my age I no longer feel I have to prove anything. But the fact that she'd returned after the treatment I gave her both surprised and excited me, and without giving her time to rest I took her to the shower to give her a thorough scrubbing. Then once she'd been cleaned up I explained a few subtleties of the game and scored a few unnatural goals. Fortunately, she'd had a chance to mend since the last time. You have to admit that I know how to dispense hospitality: within fifteen minutes of her arrival she'd been washed and sodomized. Who could offer more?

I was glad to have a new toy with which to inaugurate my new house, and I spent the night staking my claim. During the day, partly hidden by a tree, I kept an eye on the work at the quebrada without dismounting from my lady love. The next night the treatment was more of the same. Early in the morning she left me – you might say she fled me – by taking advantage of the fact that Jimmy was going to Puerto Jiménez. She hadn't lasted very long this time, and it seemed unlikely that she'd return.

Work at the quebrada went on in slow motion, and I no longer knew what to build. Since I was bored, I went off once a week, taking a trip to Jiménez every Saturday morning with fifteen different men. White, a very skilful con man, always managed to be a member of the group by working out a deal with someone. I had no qualms about leaving the place under Mario's guard, because the camp's reputation, the numerous discouraging signs, and the welcome given to our rare visitors assured its tranquillity.

We left in the jeep with Jimmy at the wheel, me alongside him, and fifteen men, the maximum I could carry, piled in the rear. There were men everywhere – on the seats, standing on the bumpers, clinging in clusters to the frame of the roof. It was an epic ride.

From time to time the jolts would make some of the men lose their hold and they had to run after the car until the next hill. To lighten the load, they'd get off at every ascent and race to the top before piling in again. The vehicle had battery problems and it never stopped. More than once a man who hadn't been fast enough was left behind in the forest. Since by the time they reached Jiménez they were covered with mud, they soon worked out a system: they'd leave camp wearing shorts or briefs and carrying their clean clothes in a plastic bag. At the crossing of the last river before Jiménez the car would stop, and they'd wash, primp and dress so as to make an impeccable entrance into the city. Our two-day celebrations were completely on me, and I was open-handed. The first thing I did was take them all to the Indija, the Jiménez brothel – a filthy shed in which four big disgusting whores worked. The men's ease in brawling was matched by their awkward-ness with the ladies. It was funny to see them, a towel in hand, lining up to take their turn. They kidded around and gambled, but when the time came to cross the threshold they blushed like boys and called the whores 'Madame'.

More than once, especially at the beginning, the impatient whores would grab them by the handle and lead them off to do their duty. Afterwards to hear the men talk you'd think they fucked better than anybody in the world. . . . Cunado boasted of his prowess in oral sex, and when I manifested disgust he said very grandly: 'For me, a whore is always a lady.'

The hell she was! After she'd been with fifty guys she was more of a stew than a lady!

Eventually, he confessed the real reason. 'It's this way. When they see how I'm hung, they all refuse.'

I finally understood his love for the mare.

A few weekends later, it was Cunado's birthday and he was solemnly led to the brothel. I was seated at the house bar with those men who'd already been serviced, when a naked whore burst into the room cursing Cunado, who followed her looking like an unhappy little boy. A towel was wrapped around his waist, and his anomaly banged around his thighs.

'Don Juan Carlos,' he said sadly, 'she doesn't want to.'

'Give him a hand,' I said to my men, who'd collapsed laughing. Such a lack of professional conscience deserved to be punished.

Eager to please their buddy, White, Chiche, Fabio and Miguel caught the lady and spread-eagled her on the floor. Keeping her pinned in that position, they signalled to Cunado and sang: 'Happy birthday to you, happy birthday to you.' Cunado – touched to tears by

259

such attentions, and his ardour multiplied tenfold by coke – rushed at his present and began to plough away furiously. The cries of the whore and the lustily bawled song drew a few rubbernecks, who kidded around as they watched the rare spectacle. Even the initially shocked barman joined in the chorus.

After that, Cunado and a good number of my men were denied entrance to the brothel, and on several occasions we had to force the door.

Every Saturday evening there was a ball in Jiménez at the Rancho de Oro or some other bar. The appearance of a military vehicle with fifteen men with shaven heads could hardly go unnoticed. Everybody admired the jeep and the men, very proud, pretended to be casual. We soon became known, and as we entered the room the singer would announce the arrival of 'the people from the Quebrada del Frances' as my men swelled with pride. I should add, however, that they weren't very polite and that their behaviour left something to be desired: abstinence, alcohol and the need to provoke drove them to squeeze every arse that passed within range. Brawls often broke out, but our number and reputation soon restored calm. The people in Jiménez weren't exactly peace-loving, but they were cowed, so we could do pretty much as we pleased.

On one occasion, we were for once quietly seated at our table when a little scuffle broke out between a man and a woman in front of us. She kept slapping his face, and the man, obviously inhibited by some vestigial gallantry, was trying to calm her without slapping her in return. Finally, in exasperation, he gave her an enormous whack that laid her out flat. Some of the other men in the bar grabbed the guy and started dragging him outside, others tried to defend him, and in a few minutes the dance-hall was an enormous battlefield as eighty men, pleased with the opportunity, were busy killing one another. Chairs, tables and bottles flew in every direction; the field spread, and the battle continued outside. A little way off, we settled into the jeep so as to have front-row seats for the show. Immediately in front of us, a woman prospector with enormous arms caught up one guy after another and knocked him out with a single punch. Everywhere around, men were going at one another helter-skelter simply for the fun of it all.

Little by little the brawl changed locale and surrounded our vehicle. The men were scratching the paint, and we tried to move them away – at first politely and then with energetic kicks in the head: the gentle-faced accountant had one of them trapped under the jeep and, gripping him by the hair, was driving his heel into his skull.

Then somebody yelled, 'Death to foreigners,' and the cry was

260

followed by 'Death to the Frenchman', and in a few minutes every-body had focused on a common enemy. Since the mob looked threatening and they were talking of overturning the jeep, I drew my gun and made them keep their distance. Jimmy and others who were armed immediately imitated me, while the rest started pushing the jeep to make it start. When we piled in, the abuse began again, and a few bottles flew through the air. Jimmy, plastered, was at the wheel and drove forward a few yards – then suddenly saw red. Wheeling round, he drove right into the thick of the crowd, and as several men screamed and jumped aside he drew his gun and fired. In two seconds, everyone was hugging the ground, and the cursing stopped. We rode off to the sound of terrified cries.

When we got to the courtyard of the hotel, where every weekend six rooms were reserved for us, I hid all the non-declared arms; a police chief can be bribed, but if a death has taken place before witnesses there isn't much he can do. Jimmy, who'd sobered up, was biting his fingernails, and the rest of the men had collapsed wherever they could to catch a little sleep while Miguel mounted guard. In the morning I went for news and learned that the cops had just ignored the whole situation. From that day on, nobody in Jiménez tangled with us – but as a safety precaution my men always grouped together.

Every weekend the celebration went on until the men collapsed dead drunk. We'd start back on Monday morning at about five, after I'd kicked awake those who were the least drunk and they'd helped me load the others into the jeep.

Once back at the mine, I set everyone to work. They could barely stand up, and it was a load of semi-corpses that I'd take from the vehicle to the hole, into which they were roughly thrown by those who hadn't taken part in the celebration.

Those men knew the scenario, because they'd lived through it themselves, and as soon as they saw the jeep they came running to unload. Stimulated by their bitterness against the revellers, they heaved them through the air and into the hole. The cold water woke the men up, but some who had been carelessly thrown didn't always make it into the water. Chiche had his head split on a boulder; and Raphael, in a complete alcoholic stupor, once floated on the surface until the men took him out half-drowned and laid him on a rock to dry.

But the spree remained a basic necessity for them. They knew that outside the camp anything went, and they kept trying to see how far they could go. On the way back one morning, when for some reason they weren't drunk, we picked up every domestic animal we came across; the men raced after the chickens and the pigs – and, as you can well imagine, that evening we ate like kings. On every trip, coming and going, I'd knock down Demesio's fences, which he'd tirelessly repair.

When Herman came back to see us, he brought a two-way radio, a gadget I considered useless, though he told me it was 'very expensive'. He was accompanied by his son, a twelve-year-old kid who had the unheard-of luck of finding a 150-gram nugget in the canoa.

Relations between Herman and me had changed, and it was difficult to discuss things; as long as I still had doubts, I was incapable of speaking normally to him. When I looked at him, I began to think that he'd set up that whole business in San José, and I wanted to kill him. He knew about the sprees in Jiménez and the fuss we kicked up, and it made him uneasy.

'Have you got any gold out?'

'Yes, a little.'

'Do you have any for me?'

'No, I produce just enough to cover camp expenses and entertainment.'

'Why are you doing so little work?'

'Come along, and I'll explain.'

I took him to the quebrada and showed him the wall of rock rising into the air about twenty feet above the hole.

'Look at that,' I said. 'It could collapse at any moment, and if it does I'm sure to lose five or six men. I don't intend to sacrifice lives because you haven't kept your fucking promises. We can't work by hand any more – we need the machines, and there'll be no production until you get the permit.'

It wasn't that I suddenly had an exaggerated respect for the law, but I didn't care to spend the rest of my life in the mountains. So far as I was concerned, the best use that could be made of the mine would be to sell it to some big company for several million dollars. But before this could be done our papers had to be in order: I didn't want any trouble with the Ministry of Geology and Mines.

Herman didn't remain in the camp long, but two weeks later he was back to repair the radio. I had quietly managed to break it, because he'd call every day and the daily check irritated me.

I was having coffee with Herman when a truck loaded with men appeared. Except for our own vehicle, it was the first one to come up that road. Giving no heed to the warning signs, the driver got out and opened the gate. Mario was in the kitchen, and I sent White to stop them, but they paid no attention and continued on. I didn't know who they were, but they were about to learn that you couldn't defy me without paying the penalty. Getting into position, I took aim at the driver so as to stop them in no uncertain manner.

The truck immediately came to a halt, and the driver dived under the dashboard. The man alongside him jumped down and shouted: 'Don't shoot. Herman! Hey, Herman!'

'Don't shoot,' said Herman in a strained voice. 'It's Adriano.'

Adriano Caracas, a half-brother of Tino, was the family terror. He'd been a mercenary in Nicaragua and had a bad reputation; his swindles, unpunished because of his name, were always in the papers. Jimmy knew him and told me he was a dangerous type. What had that snake come here for?

The men piled out of the truck, Adriano coming first. To my surprise, he was a shrimp with the well-trimmed beard of an egghead. Behind him was a heavy guy about seven feet tall. His body was going to rack and ruin but, though at first sight he seemed like any other flabby gringo, his piercing eyes indicated an unusual intelligence. That was Carano, an American sought by Interpol, a man who lent his services to the corrupt branch of the Caracas family. Next came two other gringos – bodyguards covered with tattoos, nasty bastards, probably mercenaries or escaped prisoners. Then came some ten determined-looking Ticos – henchmen. Adriano's gang in its entirety.

They were widely known, and on the Río Tigre they had just pulled off a scam that had netted several million dollars. This branch of the family was said to use the brains of Americans on the run, the most famous of whom was Robert Vesco. They granted them political exile and made sure that American extradition demands never led anywhere, and in exchange for their protection the Caracases made use of those men to swindle their countrymen with impunity. Anyone who objected ran the risk of ending in gaol or at the bottom of a ditch.

I had no idea what Adriano wanted but, though he might be the son of the president, he wasn't about to dictate the law here. Protected by his name, he'd counted on intimidating me and had therefore been far from expecting such a reception. My initial response to their arrival, my almost total lack of interest when I was told his name, and my twenty-five shaven-headed men who watched him in silence made it clear that he'd lost the game. While he talked to Herman, I remained silent. I had the Magnum in my holster and my .38 in my belt. Those – in addition to my silence and a shaven head that did nothing to soften my expression – made him uneasy, and he kept glancing at me nervously. Carano had put on dark glasses, but I could see he was also watching me out of the corner of his eye.

As I walked away, Adriano said: 'Is that the French mercenary?'

His voice trembled with hatred. Without a word having been spoken, without a blow having been struck, he'd lost face before everybody. He was white with frustrated rage. A small man he knew that here in any case even his name wouldn't keep him from being booted in the arse.

He'd come as a conqueror, but now he had Herman ask me for permission to visit the mine.

'OK,' I said, 'but I'm going with them.'

Adriano, Carano, the two gringos and Valverde – a corrupt ministry lawyer – went into the jungle. I brought up the rear. I still hadn't said a word. They all sat on a felled tree while Herman showed them the hole, but I remained standing silently behind them. After ten minutes, Adriano, still ill at ease, gave the signal to depart, and they rapidly left the jungle.

When they reassembled at their truck, I counted them and I wasn't sure they were all there. Grabbing Jimmy's carbine, I gave it to Lars.

'Go see if any of those cocksuckers stayed behind at the quebrada. If you see one, just put a bullet in his head.'

'With pleasure,' he replied. 'I never did like these sons of bitches.'

They were all aware of my order, and the silence grew heavy. Shortly afterwards, Lars returned, disappointed not to have found anyone. Everyone piled into the truck and left.

To give them a last look at my puss, I escorted them in the jeep as far as Vanegas before turning back. That was a close one, I thought. Those weren't the usual softies we'd had visiting; men like them aren't likely to retreat in the face of danger. Carano was very sharp. What they'd lacked was a leader, a real one: Adriano hid behind his name. His father must have been one hell of a guy, but Adriano was a four-flusher, a contemptible bastard who for lack of anything else counted on the power of his reputation.

As I saw it, they'd come to take over the mine. The name Caracas, the unsettling look of the bodyguards and henchmen, the presence of the expert Carano, the legal cover provided by the lawyer were enough, they'd thought, to intimidate us. However, instead of finding themselves among some terrified and resigned peasants, there they were in a paramilitary camp surrounded by men ready to obey my slightest command! Given the situation, all they could do was disguise the warlike expedition as a courtesy call. Adriano wasn't going to forget that.

Jimmy was very happy. For years he'd been considered a lackey by the entire Caracas clan, but for once he was on the right side of events.

'Adriano asked me if you'd have fired at him knowing who he was. I said yes, and that sent a chill down his back.'

In high spirits, Herman told me about his talk with Adriano.

'So I told him: "Look, Adriano, we won this mine with bullets and nobody's going to take it from us. That's why we reacted so strongly." '

I found myself thinking: who's this 'we', windbag? No doubt about it – there wasn't one Tico who was worth more than another; they were all useless.

About Easter time, I stopped all work at the quebrada. I was concerned that the cliff might collapse at any moment, and my men had become more than mere employees to me.

Every year at this time, Herman organized an outing for the men who worked for him. Malessa had a pretty good soccer team, and he now suggested by radio that we have a friendly match between it and the Quebrada del Frances men on the Rincón field. I accepted with pleasure, because my boys were tired of slaughtering one another.

The day of the match, we went down to Rincón. Half the men were in the jeep and the other half ran along behind it. The Malessa employees had set up a tent and been waiting for us since the day before. At my request, Herman had brought shoes and T-shirts bearing a simple design – a nugget surrounded by the words 'Quebrada del Frances Sports Club'.

Before the match, the two teams posed for pictures, and the contrast was amazing. On the one hand, the Malessa team – fourteen long-haired young men wearing their uniforms with ease and smiling at the photographer; on the other, the Quebrada team – twenty squat guys with shaven heads and scraggly beards giving the camera the finger and shoving to be in the front row.

The referee, a man from Rincón, frisked my team and confiscated the revolvers, knives and knuckledusters that just happened to be in our pockets. Then the game began.

For the first time, my men had football boots, and they weren't used to the studs. Several – including Miguel, who had very big feet – quickly tossed them away and played either barefoot or in rubber boots. The Malessa team was well trained and knew the rules; my people hardly knew where the ball should go, but they had aggressiveness to spare. At half-time Malessa was winning 2 to 0 – though it was 3 to 1 in our favour when it came to wounded players.

The second half was more animated, with my team using more subtle tricks. Miguel, the goalie, was mortified that somebody had scored against him, and when the game began again he discreetly grabbed the opposing forward and flattened him with a whack on the neck; carried away by the heat of action, he went for the wrong ball and put a dent in his adversary's nuts. Every time one of the Malessa team came too near our goal, the half-backs sneakily pounded him until he changed his mind. Though the referee had been bribed, he had no choice but to send some of the men off – but they went back into the game as soon as he looked away. At one point there were twenty Quebrada men on the field.

The opposing team was nevertheless very strong, and the more we knocked out of the game the more they scored. A desperate attempt by Eduardo, who ran with the ball, failed despite the fact that White and Barbas cleared the way for him. Luckily, the loss of his shorts didn't handicap Puntarenas, who – profiting from his small stature – slipped around the opposing defence and kicked the goalkeeper in the shins while their team was busy scoring another goal. Eventually the survivors of the other team refused to play, and Herman, seeing his men going down one by one, called for an end to the match. When the referee, who'd taken refuge off the field and was treating a black eye, blew the whistle for the end of the match, I was running after José the mechanic, who'd brushed me with his elbow, while with the help of some instructive kicks Mario, Cunado and Raphael were explaining something to Pablo the accountant, who'd had the courage – or thoughtlessness – to play.

When the match ended, though the score was 12 to 3 in their favour, the body count was 13 to 2 in favour of the Quebrada del Frances Sports Club.

After those memorable moments I gave the men a week off. Most remained in the south spending their pay on celebrations. Mario couldn't take it any longer and refused to remain alone at the mine with his family, so I fired him, giving his job to Puntarenas, who was glad of this new post which enabled him to look after me. Turning the camp over to him, I headed the jeep for San José with Jimmy and several of the men who wanted to spend the week in town.

As soon as I arrived, I slipped away from all of them – including Jimmy – and got in touch with Luis, the narcotics agent, who was supposed to fill me in on what had happened during my earlier arrest.

He was a bit reserved on the phone.

'I've got what you asked me for,' he said, 'but I'd rather not discuss it on the phone. Can you come over to my place this evening without anyone seeing you?'

'Sure. What time?'

'About midnight would be fine.'

There was no need to draw me a diagram: I suspected the nature of the news. That evening, we quickly got down to business.

'What I'm going to tell you is confidential, so promise me never to reveal who gave you this information!'

'I give you my word.'

'Good. I discreetly questioned the cops who arrested you, and it had nothing to do with a complaint. The order to go into action had come from Altarmira, chief of the Narcotics Division. He told them to go right to the Hotel Astoria and arrest a Frenchman – he gave a description of you – who had a package of marijuana and a revolver, and he even warned them to be careful because the guy was dangerous. As you can see, there never was a denunciation from the hotel – the order came from above. Is that what you wanted to know?'

'Exactly, and I really thank you, Luis.'

'Glad to have been able to return a favour. Don't forget – you never talked to me. Goodbye.'

So I hadn't been wrong: the bastards had really betrayed me. The only ones who'd known what hotel I was staying at were Herman and his accountant, so nobody else could have given this information to Altamira. But which of the two had done it? Pablo, as a personal revenge? Herman, as part of some scheme? I figured that both had been involved. They were probably trying to put a scare into me. As a leader, I was dangerous to them; they wanted me to act like a humble employee of the all-powerful Caracases. It was a hard blow to take, and the revelation really shook me. Damn it, why did everyone have to cheat? Well, they weren't going to get away with it – all I needed was a little time to protect my rear.

But one big question still remained: why had they done what they did? What did it get them? If they'd simply wanted to steal the mine, it would have been easy enough to leave me in the slammer. But it had been Herman's lawyer who'd obtained my release. And what good had it done them since the charges had been dismissed and I was completely clean? I didn't believe that my threats had forced them to free me, and I couldn't understand what they were up to.

During the several days I spent in San José I kept asking myself what would be the best thing to do. It had been a shock, but it wouldn't make me flee the country with my tail between my legs. I'm not the man to refuse a challenge. On the contrary – if I'm provoked, I pay back with interest. But what should my attitude be? My mine was too rich for me to risk everything by acting impulsively. Though I'd have enjoyed cutting Herman's balls off, it was premature – it would be best not to let them suspect anything, just let the situation develop and try to see where the next blow would come from. The game promised to be amusing.

I had one advantage. They didn't know that I was aware of their scheming. With time enough to prepare, I'd be the one to call the tune – as long as they gave me enough time.

At the end of the week, I left for the mountains without seeing Herman again. I simply wrote him a note telling him I was leaving and asking him to send to the mine any of my men who got in touch with him. Despite all my resolutions, I knew I was incapable of speaking naturally to him or of playacting; I wouldn't be able to keep myself from slamming the cocksucker against a wall. All that hypocritical pretence of friendship, those smiles, the invitation to his home! To get me, he'd even been willing to sacrifice Jimmy and, despite their long friendship, coolly set him up for a five-year stint in the slammer. One day or another, Herman would have to pay!

Two days before I left, a fairly serious earthquake shook the country. Whole sections of mountains had collapsed on the Pan-American Highway, and the trip from north to south would take longer than ever. The epicentre had been Golfito, and the farther down I went, the more uneasy I became about the mine. Though in San José the damage hadn't been great, I knew that regions farther south had been hard hit. The metal structure of the Palmar bridge had suffered, and it was open to traffic only a few hours a day: on the Rincón road, sulphurous sand had poured down from the big splits. The closer I got to the mine, the more damage I saw.

When I got to the camp, I was relieved to see that it didn't seem to have been touched. But then Puntarenas, highly excited, led me to the work-site, which was a disaster area: the entire cliff had collapsed into the hole, and dozens of cubic yards had plugged up the section we'd been working. Luckily, the earthquake had taken place while the mine was closed – a few days earlier and the landslide would have buried dozens of my men. Even so, it was a bad break, and from now on all hand labour was impossible. Given the shortage of water, it would take weeks for the suction machine to clean the hole, and there was still the danger that the rest of the cliff might collapse at any time.

At the moment, all I could do was wait for the machines. Using the radio, which more or less worked, I informed Herman that unless he sent them to me quickly all mining would come to a halt. He told me he was hoping to get a one-month waiver that would permit their use but, so far as I could see, nothing was happening.

To fill the days, I had several different sites opened so I could test the richness of my property at the lowest geological levels. The results were positive everywhere, and sometimes there were even indications of gold on the surface. The mine was really fantastic – if only those Malessa arseholes would let me be until I could get in touch with European companies interested in large-scale operations on Osa. If only they didn't ruin everything for me! In any case, I felt at home at the Quebrada del Frances, and I intended to settle in comfortably despite their machinations.

The work on the mess-hall continued. I was very proud of it, because it was the largest building on the peninsula – a sort of monument to my obsession with grandeur. Its roof formed a point twenty-five feet high. Meanwhile, Lars had left me – no doubt worried about the education of his son, whom exposure to my men was turning into a real hoodlum – and I'd taken over the whole house for my personal use and had a ten-foot-wide bed built, but I felt a little lonely in it. Celibacy had been all right during the first days of struggle, but I was planning to stay in the mountains and had no intention of living an ascetic life. In addition, given the present uncertainty – a real Sword of Damocles – I had no idea if the adventure would last, and I wanted to profit from it as much as I could, to refuse myself no pleasure. Little by little I planned to set up a harem in the mountains.

Puntarenas and his wife came from Osa and knew a lot of people on the peninsula. I sent them everywhere as heralds to announce that Don Juan Carlos wanted to get married and was ready to examine all propositions – providing that those propositions were pretty virgins and were no more than fifteen.

I'd once or twice seen an attractive girl, of a beauty unusual on the peninsula, pass by the camp – an adorable mestiza. Puntarenas knew her and had gone to the grandfather she lived with to announce the good news.

'Don Juan Carlos is interested in your girl.'

A few days later the old gentleman brought his granddaughter to the camp. Before leaving her, he insisted on justifying himself morally by discussing the terms of the transaction. The old man was interested in a possible marriage: after all, I had a certain local reputation and people knew that the mine was very rich. Being the father-in-law of someone as important as myself would be a social promotion for him.

'I can promise nothing,' I told him. 'First, I have to see if she's worthy of being one of my women. If she suits me, she can stay.'

'Oh, she'll give you complete satisfaction. Julia is very well brought up and has never known a man.'

I sincerely hoped so. In any case, it was a *sine qua non*, because on

269

Osa incest was common and I didn't care to take sloppy seconds after that old geezer.

He made me promise that, if by chance she didn't suit me, I wouldn't just toss her out like some slut but bring her back to him. Except for the old man's servile attitude, the haggling wasn't at all sordid. The young girl wasn't a cow being led to slaughter; she was aware of the transaction and coming of her own free will. I wasn't a matinée idol, but all she could look forward to otherwise was the unappetizing prospect of ending up as a fat Tica who worked all day and was married to a dumb farmer who gave her a child every year. My proposition was a unique opportunity to escape that misery. The old man left the same evening, after having talked my ear off all day long.

I didn't want to rush Xionara. I wasn't interested in a whore who'd wait for me in my bed, her legs spread in resignation. My shaven head didn't inspire spontaneous love, so I first wanted her to get used to me. She completely understood what was expected of her, but was nevertheless frightened because she had remained pure. The first night she slept in the house of Puntarenas and his wife, who was appointed chaperon, and the next day we all went shopping in Golfito, where I bought her some jewels and the kind of trinkets a girl her age likes. Even at the hotel, she slept in a separate room, and it wasn't until several days after we returned to the camp that she shared my bed – at her own request. I'd sent to Puerto Jiménez for a nurse, who explained the pill and the principles of contraception to her; I had no use for a pregnant girl and no intention of repopulating the peninsula.

Xionara was my moment of relaxation. During the day she was turned over to the watchful señora, who taught her to take care of my stuff and anticipate my needs. In the evening, she was mine. I had someone buy some French perfume, fancy underwear, nightgowns and other such items at the Panamanian border, where you could get that kind of thing, and I petted her the way such a jewel deserved to be petted in the mountains. She slowly got used to it all and became a woman. She took care of my home, and she even sewed a special set of pink sheets for my bed. It wasn't love, but it was pleasant because she took care of me as carefully as I took care of her. It was something sweet in the hard reality of the jungle.

Camp life went on, and finally one day Herman announced that the equipment was on the way. It was none too soon. At last I was going to be able to get busy, and the excitement of the coming action took over. The men were also pleased – they'd been accustomed to a faster pace, and time hung heavy on their hands.

As soon as the date had been set I left the camp under the supervision of Puntarenas and Xionara under the supervision of the señora. I took fifteen men and went down to pick up the equipment. We stopped at Los Modos, a bar-pulperia halfway between Rincón and the Pan-American, and we waited. We waited four days – four long days during which my unoccupied men looked for dumb things to do, ran after the local whores and got into brawls.

The pulpero was relieved to see us go when the machines arrived. The trip through the jungle and the uphill climb to the camp were rough because the rains had begun again; it took us two days. There was an excavator with a front shovel and a back scoop, a double-traction tractor, a giant canoa mounted on wheels, a pump and miles of tubing, and a lot of other things, especially food-supplies.

I didn't know a thing about machinery, but I knew enough to be surprised by the decrepitude of the principal piece, the excavator. It was a big rusty thing that must have been used to lay out the Pan-American back in 1943.

'Fabio, you're a mechanic. What do you think of it?'

'Well, to tell the truth, I wouldn't have thought of using anything like this.'

'In other words, it's an old piece of shit!'

'Well, maybe not a piece of shit, but it sure is old. It's made of cannibalized pieces of two old models patched together, but it should work.'

I hoped he was right. I hoped that Herman knew what he was doing and that those arseholes hadn't sent us a piece of junk again. On the uphill sections, the excavator was pulled by the tractor, and the men pushed the canoa. When we passed Demesio's place, out of sheer habit we tore down his patched-up fence. I couldn't get over the guy's stubbornness.

As soon as we got back, we set everything up. The excavator loaded gravel into the canoa, which was installed on the banks; the water, which could be recycled, was fed to it by a new pump hooked up to the tractor. I was pleased with the system, since to a certain extent it made up for the shortage of water.

In one afternoon the excavator took out everything that had fallen from the cliff. But the next morning, an hour after it started working on a new layer, the scoop on the excavator bent and broke. I went crazy. That cocksucker Herman was purposely trying to sabotage our work by sending me shit! From the very beginning, the son of a bitch had never done anything right.

My frustration was enormous. When I saw the power of those gadgets, I understood what I could have done with a machine in good

271

condition if it had come six months earlier. In a single day it accomplished what would have required six months of manual labour. Just imagine what an entirely new machine could have done! Herman had bought the worst sort of junk he could find, and I suspected that he had done so deliberately.

I was doubly exasperated, because after our period of inactivity I had thought we were really going to take off. That very evening, I had a conversation with Herman – or, rather, I tried to, because the transmission was bad. The discussion was stormy but, though I understood him perfectly, he couldn't make out a thing I was saying. He just about got the idea that the machine had broken down, and from the safety of his office this ball-less wonder, this coward, accused me of having been negligent about using the equipment. I was giving him the full benefit of my fury when contact was broken.

Three days later, when I telephoned him from Puerto Jiménez, Herman apologized.

'I was upset, and I'm sorry I said all that. I've got two pieces of news for you, one good, one bad. First, the good: we're going to get the papers for the concession very soon. It's all been arranged. And now the bad: there's a national arrest-warrant out for you for trafficking in drugs. But don't worry; it's not serious. The important thing is that we'll soon have the concession.'

And he told it to me just like that! In other words, I had every cop in the country on my tail and I might be arrested at any moment. Anxious to get back to the mine, I cut our conversation short. On the way, as I was once again pulling up Demesio's fence, two shots rang out, one on the heels of the other, and a .22 bullet banged into my door, barely missing me.

I was sure it was Demesio. Well, he had come along at just the right time! Jumping from the vehicle, I went to look for him with my Magnum in hand – but the coward couldn't be found, and we went home frustrated. Too bad! His stuffed and mounted head would have looked great in the dining-room, right next to the photo of Barbaroja.

That evening I did some serious thinking. I had no intention of allowing myself to be arrested like some common criminal. If Herman wanted war, he'd get it.

The next morning I sent Jimmy to San José.

'Take the jeep and go see that arsehole Herman. Tell him to stop his dumb tricks now. Tell him that if he keeps playing games I'll blow up the mine and come to settle his hash– in other words, I'll cut his balls off. While you're at it, take the boys back with you.'

I kept White, Chiche, Eduardo, Puntarenas and Miguel – the five most faithful – and sent away all the others. I wanted men I could depend on with me, because I was preparing for a siege. If Herman had hoped that I'd panic, leave everything and flee to Panama, he was in for a disappointment.

I mined the whole camp: three hundred sticks of dynamite were planted in the shacks, in the machines and on the cliff of the deposit. Every available weapon was loaded and ready. The access road was under permanent guard. In case of a nocturnal attack, I'd be warned by the dogs that slept outside the camp and patrolled all night. I now had five dogs: two Dobermanns – King and Queenie – and three mongrel hunting dogs bought from the local farmers. King and Queenie were excellent guard dogs and could scent a presence well before the others.

I was determined to be ready for any visit. If the cops showed themselves, I intended to kill as many as possible – a surprise fusillade always does damage. I'd light the fuses before starting to fight and, no matter what the outcome, nobody else would reap the rewards of my work. Under cover of the panic the explosions would create, I hoped to pull out and go settle Herman's hash. I knew that it was an unequal and desperate fight, and that I was burning all my bridges, but nobody had ever tried to get the better of me without paying the price – and Herman was not going to be an exception.

Two days later I made radio contact with the jerk, who swore he was innocent. It wasn't possible to have much of a dialogue, because the radio was barely working. He promised to fix things completely and do everything to see to it that no action was taken by the police. He was sending Jimmy back to explain to me.

During the following four days the tension was high. The men were restless and sensitive to the electric atmosphere; they weren't sure just how bad the situation was, but they knew that something was about to happen – and probably very soon.

I spent most of those days with Xionara. If the fight was to be my last, I wanted to make the most of the life remaining to me. While awaiting the resolution I didn't want my nights disturbed: I still had a lot of things to do with her.

Jimmy came back. He was sure that Herman was telling the truth when he said he'd fix everything.

'He's really afraid that you'll blow up the camp. He knows you, and what you're capable of. I think he's already backed off to protect the mine. Also, I heard in Sierpe that two cops came here to arrest you but got scared when they saw the signs.'

That news pleased me. I was proud that two cops with a warrant for my arrest had taken a three-hour boat trip, then walked in the mountains for four more hours, only to leave without so much as lifting a pinky. I could see the two of them stand in front of the warning signs and discuss the best thing to do – and then, tails between their legs, turn on their heels and start inventing the lie they'd tell their chief.

I no longer knew what to think.

It seemed to me that I'd entered into an unequal struggle that might easily go against me. I couldn't count on anyone, because, though my boys were loyal, they didn't have my motivation. It wasn't their mine they were fighting for, and I knew they'd desert me at the first sign of real trouble.

In addition, even if I should do everything I planned to, I couldn't win. A century earlier, I'd have been able to do battle and, with a good bunch of boys, carry out my revenge by putting the country to the torch. But in 1983 I didn't have a shadow of a chance. With an international warrant out for me, and Interpol on my heels, I wouldn't be safe anywhere. It was the very opposite of civilization: for an act committed in the northern hemisphere they hunted you down in the southern hemisphere – and, anyway, you couldn't kill a former president's family without people noticing.

I would avenge myself on those bastards in a foolproof way. I would see to it that they couldn't bother me, even if it killed me. I wasn't afraid of death, but I certainly wasn't going to die without settling scores with Herman.

The decision was hard, but it was the right one.

I sent Xionara back to her family with all the gifts I could make her. It was sad to terminate an affair that had begun so well. My harem had been short-lived.

I closed the mine and left it in Puntarenas' care. It was May 1983. In six months I had manually taken out 23,000 grams of gold. I left the place with a feeling of regret, because I doubted I would ever see the mine again.

EPILOGUE

18 February 1984

'Don't move! Police!'

The two guys who'd been sipping Cokes at a nearby table on the patio of the Poàs Hotel were suddenly standing in front of me.

'Don Juan Carlos?'

'Yes.'

'Your passport, please.'

I mechanically bent for my passport, which I generally carried in my boots, and panic broke out. The two guys fell back and drew their revolvers, and six others came out of nowhere and pointed their machine-guns at me. The patio of the Poàs, where I'd been drinking coffee as I waited for a friend, had suddenly become very animated. About half of the 'customers' had jumped up and taken aim at me; other cops in mufti ran in as a Black Maria ground to a halt in front of the hotel. It was really a neat trap, but they'd flatteringly overestimated me.

More than a dozen of them trembled at the end of their guns, and I was alone and unarmed. (After my earlier experiences with the San José cops I stopped carrying my gun when I was downtown.) They, of course, didn't know this, so the atmosphere was very tense. I didn't make a move, because I knew they were just waiting for an excuse to pump lead into me: the little cops were nervous. I have to admit that those three years in the jungle, where I'd given free rein to my madness and violence, had left their mark on me, and my still-shaven head didn't help. They were more frightened than I was, so with machine-guns prodding my back I let myself be led to the police wagon. On that bright morning I was undergoing my eighteenth Costa Rican arrest. It was Act 3, Scene 18 of *Quebrada del Frances*, and I knew my part by heart.

It had all happened very quickly, and under the eyes of the astonished real customers. Only Juan, the waiter, knew me and understood what was happening. Before leaving, I gave him a quick wink, to which he replied with a knowing glance. He was a friend, and he knew my lawyers. Luckily – because I was sure those bastards wouldn't let me telephone.

In the wagon the tension remained high. The big son of a bitch who

275

seemed to be in charge had got in up front with the driver. Three others climbed into the rear with me. They all kept their weapons at the ready. One of them, a young guy, was leaning against the door and pointing his machine-gun at me, his finger on the trigger. Fear made him nervous, and I found myself hoping that the idiot knew how to control himself and wasn't going to send a burst into my stomach at the first jolt.

I looked out the window, and the big ugly chief immediately belched: 'Don't look out! Keep your head down!'

Astonished, I was a little late in doing as I was told, and one of the guys in the back jumped forward and pressed the business end of his gun to my neck, forcing me to obey.

'Do as you're told,' he bawled, 'or there'll be trouble.'

Things didn't look good; there was the scent of a summary execution in the air. My eighteenth arrest might well be my last, I thought. Even though it was supposedly democratic, Costa Rica had its share of unexplained deaths, and I wouldn't be the first victim of a macabre joyride.

I tuned in on traffic noises. If the wagon left the city, I was in for it. But I had no intention of letting myself be led to the slaughter without fighting back. In the pocket of my battle fatigues I had a blackjack that had escaped their first rapid frisking and, though I couldn't hope to fight my way out with that, I wouldn't go gently. If this was the end of the road for me, I'd take a few others along; and, if all was lost, I might as well make a splashy exit.

When the wagon stopped, I had no idea where we were. The back doors clanged open, I quickly glanced around, and saw a uniformed guard some thirty yards behind us, closing the gates that had been opened to let us in. I could see the walls of a compound, administrative buildings, a few vehicles. Some cops in civilian clothes came and went in the courtyard, and I breathed more freely; I wasn't going to get a quick bullet – there were too many witnesses. At worst I was in for a beating.

The search began as soon as I got out of the wagon.

'Take off your boots, Frenchie,' said the leader.

He stood in front of me so he could enjoy the spectacle. He was a sweating stinking lump of lard – like a pig's arse, but a lot more repulsive.

The cop picked up my boots, shook them, looked inside and ran his hand through them. The only thing there was my passport, which fell to the ground. The big lump of shit picked it up and shoved it into his pocket without so much as a glance.

'Put your boots back on,' he said.

He examined the blackjack the other cop had just found and slapped it against the palm of his hand.

I didn't at all care for his face, or his smile, and I couldn't keep myself from saying to him: 'You can shove it up your arse, if you want!'

Strangely enough, he made no reply. Maybe down deep, way down deep, he liked the idea. His subordinates can't have been very fond of him, because they began to laugh. Big Arse looked nasty. I'd made another friend!

'Don't be so clever,' he advised me.

The cops surrounded me until we reached the building. I let myself be led down a corridor, and I entered the prison without making a fuss.

They let me stew in that rotten slammer for the next eight hours, with my only company a dying unconscious black man whose face and body were swollen by blows and whose hands were manacled. What a bunch of bastards!

In eight months since I had left the mine, all sorts of charges had been brought against me. You had to give them credit for imagination: trafficking in gold, counterfeiting dollars, 'intimidation' (that was really too much!), threatening to kill people, etc. In short, –I was Public Enemy Number One. I'd made the rounds of every police division in the country: Narcotics, Immigration, and OIJ (the local Gestapo); each time it was the same story and, once the initial nervousness was over, all I felt was boredom and weariness. And to think that I was a man who couldn't bear doing the same thing twice!

I was sick and tired – tired of everything and especially tired of the contemptible adversaries who made my adventure look petty and dirty. I wasn't made for legal battles, and this was the first and last time I'd try them. For eight months I'd fought shadows. As I found out the hard way, the Caracas family and the Partido del Pueblo Unido were effectively in control of the whole country: with their men in all the key posts in Costa Rica, they had the advantage in the struggle against me.

I decided that my gold mine was a poisoned gift, and that sooner or later they'd go after one another. And, besides, a gold mine is like everything else – lose one, find ten.

Such were my thoughts when Big Arse, smiling narrowly, came to tell me that my lawyers had been told of my situation and shown up. I was released. He returned my passport. I tossed him one final insult and walked out.

*   *   *

277

I was free, for the moment. But the struggle had been too unequal, and I'd lost. As soon as I'd come down from the mine I'd called a meeting of my associates: it was time to clear up the confusion. The discussion was a stormy one. I told them I was ready to sell my shares to the highest bidder, and we decided to close the mine until a buyer showed up. I could see no other solution. Since Herman was the titular owner of the property I had to clear out of there as soon as possible; I'd managed to have the arrest warrant lifted by paying bail, but while awaiting trial I wasn't supposed to leave the country.

My former partners had made a few stupid attempts to talk me into some other lucrative and illegal deals – some of them very profitable affairs – but I could clearly see what they were setting up for me. One more successful trap and they could have me locked up for life. I nevertheless pretended to accept, in order to get at the truth lurking behind their façades of honesty.

Tino took me to Colonel Julio, an arms-dealer whose references said all that needed saying. A few years earlier he'd cheated the Salvadorian Contras on a shipment of prepaid arms that never reached their destination. He'd had to lie low in the United States for a year, and still lived in a villa that had been turned into a fortress. He was the best friend of Tino, the so-called puritan.

At Julio's place, Tino – who liked to pretend he was an honest businessman – finally showed his hand. He was up to his eyeballs in arms traffic and the sale of cocaine. Taking two kilos from his attaché case, he suggested I peddle them. And while I was under arrest the cocksucker Herman had told me he couldn't get Tino to intervene because the latter had strong anti-drug principles! All the stuff he sold came from the stocks seized at Customs by the Narcotics people under the order of Colonel Altamira. I was finally coming to understand that the whole country was in the grip of the Partido del Pueblo Unido – and especially of the Caracas family.

As all that became clear to me, I realized I didn't have a fighting chance against them: the deck had already been thoroughly stacked.

However, I scored one victory against them early on. Herman had the nugget weighing more than 3500 grams, and he wouldn't sell it unless he got a very good price. That nugget was something like the symbol of the mine: I didn't want those scumbags to profit from it. Pablo, the accountant, was responsible for looking after the gold, and during my last trip to Malessa, while pretending to go over the accounts, I got him all muddled and managed to take back the nugget without him realizing what had happened. They must have given him hell!

Next, for the first time in my life I decided to fight back through the courts. I got six lawyers working on the papers of the Quebrada del Frances. I told them the whole story, though since you can't put your faith in anyone in that country I played down the grade of ore so as to avoid arousing new cupidity. Anyway, they quickly discovered that nothing in the documents corresponded to the truth; everything had been falsified from the very beginning. My partners had forged my signature, which appeared on papers I'd never even seen, and instead of being the principal stockholder I had only 30 per cent. They'd cheated on everything. My lawyers wanted to bring charges of false record-keeping, forgery, abuse of confidence, etc., but I told them to forget it. Since my adversaries held the reins of power, they'd easily win, and I didn't want to give them that satisfaction. My lawyers naïvely believed in justice, but I knew the game was lost in advance.

As it turned out, the lawyers' only usefulness was to rescue me safe and sound after numerous arrests. Once their scheme had been exposed, my former partners tried every possible way to eliminate me.

At Herman's instigation, a cop had gone down to Osa and returned with eighty complaints – true and false – against me. They built up a fat dossier itemizing acts of violence that were really ordinary enough in Osa, but that taken out of context made me look like a dangerous monster.

I went up to the capital as seldom as possible, just moving around in the south and letting the lawyers handle things. I lived on a ranch in the Talamanca foothills, a place accessible only by horseback. I never saw my men again – they were already part of ancient history – but I did hear that Barbas had sold me out by giving information to Herman.

On the ranch I was more or less safe, because I still had friends among the police. Most of the cops in the area had lined their pockets thanks to me, and they were grateful. I'd made a new concession request, because after scouting around and listening to various stories I discovered another mine – one that was a lot less rich than the Quebrada del Frances, but a lot more accessible. I'd succeeded in contacting some investors representing a Nicaraguan company that had been interested in buying the Quebrada del Frances. This time I wasn't interested in the exploitation, which was beginning to go well, but in selling the concession as soon as the papers had been granted. I'd decided to handle the paperwork myself, and the simplicity of it all had completely convinced me of Herman's inefficiency.

Unfortunately, I was hampered by the constant pressure and the surveillance of the police every time I went to San José, and I had to spend a lot of time shaking them off. In addition, the prohibition against leaving the country made it impossible for me to go to Nicaragua and deal directly with my future partners. So I finally gave up pursuing the deal.

Time was precious now because I'd begun a race against the clock. I was due to be tried on 23 February on Tax Department charges of trafficking in marijuana. Theoretically, it was only a formality, and I would emerge with my name completely cleared, but I suspected my former associates were getting ready to eliminate me from the scene once and for all.

My lawyers, who either were overconfident or had been bribed by the enemy camp, assured me there was little risk. Even if the improbable worst scenario should come to pass, they said, and I was found guilty, Costa Rican law gave me two weeks of liberty and time to appeal. Nevertheless, the judge had the right to overlook that clause in the law if he believed – and they insisted this was unlikely – that the accused represented a danger to public safety.

But as they explained this I grasped the plot hatched by my partners. By having false witnesses appear at the last minute, it would be easy to affirm that I'd urged drugs on my employees and should therefore be convicted of dealing. Then, thanks to the file of eighty complaints made against me – a file composed for exactly this reason – it would be easy to show that I was indeed a public menace. And that would be that.

Afterwards it would no longer be a matter of a simple court trial. I'd be sent directly to gaol and might very well not get out for fifteen or twenty years – assuming I ever did get out, since it would be easy to provoke an incident in which I could be killed with impunity. Even if that never happened, prison would be death for someone like me, whose whole life was based on having complete freedom.

My lawyers refused to believe in such machinations, but I knew that the trial was fixed, and its consequences would have to be lived by nobody but yours truly.

Three days before the trial I decided to leave the country clandestinely and seek asylum in Panama.

I'd been walking for two days, and I figured I couldn't be far from the border. I'd left the beach the day before, and now I was working my way through the mountains. Just as I stopped to roll my last joint a peasant appeared.

'Where are we, friend – Costa Rica or Panama?'

'Panama,' the man replied.

280

And so the Costa Rican adventure was all over. It was as simple as that. There was little chance that the peasant would ever understand why I was smiling. I waited until he'd gone, then destroyed the dynamite and buried the .44 Magnum. They had played a rôle in an adventure that henceforth belonged to the past. Goodbye, Ticos – I was really fond of you, your women, and your little girls. I gave one last thought to Jimmy, my friend, the younger brother I was leaving behind. Poor fellow! To have dreamed and struggled so hard, and all in vain. . . . One by one, I remembered the other members of my happy crew. They hadn't been much to start with, but I had got them to give their best. They'd become buddies.

And then it was time for the pleasures that could be brought with my three thousand grams of gold – my last, ephemeral souvenir of Costa Rica.

Herman, you slimy bastard, I'm going to keep my promise.